Study Guide with Map Exercises

to accompany

American History: A Survey
Volume I: To 1877

Eleventh Edition

Alan Brinkley
Columbia University

Prepared by
Harvey H. Jackson
Jacksonville State University

Bradley R. Rice
Clayton State College

Boston   Burr Ridge, IL   Dubuque, IA   Madison, WI   New York   San Francisco   St. Louis
Bangkok   Bogotá   Caracas   Kuala Lumpur   Lisbon   London   Madrid   Mexico City
Milan   Montreal   New Delhi   Santiago   Seoul   Singapore   Sydney   Taipei   Toronto

Study Guide with Map exercises for use with
AMERICAN HISTORY: A SURVEY (VOLUME I: TO 1877)
Alan Brinkley

Published by McGraw-Hill, an imprint of The McGraw-Hill Companies, Inc., 1221 Avenue of the Americas, New York, NY 10020. Copyright © 2003 by The McGraw-Hill Companies, Inc. All rights reserved.

5 6 7 8 9 0 QPD/QPD 0 9 8 7 6 5

ISBN 0-07-249052-7

CONTENTS

ABOUT THE AUTHORS

Harvey H. Jackson received his Ph.D. from the University of Georgia. With Bradley R. Rice, he wrote *Georgia: Empire State of the South,* a pictorial history. He is the author of a number of books including *Rivers of History: Life on the Coosa, Tallapoosa, Cahaba and Alabama* (1995) and *Lachlan McIntosh and the Politics of Revolutionary Georgia* (1979). Jackson has also authored, coauthored and coedited seven other volumes on various aspects of southern history. He is now working on a history of the northern coast of the Gulf of Mexico. His articles and essays have appeared in several anthologies and journals including the *Journal of Southern History* and the *William and Mary Quarterly,* Jackson is Professor and Head of the Department of History at Jacksonville State University in Jacksonville, Alabama.

Bradley R. Rice received his Ph.D. from the University of Texas at Austin. He coauthored *Georgia: Empire State of the South* with Harvey H. Jackson and wrote *Progressive Cities: The Commission Government Movement in American Cities, 1901–1920* (1977). Rice is coauthor and coeditor of *Sunbelt Cities: Politics and Growth Since World War II* (1983), and his work has appeared in several edited collections and journals including the *Journal of Urban History.* Since 1982, Rice has been editor of *Atlanta History: A Journal of Georgia and the South,* which is published quarterly by the Atlanta Historical Society. Rice is Professor of History and Assistant Vice President for Academic Affairs at Clayton State College, Morrow, Georgia.

INTRODUCTION

Every history professor has heard hundreds of students complain that history is nothing but dry, irrelevant names and dates to be memorized quickly and just as quickly forgotten. To be sure, for students to have a good framework of historical understanding, they must have a basic knowledge of some important names and dates, but history is much more than that. It is society's memory, and society cannot function without history any more than an individual could function without his or her memory. The names represent real flesh-and-blood people, both famous and common, and the dates mark the time when those people lived and worked. This Study Guide will try to lead you toward the outcome of developing a historical perspective. You will be encouraged to go beyond the bare facts to think critically about the causes and consequences of historical decisions. Careful study of this guide in consultation with your instructor will help you use the text to its best advantage. With the guide, you can constantly test yourself to make sure that you have learned from what you have read.

Each chapter of the guide is composed of several parts: objectives, main themes, glossary, pertinent questions, identification, documents, map exercise, interpretative questions, summary, and review questions. Your instructor may assign specific items from the guide that best complement his or her approach to the course, or you may be expected to use the guide on your own. It will work well with either approach. The guide is not a workbook or a shortcut. It does not recapitulate, outline, or simplify the work of Professor Alan Brinkley. Rather, it is designed to challenge you to seek a better comprehension of the text in particular and American history in general.

It is best to look over the appropriate chapter in the guide *before* you read your assignment so that you will be better attuned to what to look for as you read. The objectives and main themes that are listed at the beginning of each chapter of the Study Guide will give you a general idea of what the chapter is about. The object of your reading should be to see how the text develops these themes. The glossary contains historical terms used in the text but not fully defined therein. The identification items are names and terms covered in the text but not directly mentioned in the pertinent-questions section of the Study Guide. Of course, your instructor may add to and/or delete from these lists to meet the needs of the course.

The pertinent questions, review questions, and self tests are the heart of the Study Guide. The objective of these exercises is to provide you with a thoughtful method for self-assessment after you have read each chapter. (Page numbers are provided for the pertinent questions so that you can check your answers and review if necessary.) Some students will wish to write out their answers in full; some will jot down a few key ideas; and others will simply check themselves "in their heads." Experiment and use whichever method works best for you (assuming it is acceptable to your instructor). You should keep in mind that no general survey text could possibly cover all the pertinent questions in American history or fully explicate those it does discuss. Do not become too preoccupied with incidental supporting detail. Look for the essence of the answer, and then seek out those facts and examples that support your conclusions. With this approach, you will be prepared to answer examination questions in any format—multiple choice, true-false, fill-in, or essay. The self test at the end of each chapter will help you check to be sure that you have learned the essential information being covered.

The document exercises in each chapter provide an opportunity for you to discover how important the analysis of documents can be to the historian's task. The questions on each document should be treated much like the pertinent questions. The map exercises let you see how geography can help you form a historical perspective. Note that after every five or six chapters in the guide, there is a section of general discussion questions. These questions are designed to permit you to examine ideas that carry over from chapter to chapter, and they highlight issues raised in the "American Environment" essays.

At the end of the guide are sections that will help you write a critical book review or research paper if your instructor so requires. Such assignments will give you the opportunity to exercise the critical thinking skills and historical perspective that you have cultivated while reading the text and using this guide.

Naturally, this all seems like a drawn-out process, and at first it may well be. But as you work at it, you will find that each chapter will take less time, until finally you will have developed a system of study habits and analysis that will serve you well in this course and in many others as well.

Harvey H. Jackson

Bradley R. Rice

Objectives

A thorough study of Chapter One should enable the student to understand:

1. The history of the Native Americans before the arrival of Europeans.
2. What the New World was like at the time of Christopher Columbus.
3. The ways in which the peoples of the New and Old Worlds affected each other when their societies came in contact in the late fifteenth century.
4. The changes taking place in western Europe that resulted in widespread interest in colonization.
5. The colonial policies of each nation involved, and the effect each had on the future of the Americas.
6. The reasons for the rivalry between Spain and England during the sixteenth and seventeenth centuries, and the impact of that rivalry on international affairs.
7. The African cultures from which black slaves were taken and the early development of slavery.
8. The role of religion in European efforts to colonize the New World.
9. The ways in which the experiences of the English in Ireland influenced their efforts to colonize North America.
10. The first efforts of the English to establish a colony and the reasons for their failure.
11. The host of connections that existed between what happened in the Americas and what was happening in the rest of the world.

Main Themes

1. That the colonization of the Americas was a collision of cultures—the European and the Native American—that had been developing along completely different lines for thousands of years.
2. How a variety of ambitions and impulses moved individuals and nations to colonize the New World.
3. The way the motives of the colonizers and their experiences prior to immigrating shaped their attitudes toward Native American cultures.
4. How these same motives and experiences helped determine the sociopolitical arrangements in the new colonies.
5. The ways that the Old World influenced the history of the New.

Glossary

1. demography: The statistical study of human populations, especially with reference to size, density, distribution, and vital statistics such as sex or family size. Using computers to store, sort, and retrieve the considerable data available to them, historians have conducted complex demographic studies and shed new light on social life in early America.
2. feudalism: A political, social, and economic system that existed in Europe during the Middle Ages. Based on the ownership of land and the obligations of tenant to lord, feudalism tended to fragment power and authority. By the end of the fifteenth century, it was being replaced by

centralized governments in nation-states, but aspects of the feudal system remained in parts of Europe for centuries.

3.   high church: The party within the Church of England that retained many of the Catholic ceremonies and practices that the Puritans opposed and wished to purge from the church.

4.   capitalism: An economic system based on the investment of resources (money, capital) in various enterprises in the hope of making a profit.

Pertinent Questions

AMERICA BEFORE COLUMBUS (4-9)

1.   Identify and describe the elaborate native civilizations that developed in South and Central America and in Mexico.

2.   Why did Europeans consider the Indians they met to be "savages," regardless of their cultural achievements?

3.   Describe the way of life of the North American Indians—where they lived and how they supported themselves.

4.   What were the three largest language groups, and where did their speakers live?

5.   Describe the changes taking place among North American Indians during the century before Europeans arrived.

EUROPE LOOKS WESTWARD (9-21)

6.   Why was there little incentive for other Europeans to follow after the initial voyage to America by Norse sailors?

7.   What changes stimulated the Europeans to look toward new lands?

8.   What did Columbus hope to achieve through his voyages, and what did he actually accomplish?

9.   Why did the conquistadors seek to eliminate the underpinnings of existing American civilization? How was this destruction accomplished?

10.   Explain how the Spanish empire was built primarily through private enterprise.

11.   What were the three distinct periods that the history of the Spanish empire spans?

12.   What role did the Catholic Church play in Spanish Colonization efforts?

13.   What was the "demographic catastrophe" that struck the American Indians? What impact did it have on European colonization efforts?

14.   What did Europeans gain from the Indians that proved more important than gold?

15.   What did the intermarriage of Spanish with North Americans reveal about the Spanish colonial system and suggest about the Europeans who administered it?

16.   Describe the cultures from which African slaves were taken and brought to America.

17.   How did the African slave trade originate, and how did it evolve?

THE ARRIVAL OF THE ENGLISH (23-30)

18.   What commercial factors contributed to England's decision to seek colonies in the New World?

19.   What arguments did Richard Hakluyt present in favor of England's settling colonies?

20.   How did Martin Luther's doctrine of "faith alone" differ from John Calvin's doctrine of "predestination"?

21. How did the English Reformation differ from that of Luther and Calvin? Why did it fail to satisfy the religious desires of many English people?

22. What did the Puritans wish to accomplish, and why did they clash with James I?

23. How did the English colonization of Ireland influence the way in which the English colonized America?

24. Where did the French and Dutch establish colonies in North America, and how did their efforts differ from those of the Spanish and the English?

25. How did nationalism inspire the English to get into the race for colonies?

26. Describe the colonization efforts of Sir Humphrey Gilbert and Sir Walter Raleigh.

27. How did James I settle the rivalry between London and Plymouth merchants over the exploration of North America?

WHERE HISTORIANS DISAGREE (6-9)

28. Who were the "postivists," and why has their approach to history been rejected by most scholars today?

29. Explain the efforts that have been made to determine the population of America before Columbus.

AMERICA IN THE WORLD (22)

30. What were the Old World forces that influenced the settlement and expansion of America?

31. How does the concept of an "Atlantic World" encourage us to think of early American history as a vast pattern of exchanges and interactions among societies bordering that ocean.

Identification

Identify each of the following, and explain why it is important within the context of the chapter.

1. Tenochtitlán
2. Iroquois Confederation
3. Black Death
4. Prince Henry the Navigator
5. Amerigo Vespucci
6. Francisco Pizarro
7. Don Juan de Onate
8. Pueblo Indians
9. mestizos
10. Mali
11. John Cabot
12. enclosures
13. merchant capitalists

14. mercantilism
15. Huguenots
16. Separatists
17. "plantations"
18. coureurs de bois
19. "sea dogs"

Document

John Smith is one of the most famous names associated with the English colonization of America, and his writings did much to introduce Europeans to America and to promote English colonization efforts. The document that follows is from his General Historie of Virginia, New England, and the Summer Isles . . . (1624), a chronicle of English exploration that drew heavily on the earlier work of Richard Hakluyt. This account of a meeting in 1584 between English explorers and Indians, although seen through the eyes of the English, tells us much about Indian life before the transformation of the tribes was complete. While reading it, consider the culture and possessions of the Indians and the English attitude toward what the Indians obviously valued. Also pay particular attention to what the English noticed about the Indians, and speculate on why these things were important to them.

Till the third day we saw not any of the people, then in a little Boat three of them appeared, one of them went on shore, to whom wee rowed, and he attended vs without any signe of feare; after he had spoke much though we vnderstood not a word, of his owne accord he came boldly aboord vs, we gaue him a shirt, a hat, wine and meate, which he liked well, and after he had well viewed the barkes and vs, he went away in his owne Boat, and within a quarter of a myle of vs in halfe an houre, had loaden his Boat with fish, with which he came againe to the poynt of land, and there devided it in two parts, poynting one part to the Ship, the other to the Pinnace, and so departed.

The next day came diuers Boats, and in one of them the Kings Brother, with forty or fifty men, proper people, and in their behauiour very ciuill; his name was Granganameo, the King is called Winginia, the Country Wingandacoa. Leauing his Boats a little from our Ships, he came with his trayne to the poynt: where spreading a Matte he sat downe. Though we came to him well armed, he made signes to vs to sid downe without any shew of feare, stroking his head and brest, and also ours, to expresse his loue. After he had made a long speech vnto vs, we presented him with diuers toyes, which he kindly accepted. He was greatly regarded by his people, for none of them did sit, nor speake a word, but foure, on whom we bestowed presents also, but he tooke all from them, making signes all things did belong to him.

The King himselfe in a conflict with a King his next neighbour and mortall enemy, was shot in two places through the body, and the thigh, yet recouered: whereby he lay at his chiefe towne six days iourney from thence.

A day or two after shewing them what we had, Granganameo taking most liking to a Pewter dish, made a hole in it, hung it about his necke for a brestplate: for which he gaue vs twenty Deere skins, worth twenty Crownes; and for a Copper Kettell, fiftie skins, worth fiftie Crownes. Much other trucke we had, and after two dayes he came aboord, and did eate and drinke with vs very merrily. Not long after he brought his wife and children, they were but of meane stature, but well fauoured and very bashfull; she had a long coat of Leather, and about her privities a peece of the same, about her forehead a band of white Corrall, and so had her husband, in her eares were bracelets of pearle, hanging downe to her middle, of the bignesse of great Pease; the rest of the women had Pendants of Copper, and the Nobelmen fiue or six in an eare; his apparrell as his wiues, onely the women weare

4

their haire long on both sides, and the men but on one; they are of colour yellow, but their hayre is blacke, yet we saw children that had very fayre Chesnut coloured hayre.

After that these women had beene here with vs, there came downe from all parts great stores of people, with Leather, Corrall, and diuers kinde of dyes, but when *Granganameo* was present, none durst trade but himselfe, and them that wore red Copper on their heads, as he did. When euer he came, he would signifie by so many fires he came with so many boats, that we might know his strength. Their Boats are but one great tree, which is but burnt in the forme of a trough with gins and fire, till it be as they would haue it. For an armour he would haue ingaged vs a bagge of pearle, but we refused, as not regarding it, that wee might the better learn where it grew. He was very iust of his promise, for oft we trusted him, and he would come within his day to keepe his word. He sent vs commonly euery day a brace of Bucks, Conies, Hares, and fish, sometimes Mellons, Walnuts, Cucumbers, Pease, and diuers roots. This Author sayth, their corne groweth three times in fiue moneths; in May they sow, in Iuly reape; in Iune they sow, in August reape; in Iuly sow, in August reape. We put some of our Pease in the ground, which in ten dayes were 14. ynches high.

John Smith, <u>Works,</u> ed. Edward Arber (Birmingham, Eng.: J. Grant, 1884), pp. 306–308.

Map Exercise

Fill in or identify the following on the blank map provided. Use the map in the text as your source.

1. The routes of exploration, and the nations that sponsored these ventures.

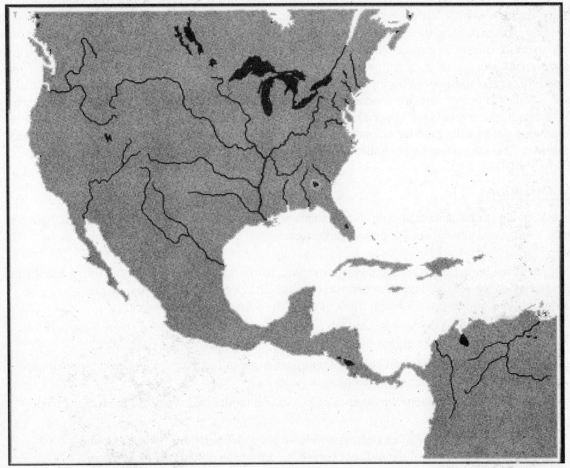

2. The centers of European settlement in North and Central America and in the Caribbean

Interpretative Questions

Based on what you have filled in, answer the following. On some of the questions you will need to consult the narrative in your text for information or explanation.

1. In light of the European rivalries of the period, and considering the various areas explored, settled, or claimed by the various European nations, what potentials existed for conflict among them?

2. Still considering the areas explored by European rivals, what opportunities existed for intercolonial trade? For trade with the Indians? What might have prevented this trade from taking place?

3. Note the location of the principal Spanish cities. Which appear to have been established for trading purposes? Which for military (strategic or defensive) purposes? Which were both military and economic?

4. Note the location of the Spanish missions. How might they have served a purpose other than religious? Why were forts often found with missions?

5. Consider the location of Spanish missions and forts. How might these have been sources of potential conflict with other European powers?

Summary

Before European explorers arrived in the Americas, Native Americans had developed their own forms of social organizations, which differed from one another in their levels of achievement. Europeans, concerned first with exploiting the New World and its peoples, regarded the natives as savages and set out to destroy their societies and replace them with a variation of European culture. Helped in this by the biological disaster brought on by smallpox and other diseases, the Europeans were able to conquer the tribes and civilizations and impose on the Indians a number of different colonial systems. To help make up for the Indians' labor lost through conquest and epidemic, Europeans brought in African slaves, who added to the cultural diversity of America. Conflicts in the old world spilled over into the New as different nations got into the race for colonies. By the end of the sixteenth century, the age of discovery was all but over, and the great era of colonization, especially English colonization, was about to begin.

Review Questions

These questions are to be answered with essays. This will allow you to explore relationships between individuals, events, and attitudes of the period under review.

1. Describe the Indian societies and their geographic distribution before the coming of the European explorers. What did these cultures contribute to the Europeans, and why, despite these contributions, did the invaders still think of the Native Americans as savages?

2. Compare and contrast the Spanish and the English motives for colonization. How were both sets of motives reflected in the organization of the colonies that each nation established?

3. How did earlier exploration and colonization experiences influence the way England, Spain, and other European nations attempted to colonize America?

4. Explain the relationship between Spanish colonists and the Indians. Why did the Indians come out the losers?

5. European colonization has often been said to have been motivated by "gold, God, and glory." Assess this interpretation of the motives behind the European colonization of America.

6.   Describe the social and cultural backgrounds of the Africans brought to America. How was this background different from the Indians? Europeans? How were the backgrounds of these people alike?

Chapter Self Test

After you have read the chapter in the text and done the exercises in the Study Guide, take the following self test to see if you understand the material you have covered. Answers appear at the end of the Study Guide.

Multiple-Choice Questions

Circle the letter of the response which best answers the question or completes the statement.

1.   The Indian Empire that dominated modern Mexico at the time of the Spanish conquest was the:
    a. Mayan.
    b. Inca.
    c. Aztec.
    d. Chaco.

2.   At the time of the Spanish conquest, the economies of most of the Native Americans in South and Central America and Mexico were based on:
    a. hunting and gathering.
    b. herding.
    c. fishing and gathering.
    d. agriculture.

3.   The eastern third of what is now the United States was inhabited by the:
    a. Woodland Indians.
    b. Plains Indians.
    c. Mountain Indians.
    d. Coastal Tribes.

4.   Indian societies in North America:
    a. made little distinction between gender roles.
    b. tended to divide tasks according to gender.
    c. put women in important political positions.
    d. did not allow women to exercise any control over social or economic matters.

5.   Paralleling the rise of commerce in Europe, and in part responsible for it was:
    a. the return of the Black Death.
    b. the invention of the compass.
    c. the revival of the African slave trade.
    d. the rise of united and powerful nation states.

6.   At least partly as a result of Columbus's voyages, Spain:
    a. got involved in the Indian slave trade.
    b. soon went to war with France.
    c. replaced Portugal as the foremost seafaring nation.
    d. opened trade with the great khan in China.

7. Through a combination of daring, brutality, and greed, the conquistadors:
   a. made possible the creation of a Spanish empire in America.
   b. brought capitalism to Mexico.
   c. founded St. Augustine.
   d. introduced African slavery into America.

8. With the Indians' conversion to Catholicism:
   a. native religions died out.
   b. most natives continued to practice their own religions.
   c. rebellions against whites ceased.
   d. Spain was able to control all southwestern tribes.

9. The first and perhaps most profound result of the meeting of native and European cultures was the:
   a. exchange of plants and animals.
   b. importation of European diseases.
   c. native adoption of European ways of waging war.
   d. intermarriage of Europeans and natives.

10. Ultimately more important to Europe than the gold and silver found in the New World was the:
    a. importation of new crops that could feed larger numbers of people.
    b. discovery of new forms of religious worship.
    c. Indian labor force.
    d. architectural knowledge gained from the Aztecs.

11. In matrilineal Indian and African societies:
    a. the father is the sole authority in the family.
    b. local gods are the basis of religious beliefs.
    c. women play a major, often dominant, role.
    d. slavery does not exist.

12. The African slave trade began:
    a. in the fifteenth century, soon after the Spanish conquest.
    b. as early as the eighth century.
    c. with the English settlement of Virginia.
    d. when the sugar industry moved to the Caribbean.

13. In the sixteenth century the market for slaves grew dramatically as a result of:
    a. the rising European demand for sugar cane.
    b. the need for labor in the tobacco fields.
    c. a desire to Christianize Africans.
    d. the English entry into the slave market.

14. Which of the following was *not* an English incentive for colonization?
    a. To escape religious strife at home.
    b. To bring the Christian religion to the Indians.
    c. To escape the economic transformation of the countryside.
    d. To find new markets for English products.

15. According to the theory of mercantilism, a nation could be made strong by:

a. exporting more than it imported.

b. building up a large standing army.

c. defeating its neighbors in war.

d. importing more than it exported.

16. Members of the Church of England who claimed that the church had not given up Rome's offensive beliefs and practices were the:

a. Baptists.

b. Presbyterians.

c. Methodists.

d. Puritans.

17. As a result of their experiences in Ireland, the English believed that:

a. all they needed to do was subdue the natives and rule them.

b. they must retain a rigid separation from the native population.

c. they could not build a complete society of their own.

d. they should intermarry with the Native Americans.

18. The country that produced the most successful fur traders and trappers was:

a. Spain.

b. Holland.

c. France.

d. Germany.

19. The first permanent English settlement was:

a. Massachusetts Bay.

b. Jamestown, Virginia.

c. Plymouth, Massachusetts.

d. St. Augustine, Florida.

20. The man to whom Queen Elizabeth granted the land on which the "lost colony" was planted was:

a. John White.

b. Walter Raleigh.

c. Humphrey Gilbert.

d. James Cobb.

True-False Questions

Read each statement carefully. Mark true statements "T" and false statements "F."

1. The Aztec capital built on the site of present-day Mexico City was Cuzco.

2. The large Indian trading center in the Mississippi River Valley near present day St. Louis was Cahokia.

3. The Iroquois Confederation consisted of tribes in the southernmost region of the eastern seaboard.

4. All Native American tribes traced their families through the father's line.

5. By the end of his first voyage Columbus knew he had not reached China.

6. Cortes might not have been able to defeat the Aztecs had it not been for an epidemic of smallpox that decimated the native population.

7. The oldest permanent European settlement in the present-day United States is St. Augustine.

8. The Catholic Church was as important in Spanish colonization efforts as the use of force and brutality.

9. Encomiendas were large estates or land grants.

10. New Mexico brought the Spanish almost as much gold and silver as Mexico did.

11. The most important native American crop taken home by the Europeans was squash.

12. Europeans felt justified in their treatment of the Indians because they considered the Indians uncivilized savages.

13. Spaniards seldom intermarried with the Native Americans.

14. Mercantilism was a theory that discouraged nations from having colonies.

15. Business partnerships operating with a monopoly from a monarch that gave them the right to trade in a particular region were charter companies.

16. The doctrine that God "elected" some people to be saved and condemned others to damnation was preached by Martin Luther.

17. The English Reformation began with a political dispute between king and Pope—not with a religious dispute over matters of theology.

18. England's first experience with colonization was in Virginia.

19. The first Europeans to settle in the Hudson River Valley were the Dutch.

20. In 1606, James I gave the exclusive right to colonize along the southeast coast of North America to a group of London merchants.

CHAPTER TWO
TRANSPLANTATIONS AND BORDERLANDS

Objectives

A thorough study of Chapter Two should enable the student to understand:

1. The differences between the Jamestown and Plymouth colonies in terms of objectives, types of settlers, early problems, and reasons for success.

2. The causes and significance of Bacon's Rebellion.

3. The background of the Massachusetts Bay colony and its founders, the Puritans.

4. The conditions in Puritan Massachusetts Bay that spawned such dissenters as Roger Williams and Anne Hutchinson.

5. The expansion of the original settlements, and the influences of the New World frontier on the colonists.

6. The significance of the Caribbean colonies in the British-American colonial system.

7. How the Spanish colonies continued to flourish and the impact this had on the British-American colonial system.

8. The efforts made by the Dutch to establish a colony, and the reasons for their failure.

9. The reasons for the founding of each of the original thirteen colonies.

10. The early economic, religious, and political factors in the colonies that tended to produce sectional differences.

11. The effect of the Glorious Revolution on the development of the American colonies.

Main Themes

1. The origins and objectives of England's first settlements in the New World.

2. How and why English colonies differed from one another in purpose and administration.

3. The problems that arose as colonies matured and expanded, and how colonists attempted to solve them.

4. The impact that events in England had on the development of colonies in British America.

Glossary

1. royal colony: A colony over which the king of England assumed control, granting it a royal charter in place of the charter it previously held. Not an act of tyranny, as often pictured, royalization guaranteed that England's laws (and English subjects' rights) would apply to the colony and colonists. A royal governor was appointed by the king to see that such laws were carried out, and a council, composed of prominent men of the colony (appointed by the king, but with the advice of local leaders), was established to advise the executive. Most important, at least to the colonists in general, was the authorization of an elected legislature (variously known as the Commons House of Assembly, the House of Burgesses, and the like) to pass local laws and deal with problems particular to the colony. This legislative activity was naturally to conform to English law and was subject to royal approval or disallowance. In time, the council came to act as the upper house of the legislature, while the commons functioned as the lower, an arrangement that, to the colonists at least, strongly resembled the relationship that existed between the House of Commons and the House of Lords in England. This system varied from colony to colony and

underwent many changes as it evolved; yet, by the end of the colonial era, most of the British-American colonies shared its basic institutional structure.

2. <u>proprietary colony</u>: A colony whose charter was granted by the king to an individual or a group (proprietors). Although the charter might place certain restrictions on the proprietors, in general they were free to run the colony as they wished—appointing governors, establishing assemblies, dividing and granting land. Because most proprietors were essentially land speculators and concerned with profit (either from the sale of land or from quitrents), they usually relaxed political and religious restrictions so as to attract colonists. But even with these concessions, proprietary governments at times proved unpopular, and opposition to them was one source of turmoil in the late seventeenth century.

3. <u>orthodox</u>: Conforming to the accepted doctrines or system of beliefs of a group, refusing to deviate or alter one's beliefs (for example, orthodox Puritans).

4. <u>antinomianism</u>: The belief that people cannot obtain salvation through good works but that "faith alone" is all that is necessary. Seventeenth-century authorities feared that antinomians would feel that it was not necessary to work for the betterment of the community and might even put themselves above the rules and regulations that governed society.

5. <u>covenant</u>: Essentially an agreement in which people are united for a specific purpose. Rooted in Protestant theology, such agreements were the basis for church governments (especially among Calvinist congregations) and, in time, influenced civil governments as well. In this way, the covenant concept helped establish the idea of government by the consent of the governed.

Pertinent Questions

THE EARLY CHESAPEAKE (34-40)

1. What conditions and circumstances that characterized the first permanent English settlements?

2. What serious difficulties did the Virginia colonists suffer from the moment they landed?

3. After the colony was established, what efforts did the Virginia Company make to attract settlers and make the colonists more happy and productive?

4. Explain the importance of tobacco in the development of the Virginia colony.

5. What led to Virginia's becoming a royal colony?

6. The survival of Jamestown was, in the end, largely the result of what?

7. What were the origins of the colony of Maryland? How did Maryland's early development differ from that of Virginia?

8. What were the origins of the political turmoil in Virginia during the 1670s?

9. How was Bacon's Rebellion related to the political unrest in Virginia, and what effect did the rebellion have on the development of that colony?

THE GROWTH OF NEW ENGLAND (40-49)

10. Describe the background of the Pilgrims and their motives for coming to America.

11. How did the Pilgrims' experience with the Indians differ markedly from that of settlers in Virginia?

12. How did the turbulent events in England generate interest in colonization among certain English Puritans? What did these Puritans hope to accomplish?

13. How did the charter of the Massachusetts Bay Company influence the colony's first government?

14. What did the Puritans believe to be their purpose in coming to America (their "mission"), and how did church and state cooperate to achieve this goal?

10. How did the colony of Connecticut originate? Rhode Island? What does this expansion ("exodus") reveal about the colony of Massachusetts Bay?

16. What was the controversy surrounding Anne Hutchinson, and what does it reveal about Puritan religious and social beliefs?

17. What factors made relations between Indians and colonists in New England such a disaster for Native Americans?

18. What were the causes and consequences of the Pequot War and King Philip's War?

19. How were the Pequot War and King Philip's War crucially affected by earlier exchanges of technology between the English and the tribes?

THE RESTORATION COLONIES (49-54)

20. How did the Stuart Restoration affect those English colonies already established in America? How did it affect attitudes about founding more settlements?

21. How did the political, economic, social, and religious institutions established in Carolina reflect the proprietors' motives for starting the colony?

22. What caused the Carolina settlements along the Ashley and Cooper Rivers to develop differently from those in the Albemarle area?

23. What sort of social order took root in the colony of Carolina? Why did it differ from that proposed under Carolina's Fundamental Constitution?

24. How did the existing Dutch settlements and institutions influence the development of New York?

25. Why did power in New York remain widely dispersed? Who shared this power?

26. What beliefs and practices characterized the Quakers, and how did their influence make Pennsylvania a unique colony?

BORDERLANDS AND MIDDLE GROUNDS (54-60)

27. What were the major British Caribbean colonies and under what circumstances were they obtained?

28. Why did British colonists in the Caribbean turn to African slaves as a source of labor? Explain.

29. In what ways were the Caribbean settlements important to the British?

30. Why was it difficult to establish a stable society and culture in the Caribbean colonies?

31. What were the principal Spanish colonies north of Mexico and what role did they play in the development of the empire?

32. Explain the relations between the Spanish in the Southwest and their French rivals.

33. How were the Spanish outposts in North America different from the English outposts along the Atlantic seaboard?

34. How did the purposes for which Georgia was founded differ from those of previous colonies? How were they similar?

35. Explain the relationships between Europeans and Native Americans in the "middle grounds."

THE EVOLUTION OF THE BRITISH EMPIRE (61-63)

36. What attempts did England make to regulate its colonies between 1660 and 1700? What moved the mother country to consider regulation at this time, and how was it enforced?

37. What were the origins of the Dominion of New England, and what was the colonial reaction to it?

38. What impact did the Glorious Revolution have on England's North American colonies?

THE AMERICAN ENVIRONMENT (42-43)

39. What were the "other pilgrims" that came to the New World with the Europeans?

40. How was "the colonization of America as much a biological invasion as a cultural one?"

Identification

Identify each of the following, and explain why it is important within the context of the chapter.

1. Powhatan
2. "adventurers"
3. "starving time"
4. A Counterblaste to Tobacco
5. John Rolfe
6. headright system
7. House of Burgesses
8. Opechancanough
9. Maryland's Act Concerning Religion
10. Sir William Berkeley
11. Oliver Cromwell
12. Green Springs group
13. Scrooby congregation
14. William Bradford
15. John Winthrop
16. Thomas Hooker
17. Fundamental Orders of Connecticut
18. Roger Williams
19. Flintlock rifle
20. Earl of Shaftesbury
21. Sir George Carteret
22. Society of Friends
23. William Penn's "Holy Experiment"
24. New Mexico
25. James Oglethorpe
26. George Trustees
27. Edmund Andros
28. William and Mary

29. Jacob Leisler

30. John Coode

Document 1

An expedition under Captain Christopher Newport began the Jamestown settlement in May 1607. In June, Captain Newport sailed for England, leaving behind 104 settlers. In September, only forty-six of them were still living. One of the survivors, George Percy, wrote an account of the terrible time at Jamestown.

> There were never Englishmen left in a foreign country in such misery as we were in this new discovered Virginia. We watched every three nights, lying on the bare cold ground, what weather soever came; and warded all the next day; which brought our men to be most feeble wretches. Our food was but a small can of barley, sodden in water, to five men a day. Our drink, cold water taken out of the river; which was at flood very salt; at low tide full of slime and filth, which was the destruction of many of our men. Thus we lived for the space of five months [from August 1607 to January 1608] in this miserable distress, not having five able men to man our bulwarks upon any occasion. If it had not pleased God to put a terror in the savages' hearts we had all perished by those wild and cruel pagans, being in that weak estate as we were; our men night and day groaning in every corner of the fort most pitiful to hear. . . . It pleased God after a while to send those people which were our mortal enemies; to relieve us with victuals, as bread, corn, fish, and flesh in great plenty, which was the setting up of our feeble men; otherwise we had all perished.

Document 2

Having read Document 1, examine the excerpt from a letter from one John Pory, written from Virginia in 1619 and printed below. What obvious changes had taken place between the times the two accounts were written? What caused these changes? In answering this question, reread the section in the text on Jamestown and Virginia, paying special attention to the incentives offered at various times by the company. How does the comparison and contrast of these two documents help to explain what was needed to succeed in Virginia? Do you feel that Pory's letter is an accurate description of what really existed in Virginia? Explain your answer.

> All our riches for the present doe consiste in Tobacco, wherein one man by his owne labour hath in one yeare raised to himselfe to the value of 2000 pounds sterling; and another by the meanes of six servants hath cleared at one crop a thousand pound English. These be true, yet indeed rare examples, yet possible to be done by others. Our principall wealth (I should have said) consisteth in servants: But they are chardgeable to be furnished with armes, apparell and bedding and for their transportation and casual, both at sea, and for their first yeare commonly at lande also: But if they escape, they prove very hardy, and sound able men.
>
> Nowe that your lordship may knowe, that we are not the veriest beggers in the worlde, our cowekeeper here of James citty on Sundays goes accowtered all in freshe flaming silke; and a wife of one that in England had professed the black arte, not of a scholler, but of a collier of Croydon, weares her rough bever hatt with a faire perle hatband, and a silken suite thereto correspondent. But to leave the Populace, and to come higher; the Governour here, who at his first coming besides a great deale of worth in his person, brought onely his sword with him was at his late being in London, together with his lady, out of his meer gettings here, able to disburse very near three thousand pounds to furnishe himselfe for his voiage. And once within seven yeares, I am persuaded (absit invidia verbo) that the Governors place here may be as profitable as the lord Deputies of Irland.

Documents 1 and 2 are from Lyon Gardiner Tyler, ed., Narratives of Early Virginia, 1606–1625 (New York: Scribner, 1907), pp. 284–285.

Document 3

In 1679, a formal synod (church council) made up of the leaders of the Puritan oligarchy under Increase Mather met in Boston and, after examining the conditions of the colony, issued the report that historian Perry Miller describes here. What conditions gave rise to the synod's attack on the way the people in Massachusetts were living? Were these Puritans concerned only with religious failings, or was there something else behind their actions? What was happening to the Puritan oligarchy at this time?

First, there was a great and visible decay of godliness. Second, there were several manifestations of pride—contention in the churches, insubordination of inferiors toward superiors, particularly of those inferiors who had, unaccountably, acquired more wealth than their betters, and, astonishingly, a shocking extravagance in attire, expecially on the part of these of the meaner sort, who persisted in dressing beyond their means. Third, there were heretics, especially Quakers and Anabaptists. Fourth, a notable increase in swearing and a spreading disposition to sleep at sermons (these two phenomena seemed basically connected). Fifth, the Sabbath was wantonly violated. Sixth, family government had decayed, and fathers no longer kept their sons and daughters from prowling at night. Seventh, instead of people being knit together as one man in mutual love, they were full of contention, so that lawsuits were on the increase and lawyers were thriving. Under the eighth head, the synod described the sins of sex and alcohol, thus producing some of the juiciest prose of the period: militia days had become orgies, taverns were crowded; women threw temptation in the way of befuddled men by wearing false locks and displaying naked necks and arms "or, which is more abominable, naked Breasts"; there were "mixed Dancings," along with light behavior and "Company-keeping" with vain persons, wherefore the bastardy rate was rising. In 1672, there was actually an attempt to supply Boston with a brothel (it was suppressed, but the synod was bearish about the future). Ninth, New Englanders were betraying a marked disposition to tell lies, especially when selling anything. In the tenth place, the business morality of even the most righteous left everything to be desired: the wealthy speculated in land and raised prices excessively; "Day-Labourers and Mechanicks are unreasonable in their demands." In the eleventh place, the people showed no disposition to reform, and in the twelfth, they seemed utterly destitute of civic spirit.

"The things here insisted on," said the synod, "have been oftentimes mentioned and inculcated by those who the Lord hath set as Watchmen to the house of Israel." Indeed they had been, and thereafter they continued to be even more inculcated. At the end of the century, the synod's report was serving as a kind of handbook for preachers: they would take some verse of Isaiah or Jeremiah, set up the doctrine that God avenges the iniquities of a chosen people, and then run down the twelve heads, merely bringing the list up to date by inserting the new and still more depraved practices an ingenious people kept on devising. I suppose that in the whole literature of the world, including the satirists of imperial Rome, there is hardly such another uninhibited and unrelenting documentation of a people's descent into corruption.

Reprinted by permission of the publishers from Errand into the Wilderness by Perry Miller. Cambridge, Mass.: The Belknap Press of Harvard University Press. Copyright ©1956 by the President and Fellows of Harvard College.

Map Exercise

Fill in or identify the following on the blank map provided. Use the map in the text as your source.

1. Colonial grants to Massachusetts Bay, Plymouth, New Haven, Hartford, Rhode Island, and the Duke of York.
2. Connecticut, New York, New Hampshire, and Maine.
3. Principal settlements in these colonies and the dates they were founded.

4. Connecticut River and Merrimack River.

5. Lake Champlain, Massachusetts Bay, Cape Cod, Narragansett Bay, and the main islands along the coast.

6. The Mason and Gorges grants.

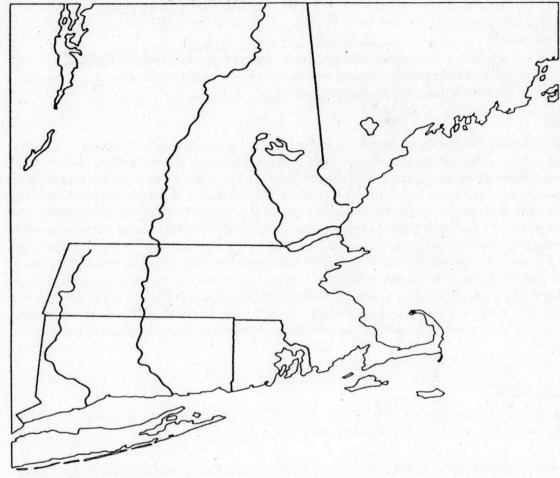

Interpretative Questions

Based on what you have filled in, answer the following. On some of the questions you will need to consult the narrative in your text for information or explanation.

1. Note the patterns of settlement in New England. What geographic features contributed to the placement of these settlements? Why did these geographic features make a difference to early settlers?

2. Looking again at the physical map of the United States, determine which settlements were in the coastal plain, which were in the piedmont, and which were along the fall line. How did the location of these settlements influence their economic growth? How would this shape the sort of societies that developed there?

3. Note the dates these settlements were established. What conclusions about the evolution of the settlements can you draw from these dates? (Consider political events as well as geographic conditions.)

4. Examine the chart of The White Population of New England, 1620–1700 located next to the map you are studying. Compare the dates of settlements with the growth of the population. Where were most colonists settling? What does this indicate about the population density of New England?

5. Note the locations of Boston, Providence, Hartford, and New Haven. What geographic features helped determine their locations? How did these features help shape the local economy of these settlements?

6. Massachusetts Bay was, or at least attempted to be, the dominant force in New England. How did that colony's land claims and expansion contribute to this? How did the location of new colonies serve to check the influence of Massachusetts Bay?

Summary

During the seventeenth century, colonies were established in British North America. This was accomplished in no small part because of exchanges between Europeans and the natives. Before 1660, most colonies began as private ventures (with charters from the king), but the motives that brought them into being were as varied as the sociopolitical systems they developed. After 1660, proprietary colonies became the norm, and charters indicated a closer tie between the "owners" of a colony and the king, who granted the charter. As a result of this colonization effort, by the 1680s England had an unbroken string of provinces stretching from Canada to the Savannah River. As the colonies matured, their inhabitants began to exhibit a concern for control of local affairs and an independence of interests that eventually came to trouble the British Empire. It was a time when colonists began to sense that they were both English and American, a dual personality that was to lead to trouble and confusion on both sides of the Atlantic. The problem was that at the very time that the American colonists were developing attitudes and institutions distinctly American, England, fully aware of the potential of its colonies, began to tighten its control of its possessions.

Review Questions

These questions are to be answered with essays. This will allow you to explore relationships between individuals, events, and attitudes of the period under review.

1. Compare and contrast Virginia and Plymouth—their origins, their goals, and their early social, political, and economic development.

2. Between 1660 and 1700, the American colonies were shaken by a series of "revolts" that, it has been contended, were the result of tensions in colonial society. Examine the protests that took place in Virginia, Maryland, Massachusetts, and New York, and then compare and contrast the internal divisions that helped spark the outbreaks.

3. By 1660, it was evident that England had become concerned about Massachusetts's lack of cooperation with the mother country's policies. Why did England view Massachusetts as a "trouble maker" (if not an outright enemy), and why, in turn, did the people of the Massachusetts Bay colony have the same opinion of England?

4. Having assessed the reasons behind England's attitude toward Massachusetts (and vice versa), explain England's policy toward the Bay colony and how the Puritans reacted to the various attempts to control them.

5. Explain the way in which England applied the principles of mercantilism to its Caribbean and North American colonies.

6. What were the "middle grounds"? What two populations tried to occupy them? How was this accomplished and what was the ultimate result of the effort?

Chapter Self Test

After you have read the chapter in the text and done the exercises in the Study Guide, take the following self test to see if you understand the material you have covered. Answers appear at the end of the Study Guide.

MULTIPLE-CHOICE QUESTIONS

Circle the letter of the response which best answers the question or completes the statement.

1. Which of the following did not shape the character of English settlements in America?
   a. The colonies were business enterprises.
   b. The colonies promoted freedom and religion.
   c. The colonies were designed to transplant society from the old world to the new.
   d. The colonies were able to develop their own political and social institutions.

2. Captain John Smith helped Jamestown survive when he:
   a. divided the duties and privileges of leadership among several members of a council.
   b. imposed work and order on the colony.
   c. ended raids perpetrated on neighboring Indian villages to steal food and kidnap natives.
   d. divided the colony's profits among the stockholders.

3. The Englishman who first cultivated tobacco in Virginia was:
   a. John Smith.
   b. Lord De La Warr.
   c. John Rolfe.
   d. Walter Raleigh.

4. The year 1619 was important in the history of Virginia because that year the colony:
   a. elected its first House of Burgesses.
   b. made its first profit.
   c. received its first royal governor.
   d. put down an Indian uprising.

5. To entice new laborers to their colony, the Virginia Company established the "headright" system to:
   a. pay the Indians for their services.
   b. import African slaves.
   c. grant land to current and prospective settlers.
   d. promise the colonists the full rights of Englishmen.

6. In 1619, two new elements were introduced into the Virginia social order. They were:
   a. women and Catholics.
   b. mestizos and blacks.
   c. blacks and women.
   d. women and mestizos.

7. Which of the following colonies allowed freedom of religion to all Christians?
   a. Massachusetts.
   b. Virginia.
   c. Plymouth.
   d. Maryland.

8. Which of the following factors contributed to the outbreak of Bacon's Rebellion?
   a. The autocratic rule of Governor Berkeley.
   b. Overrepresentation in government of the frontier settlements.
   c. The government's pursuit and destruction of Indian marauders.
   d. All of the above.

9. Bacon's Rebellion was significant because:
   a. it revealed the bitterness of competition among rival elites in Virginia.
   b. it was evidence of the continuing struggle to define the Indian and white spheres of influence in Virginia.
   c. it demonstrated the potential for instability in the colony's large population of landless men.
   d. of a. and c.
   e. of all of the above.

10. Caribbean colonies built their economies on:
    a. the slave trade.
    b. shipbuilding.
    c. export crops.
    d. fishing.

11. Many Virginians turned to slaves rather than to indentured servants for labor because Africans:
    a. already knew how to raise tobacco.
    b. did not have to be released, so there was no fear that they might become an unstable, landless class.
    c. were cheaper to purchase at the outset.
    d. were more naturally subservient and caused the master no trouble.

12. The majority of colonists who first settled in Plymouth were:
    a. members of a Puritan Separatist congregation.
    b. not members of a Puritan Separatist congregation.
    c. upper middle class Puritans from the London area.
    d. moderate Puritans who wanted only minor reforms in church practices.

13. The first governor of the Massachusetts Bay colony was:
    a. John Winthrop.
    b. William Bradford.
    c. Roger Williams.
    d. Thomas Hooker.

14. Anne Hutchinson's teaching threatened to undermine the spiritual authority of the established clergy because she:

    a. claimed believers could communicate directly with God.

    b. preached that the clergy was corrupt.

    c. denounced clergymen who were also politicians.

    d. stressed faith over good works.

15. Along the western borders of English settlement, Europeans and Indians lived together in regions where during this period:

    a. Europeans were clearly in control.

    b. neither side was able to establish clear dominance.

    c. Native Americans were clearly superior.

    d. no concessions were made and no quarter given.

16. The Restoration colonies had in common that they were all:

    a. located in the south.

    b. profitable for the crown.

    c. proprietary ventures.

    d. royal colonies.

17. Slavery in Carolina was greatly influenced by slavery in:

    a. Virginia.

    b. Barbados.

    c. St. Augustine.

    d. England.

18. The Navigation Acts were designed to:

    a. regulate commerce according to the theory of mercantilism.

    b. destroy the power of rising colonial merchants.

    c. keep the price of tobacco low.

    d. raise money to pay off England's war debts.

19. The overthrow of James II in the Glorious Revolution was:

    a. well received in New England.

    b. criticized by colonial merchants.

    c. the result of pressure on Edmund Andros.

    d. hardly felt by colonial politicians.

20. In America, the Glorious Revolution of 1688 led to changes which revealed:

    a. a colonial desire for self government.

    b. that local issues were more important than questions over the nature of the empire.

    c. that the institution of monarchy was unpopular.

    d. that the established church was unpopular.

TRUE-FALSE QUESTIONS

Read each statement carefully. Mark true statements "T" and false statements "F."

1. Virginia was a profitable colony from the start.

2. The "headright" system was used to attract colonists to Virginia.

3. Although designed to be "transplantations" from the Old World to the New, the English colonies in America nonetheless developed a distinctive society.

4. The first Africans brought to the English colonies in America arrived on a Dutch ship in 1619 and were immediately sold as slaves.

5. Bacon's Rebellion successfully overthrew the government of Sir William Berkeley.

6. The English planters who settled on Barbados were gentlemen with little ambition apart from finding an easy way of life in the islands.

7. Exchanges of agricultural technology between Indians and Europeans did not benefit Virginia.

8. Roger Williams insisted that the land on which Massachusetts was settled belonged to the Indians, not the king.

9. After New Englanders defeated the local Indians, the French refused to aid the Native Americans.

10. John Locke was the author of the Fundamental Constitution for Carolina.

11. When the English took New Amsterdam, they were able to quickly rid the colony of Dutch influences.

12. Soon after the territory was founded, the Quakers became the largest religious group in Pennsylvania.

13. The majority of colonists who came to Georgia were taken from debtors prison.

14. New Englanders liked the idea of centralized authority under the Dominion of New England.

15. The Navigation Acts increased the authority of the crown and decreased that of local governments.

16. Massachusetts was the colony that the crown could usually count on to support its policies.

17. As a result of the Glorious Revolution, religious toleration in Maryland continued.

18. The Glorious Revolution of 1688 in England had little impact in the colonies.

19. In Massachusetts, each Puritan congregation was free to choose its own minister and regulate its own affairs.

20. From the beginning, the thirteen colonies of North America thought of themselves as a single society, economy, and nation.

CHAPTER THREE
SOCIETY AND CULTURE IN PROVINCIAL AMERICA

Objectives

A thorough study of Chapter Three should enable the student to understand:

1. The disagreement among historians concerning the origins of slavery.
2. The sources of colonial labor, including indentured servants, women, and imported Africans.
3. Immigration patterns and their effect on colonial development.
4. How patterns of birth and death influenced and reflected cultural development in the colonies
5. The ways in which factors of soil and climate determined the commercial and agricultural development of the colonies, despite crown attempts to influence production.
6. The emergence of the plantation system, and its impact on southern society.
7. The New England witchcraft episode as a reflection of the Puritan society.
8. The reasons for the appearance of a variety of religious sects in the colonies, and the effect of the Great Awakening on the colonists.
9. The beginnings of colonial industry and commerce, and the early attempts at regulation by Parliament.
10. The ways in which colonial literature, education, science, law, and justice were diverging from their English antecedents.

Main Themes

1. How the colonial population grew and diversified.
2. How the colonial economy expanded to meet the needs of this rapidly growing population.
3. The emergence of a particularly American "mind and spirit."

Glossary

1. Enlightenment: The intellectual movement that dominated the late seventeenth and eighteenth centuries in Europe. Believing that the universe operated through natural laws that human beings, using their powers of reason, could understand, "enlightened" thinkers argued that once these laws were understood, people could devise means of living within them. Also called the "Age of Reason," this era was marked by an explosion of activity that brought about significant advances in science (especially natural science), education, and government. Stressing that there were certain "natural rights" (life, liberty, and property) that were given to all people—and that it was the duty of government to protect these rights from selfish individuals (those not allowing reason to control their actions)—philosophers of this age called forth many of the principles that Americans later used in their struggle with Britain. From the Enlightenment came the beliefs that freedom is the natural condition of humanity, that governments should be responsible to the governed, and that it is the right of the people to oppose a government that violates the natural rights of its citizens.

2. slavery: A legal status in which an individual is owned by another individual who controls his or her actions and benefits from his or her labor. The status is for life (unless altered by the owner) and is inherited, usually through the mother.

3. class structure: The division of society into recognizable groups. Generally based on wealth, these divisions are also affected by education, family ties, religion, and a variety of other factors recognized by the society in which the divisions exist.

4. paper money in the colonies: In an effort to overcome the lack of money in America, some colonial governments issued paper money to serve as currency. The problem, however, was to get the colonists to accept these paper bills at face value. So, to keep the bills from declining in value, some colonies employed a system (currency finance) in which paper money would be issued for only a specific purpose (for example, to buy goods that the government needed, to pay for services to the government, and so on) and would be accepted by the government, at face value, as payment for taxes or other debts owed to the colony. It was generally hoped that this would be the only exchange and that the money would not circulate; but if it did, the fact that the government would accept it as full payment was believed to be enough to keep it from depreciating greatly. In practice, however, the system did not work. The bills lost their value as they circulated, creating the inflation that opponents of paper money feared. Nevertheless, under a more controlled situation, the concept was indeed workable and, with some changes, is used today.

5. staple crop: The primary export (cash) crop of a region, the crop on which the region's economy rests. In the Chesapeake colonies, the staple was tobacco; farther south, it was rice or indigo. In later years, sugar (the staple in the Indies) was important in some areas on the mainland, but in time the classic staple—cotton—came to dominate the South's economy.

6. evangelicalism: The adherence to the belief that salvation comes through the personal recognition of one's sins, the awareness of one's inability to save oneself, and the acceptance of Christ as the only means of redemption. The process is usually a highly emotional one that culminates in the rebirth ("born again" state) of the sinner and his or her acceptance as one of the evangelical community of believers. The evangelical emphasis on the spiritual rather than the worldly was particularly appealing to the lower classes and to others (for example, women and slaves) who sought a means to affirm their personal worth. This often put evangelicals at odds with their social "betters," who regarded the evangelicals' rejection of those things that defined the social classes (fine dress, leisure activities, civil and religious ceremonies, and such) as an attack on the status and authority of ruling elites.

7. nuclear family: The social unit composed of father, mother, and children.

8. patriarchal: Having to do with a social system in which the father is the head of the family.

Pertinent Questions

THE COLONIAL POPULATION (66-77)

1. Explain the system of indentured servitude that developed in the American colonies. Why was it such an "appealing" system?

2. What impact did freed indentures have on colonial sociopolitical development?

3. Why did most indentures go to Pennsylvania and New York after 1700?

4. What factors contributed to the rapid increase in colonial population during the last half of the seventeenth century?

5. Explain the results that the limited extent of medical knowledge had on colonial society. Who benefited from this limitation?

6. How did the importance of reproduction in the labor-scarce society of colonial America affect the status and life cycle of women? How and why did the status of women in colonial America differ from region to region?

7. Describe the steps that led to the establishment of black slavery in the English-American colonies.

8. Why are the 1690s considered a "turning point in the history of the black population in America"? What had this change resulted in by 1760?

9. Explain the commerce in slaves—how it grew so extensive, more sophisticated, and more horrible.

10. What were the major non-English groups to migrate to America, and why did they come?

11. What were the general characteristics of the colonial population in the first half of the eighteenth century—its rate of growth, cultural composition, settlement patterns?

THE COLONIAL ECONOMIES (77-83)

12. Describe the economy of the Chesapeake region, and explain why it developed as it did.

13. How did the economy of South Carolina and Georgia differ from that of the Chesapeake? How was it similar?

14. Explain the commercial economy that emerged in the northern colonies alongside the agricultural one. What role did technology play in this?

15. What were the limits of colonial technology? Just how self-sufficient were American colonists?

16. What factors gave rise to colonial commercial enterprises? What obstacles did these enterprises have to overcome and what effect did their success have on the colonial economy?

17. What was the "triangular trade," and what does it reveal about colonial economics? How was this a response to British mercantile policies?

18. Explain the growing preoccupation with consumption of material goods in the British colonies and how this preoccupation was associated with social status.

PATTERNS OF SOCIETY (83-89)

19. How did the plantation system in the American South illustrate both the differences between the colonial and English class systems and the way in which colonial communities evolved in response to local conditions?

20. What were the characteristics of plantation slavery?

21. Describe the plantation as an economic unit; as a social unit.

22. What were the characteristics of communities that emerged in Puritan New England?

23. How was the family central to the Puritan community?

24. How did the experience of America affect the patriarchal family?

25. How did the witchcraft hysteria of the 1680s and 1690s result from a "gap between the expectations of a united community and the reality of a diverse and divided one"?

26. What forces gave rise to colonial "cities"?

27. Describe the "distinctive features" of urban life in colonial America.

AWAKENINGS AND ENLIGHTENMENTS (89-96)

28. What were the two powerful forces competing for the American mind in the eighteenth century?
29. What were the major religious groups in the colonies, what elements formed them, and where were they located?
30. What was the Great Awakening? Who brought it about, and what groups supported or opposed it?
31. What were the effects of the Great Awakening?
32. What was the Enlightenment? How did it differ from the Great Awakening?
33. What colonial colleges were in operation by 1763? Why was each founded, and what subjects were studied in the mid-eighteenth century?
34. What evidence was there that the influence of the Enlightenment was spreading in America?
35. Explain the working of the law in colonial
36. America—the concepts on which it was based and the way it functioned.

WHERE HISTORIANS DISAGREE (72-73)

36. How have historians differed over how and why white Americans created a system of slave labor in the seventeenth century?
37. Explain the debate among historians over how and why it was determined that people of African descent should be slaves in America?

PATTERNS OF POPULAR CULTURE

38. Why was it said of almanacs that "no book we read (except the Bible) is so much valued and so serviceable to the community?"
39. In colonial America, what needs did the almanacs fill?

Identification

Identify each of the following, and explain why it is important within the context of the chapter.

1. "seasoning"
2. middle passage
3. Royal African Company
4. "slave codes"
5. Scotch-Irish
6. Eliza Lucas
7. the Saugus works
8. Peter Hasenclever
9. Charles Carroll of Carrollton
10. Gullah

11.   town meeting
12.   "visible saints"
13.   primogeniture
14.   Salem, Massachusetts
15.   George Whitefield
16.   Jonathan Edwards
17.   New Lights/Old Lights
18.   "dame schools"
19.   Cotton Mather
20.   John Peter Zenger

Document 1

In the eighteenth century, slavery was hardly out of the ordinary. It existed in various forms throughout the world, and in Britain's North American colonies, it flourished. What was out of the ordinary was that after centuries of relative silence, around the mid-eighteenth century, people began to speak out against the system. Read the following extract, taken from John Woolman's 1762 work, Some Considerations on the Keeping of Negroes. Woolman was a Quaker. What was it in Quaker theology that might have moved him to take such a stand, and how is this revealed in what he wrote? What argument other than religion does the author offer against slavery? How might slavery be seen as harmful to society as a whole? Do you think that Woolman's appeal moved the slaveholder? Why or why not?

If we seriously consider that liberty is the right of innocent men; that the mighty God is a refuge for the oppressed; that in reality we are indebted to them; that they being set free, are still liable to the penalties of our laws, and as likely to have punishment for their crimes as other people: this may answer all our objections. And to retain them in perpetual servitude, without just cause for it, will produce effects, in the event, more grievous than setting them free would do, when a real love to truth and equity was the motive to it. . . .

He that hath a servant, made so wrongfully, and knows it to be so, when he treats him otherwise than a free man, when he reaps the benefit of his labor, without paying him such wages as are reasonably due to free men for the like service, clothes excepted; these things, though done in calmness, without any shew of disorder, do yet deprave the mind in like manner, and with as great certainty as prevailing cold congeals water. These steps taken by masters, and their conduct striking the minds of their children, whilst young, leave less room for that which is good to work upon them. The customs of their parents, their neighbors, and the people with whom they converse, working upon their minds; and they, from thence, conceiving ideas of things, and modes of conduct, the entrance into their heart becomes, in a great measure, shut up against the gentle movings of uncreated purity.

Negroes are our fellow creatures, and their present condition amongst us requires our serious consideration. We know not the time when those scales in which mountains are weighed may turn. The Parent of mankind is gracious; His care is over His smallest creatures; and a multitude of men escape not His notice. And though many of them are trodden down, and despised, yet He remembers them; He seeth their affliction, and looketh upon the spreading, increasing exaltation of the oppressor. He turns the channels of power, humbles the most haughty people, and gives deliverance to the oppressed, at such periods as are consistent with His infinite justice and goodness. And wherever gain is preferred to equity, and wrong things publicly encouraged, to that degree that wickedness takes root, and spreads wide amongst the inhabitants of a country, there is real cause for sorrow to all such whose love to mankind stands on a true principle, and who wisely consider the end and event of things.

John Woolman, Some Considerations on the Keeping of Negroes (1762).

Document 2

Georgia, for reasons other than those advanced by John Woolman, tried to prohibit slavery. But by the 1740s, the clamor for black labor was growing, and it was only a matter of time before slavery would be legal in Georgia. Below is an excerpt from "A Brief Account of the Causes that Have Retarded the Progress of the Colony of Georgia." What are the reasons given to support demands for slave labor, and why did these reasons have a greater impact on colonists than did Woolman's arguments against slavery? How does the author of this tract refute the contention that people can succeed without slaves (especially in the case of the Saltzburgers, Protestant refugees led by their minister, the Reverend Boltzius)? What other reasons are given to explain why some Georgians still opposed slavery despite its obvious benefits to white colonists?

. . . But as if the difficulties arising from indifferent lands, and discouraging tenures, were not sufficient to humble and prepare them for the other severities they have met with, they were totally prohibited the importation, use, or even sight of negroes. In spite of all endeavors to disguise this point, it is as clear as light itself, that negroes are as essentially necessary to the cultivation of Georgia, as axes, hoes, or any other utensil of agriculture. So that if a colony was designed able but to subsist itself, their prohibition was inconsistent; if a garrison only was intended, the very inhabitants were needless: but all circumstances considered, it looked as if the assistance of human creatures, who have been called slaves, as well as subject to the treatment of such, were incongruous with a system that proceeded to confer the thing, but to spare the odium of the appellation. Experience would too soon have taught them the parity of their conditions, in spite of a mere nominal difference. The only English clergymen, who were ever countenanced there, declared they never desired to see Georgia a rich, but a godly colony; and the blind subjection the poor Saltzburgers are under to the Rev. Mr. Boltzius, who has furnished such extraordinary extracts in some accounts of Georgia, published here, will be too evident from some of the annexed depositions to call for any descant.

The pretended content and satisfaction of the people of Ebenezer, without negroes, will plainly appear to be the dictates of spiritual tyranny, and only the wretched acquiescence of people, who were in truth unacquainted with the privilege of choosing for themselves.

It is acknowledged indeed that the present war, and late invasion, may furnish the enemies of the colony with the most plausible objections that could occur, against the allowance of black slaves; but these reasons have not always existed, nor have the trustees ever declared any resolution to admit them, at any other juncture. But if it plainly appears that Georgia, as a colony, cannot barely exist without them, surely an admission of them under limitations, suitable to the present situation of affairs, is absolutely necessary to its support; since want and famine must be more dreadful and insuperable invaders, than any living enemy: besides, the honorable trustees were informed by a letter from Mr. Stirling and others, of the falsehood, of the contended and comfortable situation the people of Darien were affirmed to be in; and that they were bought with a number of cattle, and extensive promises of future rewards, when they signed their petition against negroes. . . .

"A Brief Account of the Causes that Have Retarded the Progress of the Colony of Georgia," Collections of the Georgia Historical Society 2(1842): 93–94.

Document 3

Below is the report of the "confession" of Mary Osgood of Andover, Massachusetts, which was given on September 8, 1692, before a group of judges.

> She confesses that, about 11 years ago, when she was in a melancholy state and condition, she used to walk abroad in her orchard; and upon a certain time she saw the appearance of a cat, at the end of the house, which yet she thought was a real cat. However, at that time, it diverted her from praying to God, and instead thereof she prayed to the devil; about which time she made a covenant with the devil, who, as a black man, came to her and presented her a book, upon which she laid her finger, and that left a red spot: and that upon her signing, the devil told her he was her God, and that she should serve and worship him, and she believes she consented to it. She says, further, that about two years agone, she was carried through the air, in company with deacon Frye's wife, Ebenezer Baker's wife, and Goody Tyler, to five mile pond, where she was baptised by the devil, who dipped her face in the water and made her renounce her former baptism, and told her she must be his, soul and body, forever, and that she must serve him, which she promised to do.

Six weeks later, Mrs. Osgood visited the Puritan divine Increase Mather. He reported that she had recanted.

> Mrs. Osgood freely and relentingly said that the confession which she made upon her examination for witchcraft, and afterwards acknowledged before the honourable judges, was wholly false, and that she was brought to the said confession by the violent urging and unreasonable pressings that were used toward her; she asserted that she never signed the devil's book, was never baptised by the devil, never afflicted any of the accusers, or gave her consent for their being afflicted.

In the light of what you have read in your text, what do these documents tell you about religion in the Massachusetts Bay colony, the relationship between church and state in that colony, and the impact of religion on the lives of the Puritans? Reread Document 3 in Chapter Two. How might Puritan leaders have believed that witches were just another manifestation of the fall from grace that had taken place in the colony? How might the witch trials have helped to restore the power that Puritan leaders felt they had lost?

Document 4

Although they were very different sorts of men, Jonathan Edwards and George Whitefield used emotional appeals to try to make sinners realize the danger they faced and to see how necessary it was for them to put full faith in Christ and be "born again." Following is an excerpt from one of Edwards's most famous sermons, which he preached at Enfield, Connecticut, in 1741. An original and systematic theologian, Edwards presented his audience with a vivid picture of the terrors awaiting them if they did not repent; his evocations of hell produced great "breathing of distress, and weeping." Whitefield's sermons were said to have had much the same effect.

> More orthodox ministers felt that Edwards and Whitefield were appealing to the emotions rather than to the intellect and were distressed at what seemed to be a movement that ran counter to reason. What evidence can you find to support this allegation? How might Edwards and Whitefield have answered such charges?

> Your wickedness makes you as it were heavy as lead, and to tend downwards with great weight and pressure towards hell; and if God should let you go, you would immediately sink and swiftly descend and plunge into the bottomless gulf. . . .

O sinner! Consider the fearful danger you are in: it is a great furnace of wrath, a wide and bottomless pit, full of the fire of wrath, that you are held over in the hand of God. . . . You hang by a slender thread, with the flames of divine wrath flashing about it, and ready every moment to singe it, and burn it asunder. . . .

And now you have an extraordinary opportunity, a day wherein Christ has thrown the door of mercy wide open, and stands in the door calling and crying with a loud voice to poor sinners. . . .

And let everyone that is yet out of Christ, and hanging over the pit of hell, . . . now hearken to the loud calls of God's word and providence. This acceptable year of the Lord, a day of such great favours to some, will doubtless be a day of as remarkable vengeance to others. . . .

Document 5

Hugh Bryan and his wife, Catherine, were members of a small group of southern gentry who became followers of George Whitefield. Once they were "reborn," they began to reject worldly things and to concentrate on spiritual concerns, which caused them to renounce many of the things that defined the class to which they belonged. Their renunciation not only caused concern among the gentry, who saw this as an attack on their class and its authority, but also created divisions in the Bryan family. The letter was written by Bryan to his daughter, who had strayed from the path set by Whitefield. What does it tell you about the demands that evangelicalism put on individuals? What are the implications in this letter with regard to the division into and distinction among social classes in colonial America? What impact might changes such as Bryan suggested have had on political power? What does this letter reveal about the patriarchal family in the colonies and about the status of women? Reread Document 4, and consider that it was a sermon such as Edwards's except written by Whitefield, that moved Hugh Bryan.

DEAR CHILD,

Considering the continual scene of vanities before you in that town where you are, which pass under the names of neatness, and innocent diversions and amusements, I shall not be surprised to hear that my last was a disagreeable letter, enjoining unnecessary restraints, and laying you under an obligation to be singular, and consequently to be pointed at, and perhaps ridiculed; but, my dear, let such thoughts put you upon seeking to God for his directions for that true wisdom by which only you may understand his will. God will give liberally, see James I. ver. 5. if we seek with honest and holy intentions to promote his glory, in devoting our lives to his service, which only is the true end of our being. . . . The soul that seeks happiness must be open, and willing to receive reproof, as well as instruction; remember and bear constantly in mind, that in your baptismal vow, you have absolutely renounced all the vanities of this world, and that every superfluous thing is a vanity which you are to shun. All discourse which has no tendency to your own good, or to the good of others, is idle, unprofitable, and sinful, and your actions are to be governed by the same rule; therefore when you find in you an inclination to any vanities, lift up your prayer to God for strength to enable you, and resolve immediately to turn your heart to some object, or subject that may be agreeable to his will. . . .

And now, my dear, can it be a restraint on a soul thus disposed, to refrain vain songs, dancings, and fine dress, or light and unprofitable discourse and diversions? Or will no spiritual songs, hymns, and psalms of praise be more noble, and suitable, and agreeable to raise its affections to the true objects of its love? And will not a plain clean dress, profitable discourse that may inform the judgment, and such diversions only as may fit and prepare both body and soul for the true and only end of its being, namely, to glorify God, be its only delight and constant aim and happiness, even in this life? . . .

O! rest not, my dear, in the love of worldly goods; get out of this spiritual Sodom, from the vain sensual delights which pollute the soul, lest you be consumed with the wicked; flee to your most gracious redeemer, seek to him with strong and constant prayers to accept and justify you by his free grace, and sanctify your corrupt nature by his Holy Spirit, that your whole soul and body may be prepared for his service, and devoted entirely to do his will.

From your affectionate father,

H.B.

Hugh Bryan and Mary Hutson, <u>Living Christianity</u> (London: J. Buckland, 1760), pp. 21–24.

Map Exercise

Fill in or identify the following on the blank map provided. Use the map in the text as your source.

1. British North American colonies.
2. Colonial groups—southern, middle, and New England.
3. Principal settlements in each colony.
4. Principal rivers in each colony.
5. Using different colors, identify dominant imigrant groups.

Interpretative Questions

Based on what you have filled in, answer the following. On some of the questions you will need to consult the narrative in your text for information or explanation.

1. Refer to the map in the text and compare the settled areas in 1700 to those in 1760. Where did the most dramatic changes occur? What immigrant groups were most involved?

2. What was the major non-English immigrant group in the southern colonies? What circumstances led to their immigration to the New World? Why were they concentrated in the South rather than in other regions?

3. Who were the Scotch-Irish? Why did they leave their homeland, and why did they settle where they did? How would the conditions that led to their immigration and settlement have affected their attitude toward England and English colonial governments?

4. Note the location of German immigrant groups. Why did they leave their homeland, and why did they settle where they did? How would the conditions that led to their immigration and settlement have affected their attitude toward England and English colonial governments?

5. Why were the Dutch located where they were? Was this a post-1700 immigrant group? Why did they leave their homeland and settle where they did? By 1760 what changes in society in this region might you expect?

6. Note where the English are concentrated. Which are the most "English" colonies and regions? Why would the southern colonies continue to have a strong English orientation despite the presence of a large immigrant group?

Summary

After the turmoil of the late seventeenth century had subsided, it became evident that the English-American colonies and the colonists who populated them were beginning to develop characteristics that were distinctly "American." Although still essentially transplanted English subjects and still greatly influenced by European ideas and institutions, the colonists were also diverse, aggressive, and as concerned with their own success as with that of the empire of which they were part. New sources of wealth and new patterns of trade shaped the growth of the colonies, and new immigrants, not always from England, added a dimension unknown in the mother country. Although differences in geography, economy, and population gave each colony its own particular character and problems, there remained many common concerns—not the least of which was how to deal with, or avoid dealing with, British mercantile restrictions. In short, between 1700 and 1750, Britain's American colonies began to show signs of being both English and American; they were indeed "different," and it is this difference that Chapter Three explores.

Review Questions

These questions are to be answered with essays. This will allow you to explore relationships between individuals, events, and attitudes of the period under review.

1. Compare and contrast the economy of the northern colonies with that of the southern colonies. What made the two regions develop as they did? How did these economic systems reflect social systems emerging at the same time?

2. Who were these Americans? Write an essay in which you describe the diverse populations that settled the British colonies in the sixteenth and seventeenth centuries, and assess the growth of the population during this period.

3. By violating the Navigation Acts and developing their own trading patterns, were the American colonies creating their own mercantile system? Discuss this question and the implications it might have for future relations with England.

4. What role did religion play in the advance of education in America? In what way did religion also hinder education? After assessing these two relationships, show the extent to which the fruits of education (reading, writing, science, and law) flourished in America; at the same time, show how these helped to form a character that was "American."

Chapter Self Test

After you have read the chapter in the text and done the exercises in the Study Guide, take the following self test to see if you understand the material you have covered. Answers appear at the end of the Study Guide.

MULTIPLE-CHOICE QUESTIONS

Circle the letter of the response which best answers the question or completes the statement.

1. During the seventeenth century, at least three-fourths of the immigrants who came to the Chesapeake colonies came as:
    a. slaves.
    b. artisans.
    c. indentured servants.
    d. convicts.

2. The high mortality rate in the colonies had the effect of:
    a. weakening the traditional patriarchal family structure.
    b. creating significant labor shortages in New England.
    c. making it difficult for women to find husbands.
    d. keeping the birth rate low.

3. In the Puritan colonies, the principal economic and religious unit in the community was the:
    a. family.
    b. meeting house.
    c. town meetings.
    d. small farm.

4. The mid-1690s marked a turning point in the history of the black population in America because:
    a. planters from Barbados came to Carolina.
    b. slavery was introduced in Georgia.
    c. Massachusetts and Rhode Island abolished slavery.
    d. the Royal Africa Company lost its monopoly.

5. The one factor which determined whether a person was subject to the slave codes in the British American colonies was:
    a. their country of origin.
    b. the ancestry of their father.
    c. the ancestry of their mother.
    d. their African ancestry.

6. Historian Edmund S. Morgan argued that the institutionalization of African slavery in America reflected:

   a. an effort by colonial governments to attract more white indentured servants by offering them a relatively high status.

   b. the deep seated racism that white settlers had brought with them.

   c. white fears of black resistance or even revolt.

   d. economic and social needs for an easily recruited and controlled labor force.

7. The most numerous of the non-English immigrants were the:

   a. Scotch-Irish.

   b. Pennsylvania Dutch.

   c. French Huguenots.

   d. Scottish Highlanders.

8. Which of the following was <u>not</u> one of the reasons that Africans were so valuable to planters along the Carolina and Georgia coasts?

   a. They could be forced to do work that white laborers refused to do.

   b. They often came from rice-producing regions of Africa.

   c. They were more accustomed to the hot and humid climate.

   d. They could be counted on to work the fields without protest.

9. Conditions for agriculture were good in Pennsylvania because of the:

   a. cold weather and rocky soil.

   b. concentration of land ownership and the maintenance of great estates.

   c. success of German immigrants in applying European methods of intensive cultivation.

   d. oversupply of single male workers.

10. A common problem in American commerce in the seventeenth century was:

   a. the lack of a commonly accepted currency.

   b. an insufficient number of ships to carry colonial goods.

   c. too many large companies in every colony.

   d. a small, unprofitable coastal trade.

11. The maze of highly diverse trade routes that involved the buying and selling of rum, slaves, and sugar was known as the:

   a. staple system.

   b. triangular trade.

   c. middle passage.

   d. Atlantic highway.

12. During the seventeenth century, colonial plantations were:

   a. rough and relatively small.

   b. English country estates on a smaller scale.

   c. seats of an entrenched, landholding aristocracy.

   d. insignificant in the colonial economy.

13. African slaves in the colonial South:

   a. were rigidly separated from whites.

   b. were widely scattered on small farms, seldom in contact with one another.

c. often participated in various forms of organized resistance.

d. began to develop a society and culture of their own.

14. The characteristic social unit in New England was the:

    a. isolated farm.

    b. meeting house.

    c. town.

    d. plantation.

15. In colonial New England, tensions between expectations of a cohesive, united community and the reality of an increasingly diverse and fluid one led to:

    a. a general economic decline.

    b. the witch trials.

    c. a decline in piety.

    d. the rise of the merchant class.

16. Which of the following was <u>not</u> a function of a colonial American city?

    a. They were trading centers.

    b. They were centers of industry.

    c. They were intellectual centers.

    d. They were areas of few social distinctions.

17. In matters of religion, Americans were:

    a. less tolerant than their English counterparts.

    b. more tolerant than their English counterparts.

    c. more inclined to be members of an Anglican congregation.

    d. unconcerned about piety, especially in New England.

18. Which of the following was <u>not</u> a reason for the decline of piety in colonial America?

    a. Denominationalism.

    b. Rise of towns.

    c. Corrupt ministers.

    d. The importation of Englightenment ideas.

19. The Great Awakening was:

    a. an effort to alert colonists to British efforts to control them politically.

    b. the way the Englightenment influenced American education.

    c. the opening of new commercial opportunities in the West.

    d. the first great American revival.

20. During the first half of the eighteenth century, colonial legislatures were generally:

    a. able to act independently of Parliament.

    b. controlled by the governor.

    c. free from class distinctions.

    d. a reflection of democracy in their respective colonies.

TRUE-FALSE QUESTIONS

Read each statement carefully. Mark true statements "T" and false statements "F."

1. After the 1650s, natural increase became the most important source of population growth in New England.

2. In colonial America few women remained unmarried for long.

3. The survival rate for children was higher in the South than in any other section.

4. Because women were scarce in colonial America, they were not bound by patriarchal authority.

5. The "middle passage" was the route taken by settlers trying to get to the Ohio Valley.

6. Africans were enslaved from the time of their arrival.

7. The earliest non-English European immigrants to arrive in the British-American colonies were the Huguenots.

8. Between 1700 and 1775 the colonial population increased from under 300,000 to over 2 million.

9. During the colonial era most colonists were self-sufficient farmers.

10. The largest industrial enterprise in English North America employed fewer than 100 workers.

11. Although colonial urban centers were small, most of the activities associated with cities were carried out there.

12. A great landowner in colonial America was powerful on his estate, but generally had no influence beyond the boundary of his property.

13. Southern society was fluid and therefore not highly stratified.

14. There were no significant slave rebellions during the colonial era.

15. The rigid patriarchal structure of the Puritan family limited opportunities for younger male members to strike out on their own.

16. In New England, what happened at Salem was unique because very few Puritans believed in witches.

17. During the colonial era there was a growing preoccupation with the consumption of material goods and these possessions were directly associated with social status.

18. With access to "dame schools," American women enjoyed a higher degree of literacy than did men.

19. Most of the early colleges in America were started for religious reasons.

20. In the John Peter Zenger case, the court held that criticism of the government was not libelous if factually true.

CHAPTER FOUR
THE EMPIRE IN TRANSITION

Objectives

A thorough study of Chapter Four should enable the student to understand:

1. The primary reasons for the growth of the differences between colonial Americans and the British government that resulted in a clash of interests.

2. The colonial attitudes toward England and toward other colonies before the Great War for empire.

3. The causes of the Great War for empire, and the reasons for the French defeat.

4. The effects of the war on the American colonists and on the status of the colonies within the British Empire.

5. The options available to the British for dealing with the colonies in 1763, and the reasons for adopting the policies that they chose to implement.

6. The importance of the series of crises from the Sugar Act through the Coercive Acts, and how each crisis changed colonial attitudes toward the mother country.

7. The change in American attitudes toward Parliament, the English constitution, and the king. What such slogans as "No taxation without representation" really meant.

8. The significance of the convening of the First Continental Congress, and what it accomplished.

9. Lexington and Concord—who fired the first shot, and does it really matter?

Main Theme

How it was that colonists who, for the most part, had enjoyed benefits unattainable by their European counterparts, rose in rebellion against the nation that was responsible for their circumstances.

Glossary

1. imperialism: The policy of extending a nation's sovereignty to include possessions beyond the boundaries of the nation (colonies). In the seventeenth and eighteenth centuries, this was directly associated with mercantilism.

2. sovereignty: Supreme power, independent of and unlimited by any other force, as in a sovereign state.

3. old colonial system: The period extending from the mid-seventeenth century to the mid-eighteenth century, characterized by the acts, regulations, and enforcement institutions used by Britain to govern its colonies. Influenced by the theory of mercantilism, England first tried to direct colonial commerce through the mother country and regulate it through the Board of Trade and Plantations. But finding that the colonies (and, as a result, the empire) prospered under a less restrictive system, England eased enforcement, and the policy of "salutary neglect" (neglect for the good of all) emerged. It has been argued that had the British not altered this policy during and after the Great War for the empire, the American Revolution might not have taken place as it did, so content were the colonists with the economic freedom and relative self-government that the "old colonial system" provided.

4. new colonial system: The system that emerged after 1763 (although there is evidence that the change was taking place in the 1740s) when the British government decided to reorganize the colonial system on more efficient (and profitable) lines. What it did was to alter the relationship between colonies and the mother country, stressing the supremacy of the latter just at the time that most North American provinces were feeling more secure and self-confident than ever before. Characterized by a series of acts that not only taxed the colonies, but also attempted to enforce collection, this "new" system stood in stark contrast to the "old" and raised fears in the colonies that if these actions were not opposed, even worse would follow. From the British standpoint, however, the "new colonial system" was simply an effort to get the colonies to pay for their own administration and to discourage the illegal trade that had flourished during the period of salutary neglect—neither of which concept the mother country felt was unreasonable.

5. commonwealth: A political body governed by its own elected representatives.

6. federation: A union of sovereign powers in which each unit retains the power to control its own local affairs.

7. right of revolution: A concept found in the writings of John Locke which holds that if a government denies its people their natural rights, those people have the right—indeed, the duty—to rise up against the oppressive government, overthrow it (by force if necessary), and establish a more responsive government in its place. This, Locke contended, was what had taken place during the Glorious Revolution. It was also, Thomas Jefferson later contended, what brought about the American Revolution.

8. Whig: The name given the English political faction responsible for the Glorious Revolution. Basing its power in Parliament, it opposed arbitrary rule by the monarch, calling instead for the country to be governed by the representatives chosen by those people qualified to vote (essentially an electorate limited to the upper-class males). In America, many who protested against England's new colonial system adopted the name Whig, to indicate that they, too, opposed arbitrary rule and believed that government should rest in the hands of the people's representatives. Their point, however, was that the British government (specifically Parliament at first and later the king) was attempting to govern without legitimate authority and that the true representatives of the people in the colonies were the colonial assemblies. In this way, colonial opponents of British policies called attention to their belief that their protests were part of the tradition of opposition to tyranny on which the very government they protested claimed to have been founded.

9. Loyalists (Tories): Americans who, for many and varied reasons, remained loyal to the king and were called Tories by American Whigs. The name Tory came from the English political faction that supported the king and was less willing to see Parliament (especially the House of Commons) rise to power. American Tories rejected this classification, calling themselves Loyalists instead. In fact, some Loyalists argued that the real threat to liberty was not the king and Parliament, but groups, such as the Sons of Liberty, that carried out their programs through threats and violence. By opposing such people, the Loyalists contended, they were the ones who stood firm against arbitrary rule and for representative government—in short, that they were the true Whigs.

10. democracy: A system of government in which the ultimate power to govern resides with the people, and they exercise that power directly. Although not the prevailing system in colonial America (it is actually viewed with horror by colonial elites), elements of democracy were found in such institutions as church covenants and town meetings.

11.   republic: A government in which, as in a democracy, the power to govern lies with the people, but the people exercise this power through elected representatives. Colonial elites distrusted this form as well, especially when low qualifications to vote threatened to allow mass participation. Nevertheless, this system was more acceptable than direct democracy was. For example, examine the colonial legislatures.

Pertinent Questions

A LOOSENING OF TIES (100-101)

1.   How did the relationship between king and Parliament change during the early eighteenth century? What role did the prime minister play in this change?

2.   How were the American colonies administered by Britain, from Britain, during this period? What was the effect of this policy?

3.   How did British officials in the colonies carry out (or fail to carry out) their duties, and what was the effect of their activities?

4.   How was England's hold on the colonies weakened between 1700 and 1775?

5.   What factors helped promote colonial divisions during this period?

6.   What was the Albany Plan, and what did it reveal about colonial unity.

THE STRUGGLE FOR THE CONTINENT (101-105)

7.   To what areas of North America had the French laid claim by 1750?

8.   How did the French attempt to secure their hold on the vast areas they claimed?

9.   What could the French and the English offer the Indians who lived in the continental interior? What did the French offer that was "often more important" than what the British promised, and what made it so significant?

10.   What were the causes and results of Anglo-French conflicts between 1686 and 1748? What role did the American colonies of each play in these?

11.   What caused the Great War for the empire, and why is it called by that name?

12.   How did the Great War for the empire become a "truly international conflict," and how did Britain carry out its part in the struggle?

13.   What role did the French and British colonies play in this war?

14.   What were the terms of the Peace of Paris of 1763?

THE NEW IMPERIALISM (105-111)

15.   What dilemma faced London policymakers at the end of the Great War for the Empire?

16.   What arguments were raised for and against the post-1763 "territorial imperialism," and how did this new policy alter British attitudes toward the colonies?

17.   What initial policy changes occurred when George III ascended the throne, and what were the king's motives for these changes?

18.   How were the policy changes cited in question 17 reflected in the acts passed under the Grenville administration? Deal with the specific acts as well as general policy objectives.

19.   What was it about post-1763 British policy that would cause colonists in every section to see the disadvantages rather than the advantages of being part of the British Empire?

STIRRINGS OF REVOLT (111-119)

20.   Why did the Stamp Act so antagonize the American colonists?

21.   Who sounded the "trumpet of sedition" in Virginia over the Stamp Act? What reasons, other than those stated in the resolutions proposed, contributed to this action? What was the effect of this, and what were the results?

22.   How did actions by the Stamp Act crowd raise questions of whether protests in the colonies represented more than opposition to British policies?

23.   What was England's response to the American protests over the Stamp Act. Explain the policies of Charles Townshend and of Lord North differ.

24.   What role did Samuel Adams play in the American protests? How did his view of the need for American independence differ from those of most other colonial leaders at the time?

25.   How did the colonial view of the nature of the British Empire differ from the view by George III and his supporters?

26.   What was the "political outlook" that gained a following in America and ultimately served to justify revolt?

27.   Why was the Tea Act seen by many Americans as a threat to themselves and their institutions?

28.   What were the Coercive Acts? How did the Quebec Act help to unite the colonies with Boston in opposition to these acts?

COOPERATION AND WAR (119-122)

29.   What role was played by committees of correspondence in the American protests?

30.   What were the five major decisions made at the First Continental Congress, and what was their significance?

31.   What British leaders spoke out in support of the American cause, and what were their reasons for doing so?

32.   What were the circumstances that led to the fighting at Lexington and Concord?

PATTERNS OF POPULAR CULTURE (118)

33.   How and why did taverns become a central institution in colonial American social life?

34.   What circumstances and events helped make taverns central to political life as well?

Identification

Identify each of the following, and explain why it is important within the context of the chapter.

1.   Robert Walpole

2.   Board of Trade and Plantations

3.   Treaty of Utrecht

4.   King George's War

5.   Edward Braddock

6.   William Pitt

7.   James Wolfe

8.   Proclamation of 1763

9.   Sugar Act of 1764

10.   Paxton Boys

11.   Regulators
12.   Sons of Liberty
13.   Declaratory Act
14.   Mutiny Act
15.   Townshend Duties
16.   Boston Massacre
17.   Massachusetts Circular Letter
18.   John Adams
19.   The English Constitution
20.   "virtual" representation
21.   Gaspee incident
22.   The Tea Boycott
23.   Intolerable Acts
24.   Continental Association
25.   Conciliatory Propositions

Document 1

Below is an extract from the resolutions of the Stamp Act Congress, passed in 1765. Note the line of argument. How do the resolutions reflect attitudes toward local control of local affairs developed over the preceding century?

I. That His Majesty's subjects in these colonies owe the same allegiance to the Crown of Great Britain that is owing from his subjects born within the realm, and all due subordination to that august body the Parliament of Great Britain.

II. That His Majesty's liege subjects in these colonies are intitled to all the inherent rights and liberties of his natural born subjects within the kingdom of Great Britain.

III. That it is inseparably essential to the freedom of a people, and the undoubted right of Englishmen, that no taxes be imposed on them but with their own consent, given personally or by their representatives.

IV. That the people of these colonies are not, and from their local circumstances cannot be, represented in the House of Commons in Great Britain.

V. That the only representatives of the people of these colonies are persons chosen therein by themselves, and that no taxes ever have been, or can be constitutionally imposed on them, but by their respective legislatures. . . .

Document 2

The following excerpt is from the Declaratory Act of 1766. In it, how does Parliament refute American claims? How does the Declaratory Act reflect the English view of the nature of the empire as opposed to the view held by most colonists?

Whereas several of the houses of representatives in his Majesty's colonies and plantations in America have of late, against law, claimed to themselves or to the general assemblies of the same, the sole and exclusive right of imposing duties or taxes upon his Majesty's subjects in the said colonies and plantations; and have, in pursuance of such claim, passed certain votes, resolutions, and orders, derogatory to the legislative authority of parliament, and inconsistent with the dependency of said colonies and plantations upon the crown of Great Britain: . . . be it declared . . . That the said colonies and plantations in America have been, are, and of right ought to be subordinate unto the dependent upon the imperial crown and parliament of Great Britain; and that the King's majesty, by and with the advice and consent of the lords spiritual and temporal and commons of Great Britain in parliament assembled, had, hath, and of right ought to have full power and authority to make laws and statutes of sufficient force and validity to bind the colonies and people of America, subjects of the crown of Great Britain, in all cases whatsoever.

Document 3

Below is a series of resolutions passed by a Whig committee in the Altamaha River village of Darien on the southern frontier of Georgia. How do these resolutions compare with those of the Stamp Act Congress? What new issues arose between 1765 and 1775? Which of these resolutions address purely local concerns, and which deal with intercolonial matters? What does this diversity of demands tell you about the nature of the protests against Great Britain?

Notice resolution number 5. Would you expect such a statement from people who included in their number some of the region's more prominent planters? What does this tell you about the Whigs' awareness of the paradox of Americans struggling against an "unjust system of politicks adopted . . . to subject and enslave us" (resolution number 2) while subjecting and enslaving blacks?

DARIEN (GEORGIA) RESOLUTIONS.

In the Darien Committee, Thursday, January 12, 1775.

When the most valuable privileges of a people are invaded, not only by open violence, but by every kind of fraud, sophistry, and cunning, it behoves every individual to be upon his guard, and every member of society, like beacons in a country surrounded by enemies, to give the alarm, not only when their liberties in general are attacked, but separately, least a precedent in one may affect the whole. . . . Every laudable attempt . . . in a constitutional manner, hath been hitherto frustrated, by the influence and authority of men in office, and their numerous dependants, and in every other natural and just way, by the various arts they have put in practice. We, therefore, the Representatives of the extensive District of Darien in the Colony of Georgia, being now assembled in Congress, by the authority and free choice of the inhabitants of the said District, now freed from their fetters, do Resolve,

1st. That the unparalleled moderation, the decent, but firm and manly conduct of the loyal and brave people of Boston and Massachusetts Bay, to preserve their liberty, deserves not only the applause and thanks of all America, but also, the imitation of all mankind. But, to avoid needless repetitions, we acquiesce and join in all the Resolutions passed by the Grand American Congress in Philadelphia last October. We thank them for their sage counsel and advice, and most heartily and cheerfully accede to the Association entered into by them, as the wisest and most moderate measure that could be adopted in our present circumstances to reconcile and firmly unite Great Britain and the colonies, so indispensably necessary to each other, by the surest and best basis-- mutual interest.

2nd. That in shutting up the Land Offices, with the intention of raising out quit-rents, and setting up our Lands at publick sale, representations of the Crown tract have not been duly considered (and attended to) in all its consequences to this vast Continent: That it is a principal part of unjust system of politicks adopted by the present Ministry, to subject and enslave us, and evidently proceeds from an ungenerous jealousy of the Colonies, to prevent as much as possible that population of America, and the relief of the poor and distressed Britain and elsewhere, for whom a kind Providence has opened a new-world from their merciless oppressor, when the old is overrun with such monsters: That monopolizing our Lands into few hands, is forming and encouraging petty tyrants to lord it over us, or reside in any other part of the world in extravagance, luxury, and folly, by the fruit of our labour and industry--such oppressions, neither we nor our fathers were able to bear, and it drove us to the wilderness: And that all encouragement should be given to the poor of every Nation by every generous American.

3rd. That Ministerial Mandates, under the name of Instructions, preventing the legal Representative of the people to enact laws suiting their own respective situation and circumstances, are a general grievance, and more especially in this young Colony, where our internal police is not yet well settled; and as a proof of the intention of these restrictions, when time and opportunity offers, we point out particularly, amongst many others of like nature, the not suffering us to limit the term of our Assembly, or passing a quit-rent law, to ascertain and fix the most valuable part of our property.

4th. That an over proportion of Officers, for the number of inhabitants, and paying their salaries from Britain, so much cast up to us by Court parasites, and for which we are so often charged with ingratitude, are in truth real and great grievances, rendering them insolent, and regardless of their conduct, being independent of the people who should support them according to their usefulness and behaviour, and for whose benefit and conveniency alone they were originally intended. That besides these exorbitant salaries, which enables them all to act by Deputies, whilst they wallow in luxury themselves, their combining to raise their exorbitant and illegal fees and perquisites, by various acts upon the subject, to an alarming height, are more dangerous to our liberties than a regular Army; having the means of corruption so much in their power, the danger of which is imminently exemplified in the present unhappy state of our brethren and fellow-subjects in Britain, and even in the late conduct of this Colony. To prevent therefore as much as in us lies these direful effects, we do resolve never to choose any person in publick office, his Deputy, Deputy's Deputy, or any expectant, to represent us in Assembly, or any other publick place, in our election, hoping the example will be followed throughout this Colony, and all America.

5th. To show the world that we are not influenced by any contracted or interested motives, but a general philanthropy for all mankind, of whatever climate, language, or complexion, we hereby declare our disapprobation and abhorrence of the unnatural practice of Slavery in America, (however the uncultivated state of our country, or other specious arguments may plead for it,) a practice founded in injustice and cruelty, and highly dangerous to our liberties, (as well as lives,) debasting part of our fellow-creatures below men, and corrupting the virtue and morals of the rest; and is laying the basis of that liberty we contend for (and which we pray the Almighty to continue to the latest posterity) upon a very wrong foundation. We therefore resolve, at all times to use our utmost endeavors for the manumission of our Slaves in this Colony, upon the most safe and equitable footing for the masters and themselves.

Peter Force, ed., American Archives, 6 vols. (Washington, D.C.: 1837–1846), 4th ser., 1:1137.

Map Exercise

Fill in or identify the following on the blank map provided. Use the map in the text as your source.

1.   Britain's North American colonies.
2.   Other territory claimed by Britain.
3.   Spanish claims.
4.   Provincial capitals (British and Spanish).
5.   Other principal colonial towns.
6.   Non-Indian settlement before 1700.
7.   Non-Indian settlement between 1700 and 1763.
8.   Frontier line in 1763.

9. Proclamation Line of 1763.

10. Principal rivers, the Great Lakes, and the Appalachian Mountains.

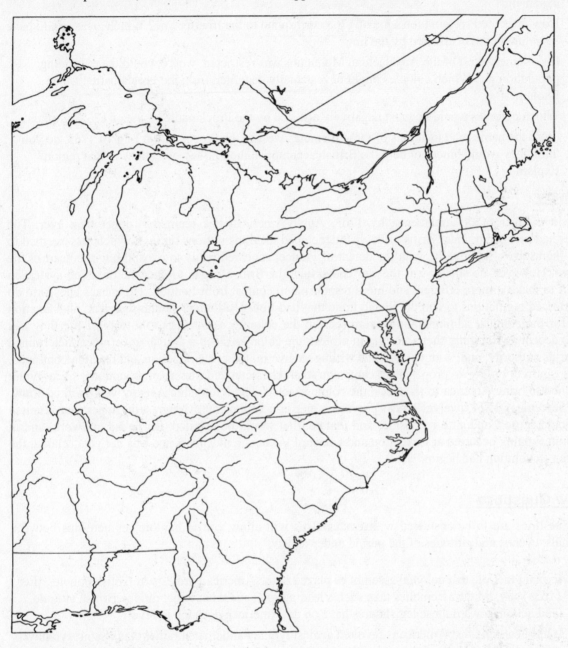

Interpretative Questions

Based on what you have filled in, answer the following. On some of the questions you will need to consult the narrative in your text for information or explanation.

1. Compare the non-Indian settlement after 1700 to that which occurred before 1700. Where did most of this expansion take place? Now refer back to the map in the previous chapter of the text. Which immigrant groups were most involved in this expansion?

2. Note the frontier line in 1763 and consider how much territory east of this line had been settled. How would this settlement pattern support Britain's post-1763 policy concerning Western expansion?

3. How does the Proclamation Line of 1763 correspond to the frontier line? Which areas would have been immediately affected by the line?

4. If settlement west of the Appalachian Mountains was restricted, where would the expanding population go? Which colonies might have actually benefited from the Proclamation Line? Explain.

5. Which colonies would be most negatively affected by the Proclamation Line of 1763? Explain.

6. From the names and locations of the settlements west of the Proclamation Line of 1763, do you think they would hinder or help the British accomplish their policy objectives in that region? Explain.

Summary

Despite a number of disagreements, by 1763, Anglo-American ties seemed stronger than ever. The colonies had prospered under British rule, had developed local institutions through which they seemed to govern themselves, and finally, with the defeat of France, appeared ready to expand into the heart of the continent. However, no sooner was the war ended than the British began to alter the pre-1763 system in an effort to make it more efficient and more responsive to control from London. The means chosen to do this (enforced regulations to end the illegal trade that had flourished under salutary neglect, plus taxation to pay for the colonial administration) were seen in the colonies as threats to the way of life they had come to accept as rightfully theirs. Rising in protest, the colonies faced a British government determined to assert its authority, and, with neither side willing to give in, the cycle of action and reaction continued. Finally, spurred on by a propaganda campaign that characterized the mother country as a tyrant determined to bring America to its knees, the colonies acted. The Intolerable Acts proved the final straw, and in September 1774, twelve British provinces met in a Continental Congress in hopes that a united front would cause London to reconsider and that conflict would be avoided. But it did not work, and in the spring, fighting occurred at Lexington and Concord. Although independence was not yet declared, the American Revolution had begun.

Review Questions

These questions are to be answered with essays. This will allow you to explore relationships between individuals, events, and attitudes of the period under review.

1. Explain the role that colonial assemblies played in the American protests of British policies after 1763. Why did the assemblies take such a leading role, and what effect did the British attitude (and action) toward these legislatures have on the American decision to revolt?

2. It has been said that Americans revolted against tyranny anticipated rather than against tyranny inflicted. Define tyranny as you believe an eighteenth-century American might have, and then assess this point of view.

3. From the outset, Massachusetts was the leader of the anti-British protest studied in this chapter. Why? What was it in the economic, political, and intellectual climate of that colony that made it such a hotbed of revolution? What part did Puritanism play in shaping this climate?

Chapter Self Test

After you have read the chapter in the text and done the exercises in the Study Guide, take the following self test to see if you understand the material you have covered. Answers appear at the end of the Study Guide.

MULTIPLE-CHOICE QUESTIONS

Circle the letter of the response which best answers the question or completes the statement.

1. By the 1750s colonial legislatures had come to see themselves as:
   a. little parliaments.
   b. agents of the royal governor.
   c. powerless.
   d. agents for democratic reform.

2. A conference of colonial leaders gathered in Albany, New York, in 1754 to discuss a proposal by Benjamin Franklin to:
   a. establish "one general government" for all of the colonies.
   b. negotiate a treaty with the French.
   c. expand a system of intercolonial roads.
   d. extend the operation of the colonial postal service.

3. Both the French and the English were well aware that the battle for control of North America would be determined in part by:
   a. who had the Dutch on their side.
   b. whose king was the best military commander.
   c. which group could win the allegiance of native tribes.
   d. whose armies could best fight "Indian" fashion.

4. The British victory in the Great War for the empire:
   a. expelled France and Spain from North America.
   b. gave England control of the settled regions of North America, including Canada and Florida.
   c. resulted in the defeat of all North American Indian tribes.
   d. resulted in less contact between Britain and America.

5. Prior to the Great War for the empire, the Iroquois Confederacy:
   a. traded exclusively with the English.
   b. traded exclusively with the French.
   c. maintained their autonomy by avoiding a close relationship with both French and the English.
   d. traded only with the five tribes that made up the Confederacy.

6. Which of the following did not occur during the Great War for the empire?
   a. Americans were reimbursed for supplies requisitioned in their British colonies.
   b. Colonial assemblies were in charge of recruitment in their respective colonies.
   c. The French lost the city of Quebec.
   d. Most of the fighting was done by colonial militia.

7. For which of the following was the result of the Great War for the empire a disaster?
   a. English frontiersmen and traders.
   b. Colonial merchants.
   c. The Iroquois Confederacy.
   d. The Royal Africa Company.

8. The English decision to reorganize the British Empire after 1763 was the result of:
   a. colonial demands for more efficient government.
   b. problems in the merchant community and their desire for regulation.
   c. colonial unrest, which the British government planned to put down before it become serious.
   d. a need to administer an empire that was now twice as large as it had been.

9. In an effort to keep peace between frontiersmen and Indians and provide for a more orderly settlement of the West, the British government:
   a. forbade settlers from crossing the mountains that divided the Atlantic coast from the interior.
   b. gave Indian tribes and confederations colonial status.
   c. allowed interior settlement only if settlers bought land from the tribes.
   d. put forts in the Ohio Valley to protect settlers there.

10. Which of the following was a consequence of the policies of the Grenville ministry?
    a. British tax revenues in the colonies increased ten times.
    b. Colonists effectively resisted and paid little tax.
    c. Many colonial merchants went out of business.
    d. Colonial assemblies assumed the responsibility for taxing their individual colonies.

11. The Regulator movement of 1771 consisted of:
    a. Pennsylvania frontiersmen who demanded attention from the colonial government for their defense needs.
    b. farmers of the Carolina upcountry who protested lack of representation and forcibly resisted tax collection.
    c. northern merchants who refused to comply with the restrictions of the Grenville program.
    d. western farmers who protested the Proclamation of 1763.

12. British policies after 1763:
    a. destroyed the economy of the American colonies.
    b. stripped colonial assemblies of their authority.
    c. created a deep sense of economic unease, particularly in colonial cities.
    d. actually helped the colonial economy.

13. Colonists argued that the Stamp Act was not proper because:
    a. it affected only a few people, so the burden was not shared.
    b. the money raised would not be spent in the colonies.
    c. colonies could be taxed only by their provincial assemblies.
    d. the tax was too high.

14. British authorities decided to repeal the Stamp Act primarily because of the:
    a. passage of the "Virginia Resolves."
    b. well-reasoned petitions of the Stamp Act Congress.
    c. intimidation tactics employed by the Sons of Liberty.
    d. economic pressure caused by a colonial boycott of English goods.

15. Colonists were most upset over the Mutiny Act (Quartering Act) of 1765 because it:
    a. required that the colonies pay the soldiers expenses.
    b. quartered troops in private residences.
    c. required colonies to draft citizens to serve in the Army.
    d. punished innocent civilians for the vague crime of "mutiny."

16. Colonial "committees of correspondence" were created to:
    a. keep colonial intellectuals in contact with each other.
    b. publicize grievances against England.
    c. improve the writing skills of young gentlemen.
    d. correspond with English radicals who supported the American cause.

17. American complaints concerning lack of representation made little sense to the English who pointed out that:
    a. over eighty percent of the population of Great Britain was entitled to vote for members of Parliament.
    b. each colony was represented by an agent and a designated member of Parliament.
    c. each member of Parliament represented the interests of the whole empire rather than a particular individual or geographical area.
    d. American participation in parliamentary discussions would bind them to unpopular decisions.

18. Colonists felt that when the English constitution was allowed to function properly, it created the best political system because it:
    a. distributed power among the three elements of society—the monarchy, the aristocracy, and the common people.
    b. created a republican government.
    c. created a democracy.
    d. put power in the hands of those best suited to govern.

19. The Coercive Acts or "Intolerable Acts":
    a. isolated Massachusetts from the other colonies.
    b. made Massachusetts a martyr in the eyes of other colonists.
    c. created no concern among any group other than merchants.
    d. increased the power of colonial assemblies.

20. Which of the following was not a step taken by the First Continental Congress?
    a. It adopted a plan for a colonial union under British authority.
    b. It endorsed a statement of grievances.
    c. It called for military preparations.
    d. It called for a series of boycotts.

TRUE-FALSE QUESTIONS

Read each statement carefully. Mark true statements "T" and false statements "F."

1. By the 1750s most Americans felt little loyalty to the British crown.

2. The French were able to forge good relations with the Indian tribes because they were more tolerant of the Indian way of life than the British were.

3. Before the Great War for the empire, England, France, and Spain had been at peace with each other for nearly half a century.

4. The Seven Years' War, the French and Indian War, and the Great War for the Empire are all the same war.

5. After the Peace of Paris of 1763, the English were inclined to let the colonies go their own way, with few restrictions.

6. England was fortunate that King George III was young, bright, and surprisingly mature for his age.

7. Because they needed protection, colonists in both the East and the West were glad to have regular British troops stationed permanently in America.

8. The Paxton Boys and the Regulator movement revealed that colonists in the West believed they were not being treated fairly by colonists in the East.

9. The Stamp Act was particularly ill-designed by the British, for it evoked opposition from some of the most powerful and strategically placed members of the colonial population.

10. Colonists were concerned over the immediate impact of the Stamp Act, not its long-range implications.

11. Parliament repealed the Stamp Act and in the Declaratory Act it declared that it would not tax the colonies in this way again.

12. Colonists responded to the Townshend Duties with agreements not to import the taxed goods.

13. Americans wanted their representatives to "actually" represent them, while the British claimed the Parliament represented all British citizens, no matter where they lived.

14. Among the basic principles held by Americans was the belief that people should be taxed only with their own consent.

15. The British soldiers involved in the "Boston Massacre" were convicted of murder and hung.

16. Women, especially southern women, took no part in the protests and boycotts rising from the Coercive Acts.

17. By the time the First Continental Congress convened in 1774, a growing majority of Americans agreed upon the necessity of a declaration of independence.

18. Lord North assumed that most colonists would welcome the Tea Act of 1773 because it made tea cheaper.

19. Those who attended the Continental Congress did not intend for it to be a continuing organization.

20. The fighting at Lexington and Concord caused many who previously had little enthusiasm for the rebel cause to rally to it.

GENERAL DISCUSSION QUESTIONS FOR CHAPTERS ONE–FOUR

These questions are designed to help you bring together ideas from several chapters and see how the chapters relate to one another.

1. Compare and contrast the English, Spanish, and French colonial systems—their functioning, their successes and failures, and their impact on the Native American population.

2. Why was labor such a problem for colonists in the seventeenth century? How was this problem addressed in the middle and the New England colonies? What effect did these efforts to solve the labor shortage have on the social and economic systems of these regions?

3. During the years before the Revolution, the "transplanted English" became Americans and developed characteristics that made them different from their counterparts in the mother country. What was this "American character"? Look at the social, economic, religious, and political institutions that grew up in colonial America, as reflected in the illustrations in your text, and from these pictures, identify the elements that combined to produce the American character. Once this is done, write an essay in which you explain just what made the American unique.

4. Colonists who first came to America came in search of rather specific things. Some found what they wanted; others did not. But most stayed to create a new life for themselves. What happened to their initial dreams? Examine the goals set by those who first came to Massachusetts Bay and those who first came to Virginia, and compare those goals with what their descendants were seeking in the 1770s. What had happened? How had the dreams of the early 1600s become the issues of the 1770s, and what do these changes tell you about the impact America had on European ideas and institutions?

5. Examine the unrest in the American colonies during the late seventeenth and early eighteenth centuries, and compare the causes of that turbulence with those that led to the colonial protests of the 1760s and 1770s. What parallels do you find? What are the differences? Considering what you have discovered, do you feel the American Revolution was the result of the events that immediately preceded it, or did it result from attitudes long held by colonists? Explain your conclusions.

6. Explain how the colonization of America was as much a biological invasion as a cultural one, and discuss how this was critical to the success of the English.

CHAPTER FIVE
THE AMERICAN REVOLUTION

Objectives

A thorough study of Chapter Five should enable the student to understand:

1.   The history debate concerning the nature of the American Revolution and the reasons for disagreement.

2.   American war aims and the problems experienced by the Revolutionary governments in carrying on a protracted war.

3.   The aim of the Declaration of Independence, the reasons for its issuance, and its influence throughout the world since 1776.

4.   The indispensible contributions of George Washington to the successful outcome of the Revolution.

5.   The diplomatic triumph for American negotiators embodied in the Treaty of Paris.

6.   The impact of the Revolution on women, African-Americans, Native-Americans, and other minorities.

7.   The types of governments created by the new states, and the important features in their governments.

8.   The features of the Articles of Confederation, and the reasons for its creation.

9.   The problems faced by the government under the Articles of Confederation and how they were addressed.

10. How America's revolution, and the whole modern notion of revolution, was to a large degree a product of the ideas of the Enlightenment.

Main Themes

1.   How the thirteen American colonies were able to win their independence from one of the most powerful nations on earth.

2.   How the American Revolution was not only a war for independence, but also a struggle to determine the nature of the nation being created.

3.   How Americans attempted to apply Revolutionary ideology to the building of the nation and to the remaking of society.

4.   The problems that remained after, or were created by, the American Revolution.

5.   That the American Revolution was the first and in many ways the most influential of the Enlightenment-derived uprising against established orders.

Glossary

As you have seen, interpretation is a significant element in the study of history. Below are some of the major "schools" of historical interpretation that have dealt with the colonial, Revolutionary, and early national periods in American history. A knowledge of the positions of these schools will help you understand the sections in your text entitled "Where Historians Disagree."

1. <u>Nationalists:</u> This group, writing mainly in the nineteenth century, was greatly influenced by the spirit of nationalism (a strong belief in, and devotion to, the nation; a willingness to put national interests first; a glorification of the national character) that prevailed at that time. To them, the Revolution had been a struggle of an oppressed people against a tyrannical king determined to subject them to his will. Seen in heroic terms, patriot leaders were pictured as champions of liberty who had brought the nation through the Revolution and the "critical period" that followed and who had given us the most perfect blueprint for government yet devised—the Constitution.

2. <u>imperial school:</u> Following on the heels of the Nationalists, and in many ways as a reaction to them, the Imperial school placed the thirteen American colonies within the context of the whole British Empire. Writing for the most part in the late nineteenth and early twentieth centuries, and influenced by America's growing international involvement, the Imperial school concluded that Britain's colonial policy, when considered as a whole, had been far from oppressive. Instead, it had been beneficial to colonies and mother country alike, which seemed to suggest that the American Revolution could not have been solely an attack on British policies.

3. <u>progressive historians:</u> This group added to the imperial school's interpretation by focusing on the struggles for power among the colonists themselves, struggles that had made use of the tensions aroused by Britain's colonial policies. Stressing economic and social conflicts that had manifested themselves in politics, the progressives saw the war, and the period that followed, as an era in which the crucial questions had been not only that of home rule, but also that of "who would rule at home." Although they failed to agree on the meaning of the outcome of the latter struggle, the progressive historians forced Americans to realize that their Revolution had touched the entire fabric of society.

4. <u>consensus school:</u> Disagreeing with the emphasis (and, in some cases, with the evidence) produced by the progressives, the consensus school argued that what had really shaped America was not the social, economic, and political conflicts on which the progressives dwelled, but the remarkable degree of agreement that had existed. Had it not been for this consensus on such issues as representative government, popular participation, economic opportunity, and social mobility, the Revolution could not have succeeded. It was to preserve the liberties gained during salutary neglect, liberties threatened by England's new colonial system, that the Revolution had been fought. After the Revolution, the Constitution had been written to guarantee that these hard-won liberties would continue to be enjoyed by all American citizens.

5. <u>New Left or neoprogressives:</u> At present, no single school of interpretation has taken hold. Instead, historians seem to be combining elements of past interpretations in an effort to find a more satisfactory view of the past. Influenced by the disruptions of the 1960s, a group of scholars, designated the New Left, has sought and found evidence of deep social and economic divisions that were overlooked in previous works. Joining the New Left in its search, but less radical in its interpretation of the evidence, is a group whose emphasis seems to hark back to the days of the progressives. However, armed with new means of analysis (especially computers), these historians have been able to digest more complex data on economic growth and sociopolitical patterns than have their namesakes. What has begun to emerge is something of a meeting of the consensus and progressive schools, which, by using a variety of research techniques, may give us a clearer understanding of the forces that shaped early America.

The following are other terms with which you need to be familiar.

6. <u>rebellion:</u> The rising against a power or government; organized resistance.
7. <u>revolution:</u> A successful rebellion, in which one form of government or one ruling group is replaced by another.

8. constitution: The fundamental laws and principles by which an organization (nation, state, and such) is governed. In America, after the Revolution had begun, the state constitutions were written so as not to rely on tradition and previous legal practices as guides for governing.

9. confederation: A group of sovereign states that unite for specific purposes (defense, foreign policy, trade, and so on), yet otherwise act as independent bodies.

10. speculation: The practice, especially prevalent in western land dealings, in which an individual or a company (the speculator) purchased large blocks of land at a low price per acre (often on credit), divided the land into small units, and resold the property at a higher price per acre. This made many speculators rich, but the land did go to the farmers who could not have afforded large purchases.

11. inflation: The economic condition caused by an oversupply of money (generally paper) in a market undersupplied with goods to buy. The result is high prices and a corresponding reduction in the value (buying power) of money. If the inflation is prolonged, a serious disruption of the economy might occur.

12. depression: The reverse of inflation, caused by a reduction of the money supply that retards economic activity, drives prices down, and results in business failures and unemployment.

Pertinent Questions

THE STATES UNITED (126-131)

1. List the divisions within the Second Continental Congress, and give the aim of each faction. How did the factions attempt to gain their ends?

2. How did the pamphlet Common Sense address the problem of the aim of the war, and what was its impact on American opinion?

3. What were the philosophical roots of the Declaration of Independence, and what effect did the Declaration have on the struggle?

4. What were the characteristics of the governments—state and national—set up by Americans to conduct the war?

5. What problems did the Americans face in providing the necessary supplies and equipment for the war and in paying for them?

6. How were the problems in question 5 overcome, at least initially?

THE WAR FOR INDEPENDENCE (131-141)

7. What were the American advantages in the struggle, and why was George Washington selected as the best person to make the most of these advantages?

8. What were the initial setbacks in the war during 1776, and what was the significance of the Battles of Trenton and Princeton in this regard?

9. What was the initial plan for the British campaign of 1777? How was this altered, and what effect did this alteration have on the outcome?

10. What were the American diplomatic goals at the start of the war? What problems did they face, and what efforts were made to overcome them?

11. How did the victory at Saratoga affect American diplomatic efforts? How did England and France respond to this news? What was the result?

12. Why did the British decide to launch a campaign against the southern colonies in 1778? What advantages and disadvantages did each side have in this region?

13. How was the campaign in the South conducted, and why was the victory at Yorktown so significant for the Americans?

14. How was Spain an obstacle to the American hopes for peace with independence? How did this affect American diplomacy before the Battle of Yorktown?

15. What were the provisions of the Treaty of Paris in 1783, and how did the Treaty affect relations among the United States, France, and Spain?

WAR AND SOCIETY (141-146)

16. Who were the Loyalists? What elements in America remained loyal to the king, and for what reasons?

17. What happened to the Loyalists? Why was theirs a "tragic story," at least in some cases?

18. What effect did the war have on other minorities? How was its significance to African-Americans both limited and yet significant?

19. What impact did the American Revolution have on Native Americans?

20. How did the Revolution affect the way American women thought about their status, and what changes resulted from this new awareness?

21. What changes did the Revolution produce in the structure of the American economy?

THE CREATION OF STATE GOVERNMENTS (147-148)

22. What was it about the concept of a republican government that so appealed to Americans?

23. How did Americans propose to avoid what they considered to be the problems of the British system they were repudiating?

24. What was unique about the constitution drawn up by Massachusetts?

25. How did these new constitutions deal with the question of religious freedom? How did they deal with slavery?

THE SEARCH FOR A NATIONAL GOVERNMENT (149-155)

26. What type of government did the Articles of Confederation create? What were its major features?

27. Why was the Confederation organized as it was? What caused the delay in its ratification, and how were the obstacles to its ratification overcome?

28. How did the Treaty of Paris of 1783 fail to resolve, or in some cases help to create, strain between the United States, England, and Spain?

29. Above all, what commercial arrangements did American shippers and traders want after the war had ended? Why did they feel this was needed, and how successful were they in accomplishing their aims?

30. What postwar problems existed between the United States and Spain? What attempts were made to solve the problems, and why did these attempts fail?

31. How did the Confederation Congress attempt to solve the problem of the status of western territory that the states had ceded to it? Which interest groups favored which plans for the sale and distribution of land?

32. How did the Confederation deal with the Indians who also claimed the western land?

33. What were the sources of the Confederation's postwar economic problems, and how did the government attempt to solve them? What were the results?

34. How was paper money seen as a solution to the economic problems of one element in American society? Who opposed this and why?

35. How did the action of Daniel Shays and his followers relate to the economic problem of the Confederation period? What was the significance of the movement he led?

WHERE HISTORIANS DISAGREE (128-129)

36.   What are the major interpretations of the origins of the American Revolution that have been advanced by historians?

37.   Note the various schools of historical interpretation in the glossary of this chapter of the Study Guide. Which historians highlighted in "Where Historians Disagree" fit into which schools?

THE AMERICAN ENVIRONMENT (152-153)

38.   Explain how different versions of the cadastral system have "profoundly different consequences for the way colonial lands and societies developed."

39.   How did the government of the United States determine which cadastral system was most appropriate for the new republic?

AMERICA IN THE WORLD (140-141)

40.   What Enlightenment ideas most influenced America's revolution?

41.   How did Enlightenment ideas and the American Revolution inspire other people to oppose unpopular regimes? Where did these revolutions occur?

Identification

Identify each of the following, and explain why it is important within the context of the chapter.

1.   Olive Branch Petition
2.   Prohibitory Act
3.   Conway Cabal
4.   Benedict Arnold
5.   Sir William Howe
6.   John Burgoyne
7.   "militia diplomats"
8.   Joseph and Mary Brant
9.   Caron de Beaumarchais
10.   Sir Henry Clinton
11.   Lord Cornwallis
12.   Francis Marion
13.   Nathanael Greene
14.   Lemuel Hayes
15.   Dragging Canoe
16.   camp followers
17.   Judith Sargent Murray
18.   Vindication of the Rights of Women
19.   Virginia Statute of Religious Liberty
20.   small states/large states
21.   township
22.   Ordinance of 1784

Document 1

The following is taken from "Letters Addressed to the Inhabitants of the Province of Massachusetts Bay," written by Daniel Leonard and published in the <u>Massachusetts Gazette</u> on January 9, 1775. Leonard was one of the most aristocratic and successful lawyers of the period, but his views on the activities of the American Patriots and his loyal support of the crown eventually made him an outcast in his own colony. In the series of "letters" published in late 1774 and early 1775, he argued his case, and although his warnings were not heeded, he left behind one of the best statements of the Loyalist period.

Read carefully what Leonard wrote. What type of government did he want? How did this government's form, and the way that he proposed it should work, differ from the views held by American Whigs? How did Leonard answer what he felt to be the most important of the colonial grievances? Did he feel a problem really existed? Why or why not? Was Leonard so pro-British that he had no regard for America and its future? What did he suggest might be the future relationship between colonies and mother country? Do you think he considered himself an American or an Englishman? Why? And, finally, what does Leonard's position tell you about the differences between Loyalist and Whig?

ADDRESSED

To the Inhabitants of the Province of Massachusetts Bay,

January 9, 1775.

MY DEAR COUNTRYMEN,

The security of the people from internal rapacity and violence, and from foreign invasion, is the end and design of government. The simple forms of government are monarchy, aristocracy, and democracy; that is, where the authority of the state is vested in one, a few, or the many. Each of these species of government has advantages peculiar to itself, and would answer the ends of government, were the persons intrusted with the authority of the state, always guided, themselves, by unerring wisdom and public virtue; but rulers are not always exempt from the weakness and depravity which make government necessary to society. Thus monarchy is apt to rush headlong into tyranny, aristocracy to beget faction, and multiplied usurpation, and democracy, to degenerate into tumult, violence, and anarchy. A government formed upon these three principles, in due proportion, is the best calculated to answer the ends of government, and to endure. Such a government is the British constitution, consisting of king, lords and commons. . . . It is allowed, both by Englishmen and foreigners, to be the most perfect system that the wisdom of ages has produced. . . . An Englishman glories in being subject to, and protected by such a government. The colonies are a part of the British empire. . . .

This doctrine is not new, but the denial of it is. It is beyond a doubt, that it was the sense both of the parent country, and our ancestors, that they were to remain subject to parliament. It is evident from the charter itself; and this authority has been exercised by parliament, from time to time, almost ever since the first settlement of the country, and has been expressly acknowledged by our provincial legislatures. It is not less our interest, than our duty, to continue subject to the authority of parliament. . . .

If there be any grievance, it does not consist in our being subject to the authority of parliament, but in our not having an actual representation in it. Were it possible for the colonies to have an equal representation in parliament, and were refused it upon proper application, I confess I should think it a grievance; but at present it seems to be allowed, by all parties, to be impracticable, considering the colonies are distant from Great Britain a thousand transmarine leagues. If that be the case, the right or privilege, that we complain of being deprived of, is not withheld by Britain, but the first principles of government, and the immutable laws of nature, render it impossible for us to enjoy it.

Daniel Leonard, "To the Inhabitants of the Province of Massachusetts Bay, January 9, 1775," in Novanglus and Massachusettensis (Boston: Hews and Gross, 1819), pp. 168–173.

Document 2

Read the Declaration of Independence, in the Appendices to your text. This is a statement of the causes for the colonists' rebelling against England. How do these causes set down by Jefferson compare with those you have identified in your earlier reading?

The Declaration of Independence also suggests the type of society that Americans hoped would result from this struggle. Identify the major characteristics of the independent nation that Jefferson hoped would be created.

Document 3

Having read, in the text and in other documents, of the aims, interests, and ideals of the American patriots, now read the Virginia Statute of Religious Liberty: An Act for Establishing Religious Freedom. Written by Thomas Jefferson, the statute was passed by the Virginia General Assembly in October 1785. It was the first and clearest legislative expression of the idea of complete religious freedom in America. How does it reflect the principles for which Americans said they had fought the Revolution?

I. WHEREAS Almighty God hath created the mind free; that all attempts to influence it by temporal punishments or burthens, or by civil incapacitations, tend only to beget habits of hypocrisy and meanness, and are a departure from the plan of the Holy author of our religion, who being Lord both of body and mind, yet chose not to propagate it by coercions on either, as was in his Almighty power to do; . . . that our civil rights have no dependence on our religious opinions, any more than our opinions in physics or geometry; that therefore the proscribing any citizen as unworthy the public confidence by laying upon him an incapacity of being called to offices of trust and emolument, unless he profess or renounce this or that religious opinion, is depriving him injuriously of those privileges and advantages to which in common with his fellow citizens he has a natural right; . . . and finally, that truth is great and will prevail if left to herself, that she is the proper and sufficient antagonist to error, and has nothing to fear from the conflict, unless by human interposition disarmed of her natural weapons, free argument and debate, errors ceasing to be dangerous when it is permitted freely to contradict them.

II. Be it enacted by the General Assembly, that no man shall be compelled to frequent or support any religious worship, place or ministry whatsoever, nor shall be enforced, restrained, molested, or burthened in his body or goods, nor shall otherwise suffer on account of his religious opinions or belief; but that all men shall be free to profess, and by argument to maintain their opinion in matters of religion, and that the same shall in no wise diminish, enlarge or affect their civil capacities.

III. And though we well know that this Assembly, elected by the people for the ordinary purposes of legislation only, have no power to restrain the acts of succeeding Assemblies . . . yet as we are free to declare, and do declare, that the rights hereby asserted are of the natural rights of mankind, and that if any Act shall hereafter be passed to repeal the present, or to narrow its operation, such Act will be an infringement of natural right.

Document 4

The following is an excerpt from the Articles of Confederation, approved by all the states by 1781. How does it reflect the principles for which Americans said they were fighting the Revolution? What goals and objectives of the Revolution still remained to be achieved?

1. [Article II] "Each state retains its sovereignty, freedom and independence, and every Power, Jurisdiction and right, which is not by this confederation expressly delegated to the United States, in Congress assembled."

2. [Article IV] The free inhabitants of each state "shall be entitled to all privileges and immunities of free citizens in the several states" and "full faith and credit" shall be given by each state to the judicial and other official proceedings of other states.

3. [Article V] Each state shall be represented in Congress by no less than two and no more than seven members, shall pay its own delegates, and shall have one vote (regardless of the number of members).

4. [Article VI] No state, without the consent of Congress, shall enter into diplomatic relations or make treaties with other states or with foreign nations, or engage in war except in case of actual invasion.

5. [Article VIII] A "common treasury" shall be supplied by the states in proportion to the value of their land and improvements; the states shall levy taxes to raise their quotas of revenue.

6. [Article IX] Congress shall have power to decide on peace and war, conduct foreign affairs, settle disputes between states, regulate the Indian trade, maintain post offices, make appropriations, borrow money, emit bills of credit, build a navy, requisition soldiers from the states, etc.--but nine states must agree before Congress can take any important action.

7. [Article X] A "Committee of the States," consisting of one delegate from each state, shall act in the place of Congress when Congress is not in session.

8. [Article XIII] No change shall be made in these Articles unless agreed to by Congress and "afterwards confirmed by the legislatures of every state."

Document 5

Below is the charge to the jury given by the chief justice of Massachusetts, who in 1783 presided over the case of Quork Walker, a slave who was suing his master. How does it reflect the principles for which Americans said they had fought the Revolution?

As to the doctrine of slavery and the right of Christians to hold Africans in perpetual servitude, and sell and treat them as we do our horses and cattle, that (it is true) has been heretofore countenanced by the Province Laws formerly, but nowhere is it expressly enacted or established. It has been a usage--a usage which took its origin from the practice of some of the European nations, and the regulations of British government respecting the then Colonies, for the benefit of trade and wealth. But whatever sentiments have formerly prevailed in this particular or slid in upon us by the example of others, a different idea has taken place with the people of America, more favorable to the natural rights of mankind, and to that natural, innate desire of Liberty, with which Heaven (without regard to color, complexion, or shape of noses) has inspired all the human race. And upon this ground our Constitution of Government, by which the people of this Commonwealth have solemnly bound themselves, sets out with declaring that all men are born free and equal--and that every subject is entitled to liberty, and to have it guarded by the laws, as well as life and property--and in short is totally repugnant to the idea of being born slaves. This being the case, I think the idea of slavery is inconsistent with our own conduct and Constitution; and there can be no such thing as perpetual servitude of a rational creature, unless his liberty is forfeited by some criminal conduct or given up by personal consent or contract.

Document 6

The following is an excerpt from the Northwest Ordinance of 1787. How does it reflect the principles for which Americans said they had fought the Revolution?

1. Congress shall appoint a governor, a secretary, and three judges for the Northwest Territory. These officials shall adopt suitable laws from the original states. When the territory has "five thousand free male inhabitants of full age," they shall be allowed to elect representatives. These representatives, together with the governor and a legislative council of five, shall form a general assembly to make laws for the territory.

2. The inhabitants shall be entitled to the benefits of trial by jury and other judicial proceedings according to the common law.

3. Religion, morality, and knowledge being necessary to good government and happiness of mankind, schools, and the means of education shall forever be encouraged.

4. There shall be formed in the said territory not less than three nor more than five States. . . . And, whenever any of the said States shall have sixty thousand free inhabitants therein, such State shall be admitted, by its delegates, into the Congress of the United States, on an equal footing with the original States.

5. There shall be neither slavery nor involuntary servitude in the said territory, otherwise than in the punishment of crimes whereof the party shall have been duly convicted.

Map Exercise

Fill in or identify the following on the blank map provided. Use the map in the text as your source.

1. States with western land claims.
2. States without western land claims.
3. Western lands claimed by the respective states and the dates these lands were ceded.
4. Claims that were disputed.
5. British, French, and Spanish possessions.
6. Major rivers and lakes.

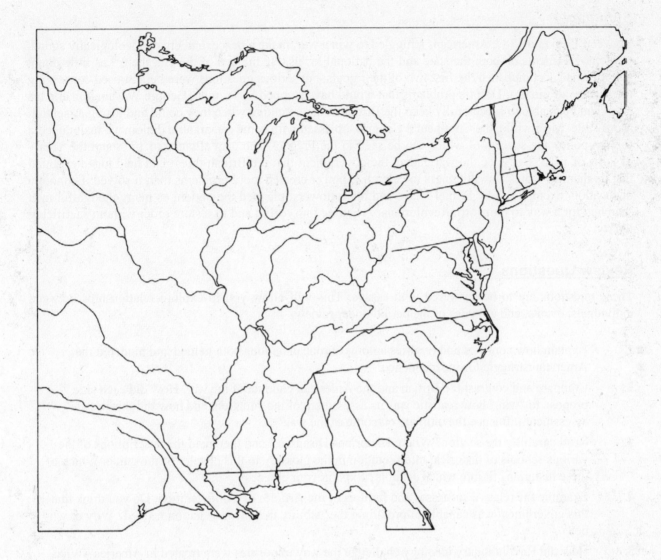

Interpretative Questions

Based on what you have filled in, answer the following. On some of the questions you will need to consult the narrative in your text for information or explanation.

1. Why was the question of western land claims so important in the ratification of the Articles of Confederation? What advantages were to be gained from western lands?

2. How did the Ordinance of 1784 propose to deal with the lands ceded to the national government? What is significant about this with regard to the political development of the West?

3. How did the Ordinance of 1787 (the "Northwest Ordinance") differ from the Ordinance of 1784? What factors caused these differences?

4. Note the territory held by Spain. How did Spanish holdings (especially along the Gulf of Mexico) threaten the westward movement of Americans?

Summary

Between 1775 and 1787, Americans struggled to win a war, make a peace, and create ideologically sound, stable governments on both the state and the national levels. By the end of the era, there was little doubt that they had accomplished the first two of their goals, but serious questions were being raised concerning the success of the last. Despite problems that would have stopped lesser men, George Washington and his army had been able to successfully keep the British at bay, winning when they could and losing as seldom as possible. Meanwhile, the Continental Congress, blessed with some remarkable diplomats, maintained a foreign policy the success of which can be seen in the Franco-American alliance of 1778 and the Treaty of Paris of 1783. But once the war ended, the government that the British threat had held together found that its member states' unwillingness to centralize power created more problems than it solved. Economic dislocation, exemplified by Daniel Shays and his followers, plagued the nation, as many thoughtful men searched for a way to transform Revolutionary rhetoric into reality and to restore order without sacrificing liberty.

Review Questions

These questions are to be answered with essays. This will allow you to explore relationships between individuals, events, and attitudes of the period under review.

1. Explain how conflicts and rivalries among European nations both helped and hindered the American struggle for independence.

2. Compare and contrast the British and the American conduct of the war. How did each side propose to "win," how realistic was its assessment of the situation, and how did this prewar assessment influence the ultimate outcome of the war?

3. Read carefully the section "Where Historians Disagree," and then read the descriptions of the various schools of historical interpretation in the glossary to this chapter of the guide. Which of these historians fit into which schools? Explain your choices.

4. Examine the relative successes and failures of the Articles of Confederation. Do you think that this government was capable of providing the stability that the new nation needed? Why or why not?

5. How did Revolutionary ideology challenge the way minorities were treated in America? What changes in this treatment resulted from this challenge, and why did some minorities find their circumstances improved while others did not?

6. Explain how the political ideology that was the foundation of the American Revolution influenced the writing of state constitutions and the Articles of Confederation.

Chapter Self Test

After you have read the chapter in the text and done the exercises in the Study Guide, take the following self test to see if you understand the material you have covered. Answers appear at the end of the Study Guide.

MULTIPLE-CHOICE QUESTIONS

Circle the letter of the response which best answers the question or completes the statement.

1. Thomas Paine's <u>Common Sense</u> is an important work because it:
    a. helped Americans reconcile their differences with England.
    b. persuaded Americans that no reconciliation with Britain was possible.

c. supported the concept of the English constitution.

d. argued that Parliament, not the King, was the enemy.

2. The Declaration of Independence stated that governments were formed to:

a. give men an opportunity to exert power.

b. reward loyal servants of the state.

c. promote democracy.

d. protect a person's life, freedom, and right to pursue happiness.

3. Most of America's war materials came from:

a. American manufacturers.

b. the seizure of British forts and the surrender of British armies.

c. the capture of supply ships by American privateers.

d. foreign aid.

4. Britain enjoyed all of the following advantages in the Revolution except:

a. the greatest navy and the best-equipped army in the world.

b. superior industrial resources.

c. greater commitment to the conflict.

d. a coherent structure of command.

5. The Articles of Confederation actually:

a. confirmed the weak, decentralized system of government already in operation.

b. drew the stages together into a strong government.

c. put power in the hands of the military.

d. put power in the hands of the executive and his appointees.

6. Congress financed the revolution by:

a. selling bonds.

b. minting gold and silver coins.

c. borrowing from other nations.

d. taxing the wealthy.

7. The choice of George Washington as commander in chief was a good one because of his:

a. knowledge of military affairs.

b. image among the people, who trusted and respected him.

c. successful military experience in the Great War for the empire.

d. relaxed, informal way with his men.

8. At the end of 1776 the American army under Washington had:

a. won no victories, major or minor.

b. become badly divided and scattered.

c. retreated into western Pennsylvania.

d. won two minor victories and remained intact.

9. Which of the following was not part of the British strategy to cut the United States in two in 1777?

a. To move forces up the Hudson from New York City.

b. To prepare a two-pronged attack along the Mohawk and the upper Hudson.

    c. To capture Charleston.

    d. To bring an army down from Canada to meet the one coming up from New York.

10. John Burgoyne's surrender at Saratoga:

    a. convinced the French that they should help the Americans.

    b. caused the British to consider giving up the fight.

    c. made George Washington a military hero.

    d. had little effect on the war in the long run.

11. After 1777 the British decided to focus their efforts in the South because:

    a. there was less population there.

    b. they believed there were more Loyalists there.

    c. they thought slaves would help them.

    d. they had more Indian allies there.

12. The treason of Benedict Arnold:

    a. shocked George Washington.

    b. came as no surprise since he was not highly regarded.

    c. led to the surrender of the fort at West Point.

    d. resulted in Arnold's hanging.

13. The British were forced to surrender at Yorktown because:

    a. French troops and a French fleet helped trap the British.

    b. Washington was able to defeat the British in the field.

    c. Americans were finally better trained than the British.

    d. the British commander underestimated the size of Washington's army.

14. Even though the British wanted to end the war, the French were reluctant to negotiate because:

    a. they feared the Americans might take Canada.

    b. British agents were at work among the common folk of Paris.

    c. they were committed to staying in the war until Spain got Gibraltar.

    d. Spain was insisting on getting the Virgin Islands.

15. Of all the Loyalists groups in America, the one which suffered most as a result of the Revolution was:

    a. western farmers.

    b. slaves.

    c. traders and trappers.

    d. Anglicans.

16. White residents in South Carolina and Georgia were more restrained in their revolutionary expressions than were counterparts in other colonies because there were:

    a. primarily rice planters, unaffected by British restrictions.

    b. Anglican and loyal to the Church of England.

    c. fearful that talk of rebellion would inspire slaves to revolt.

    d. closely tied to families back in England.

17. During the Revolution women took on new responsibilities. After the war:

    a. things generally went back to the way they were before and few concrete reforms occurred in the status of women.

b. women were able to translate wartime gains into peacetime reforms.

c. women were recognized and honored for their contributions with new careers.

d. women got the right to vote in most northern colonies.

18. In spite of rhetoric proclaiming "all men are created equal," slavery survived in America for nearly a century after the Revolution because whites:

a. harbored racist assumptions about the natural inferiority of blacks.

b. never considered it immoral or wrong.

c. feared free blacks would return to Africa.

d. refused to consider plans to compensate slaveholders for gradual emancipation of slaves.

19. If postwar Americans agreed on nothing else, they agreed that:

a. there should be no property qualifications to vote.

b. states should have democratic governments.

c. new governments should be republican.

d. some men were born to govern and some were born to follow.

20. Under the Articles of Confederation, the only institution of national authority was the:

a. Supreme Court.

b. Congress.

c. President of the United States.

d. Senate.

TRUE-FALSE QUESTIONS

Read each statement carefully. Mark true statements "T" and false statements "F."

1. By the military standards of later wars, the American Revolution was a relatively modest one in that technology was more primitive, and hence, less deadly.

2. When the fighting began, most Americans wanted the colonies to be independent from Great Britain.

3. The rebelling colonies had access to sufficient local resources to fight a successful revolution.

4. After declaring independence, colonies began calling themselves states, a reflection of the belief that each of them represented in some respect a separate and sovereign entity.

5. The British lacked the resources to conduct a war on the American continent.

6. At the outset of the war, American leaders hoped that Canada would become the fourteenth state.

7. The surrender of Burgoyne at Saratoga had no effect on the Iroquois Confederacy, since most of the Indians supported the American cause.

8. By the spring of 1776 it was clear to the British that the conflict was not a local one centered around Boston.

9. The British victory at Saratoga kept the French out of the conflict.

10. There is no actual proof that Benedict Arnold committed treason.

11. As a result of the treaty of Paris of 1783, the new American nation's western boundary was the Blue Ridge Mountains.

12. At least one fifth, and maybe as many as one third, of the American colonists were loyal to Britain during the Revolution.

13. Native Americans were pleased with the outcome of the Revolution because it reduced the desire of colonists for western land.

14. After the Revolution the future role of women in the republic was hardly discussed at all.

15. The first state constitutions written during the American Revolution generally reduced the power of the executive.

16. In the newly created states, the privileges that churches enjoyed in the colonial era were largely stripped away.

17. After independence, the United States quickly and easily persuaded Great Britain to abide by the terms of the treaty of 1783.

18. The system for surveying and selling western lands set up under the Ordinance of 1785 favored small farmers.

19. The Northwest Ordinance of 1787 laid out the requirements for western territories to become states.

20. During the period under consideration in this chapter, Congress did nothing to limit the expansion of slavery.

CHAPTER SIX
THE CONSTITUTION AND THE NEW REPUBLIC

Objectives

A thorough study of Chapter Six should enable the student to understand:

1. The groups that advocated a stronger national government and how they, probably a minority, were able to achieve their objective.

2. The origin of the Constitutional Convention, who the delegates were, how well they represented the people, and how they were able to achieve a consensus.

3. The historical debate concerning the motives of the delegates to the Constitutional Convention.

4. Federalism and how the Constitution is designed to make it work.

5. The importance of The Federal Papers in the ratification struggle, and their significance in the years since.

6. The effectiveness of George Washington's solutions to the problems of the presidency, and how Washington, as its first occupant, affected the office and the nation.

7. The financial program of Alexander Hamilton, and its contribution to the success of the new government.

8. The ways in which the weak new nation coped with international problems, and the importance of such events as Washington's decision for neutrality and the "quasi-war" with France.

9. The emergence of political parties, their political philosophies, and their influence through the election of 1800.

Main Themes

1. How and why the Constitution replaced the Articles of Confederation.

2. How differing views of what the nation should become led to the rise of America's first political parties.

3. The way in which the new United States was able to establish itself as a nation in the eyes of foreign powers and of its own people.

4. The rise and fall of the Federalist Party.

Glossary

1. national bank: A private (as opposed to government) institution into which government revenue is deposited. This bank issues currency, grants loans, and generally encourages commercial activity while stabilizing the economy.

2. tariff: A tax on goods imported or exported by a country; in the United States, a tax on imported goods.

3. protective tariff: A tax on goods that are brought into the country and compete with that country's own products. It is designed to drive up the cost of foreign goods and protect native manufacturers from disruptive competition.

4. federalism: A system of government in which powers are divided between a central government and local governments, giving each authority in its own sphere. The extent of and the limitations on this authority are defined in a constitution, which in the United States, also reserves certain powers to the people. It was such a system that many argued existed under the British Empire,

whereas others insisted that a true "federal" system existed under the Articles. This latter group further argued that the Constitution of 1787 put too much power in the hands of the central government and hence created a national rather than a federal government.

5.   implied powers: Powers that are not clearly defined in the Constitution, but, by implication, are granted to the government. Those who believe in the existence of such powers favor a "loose" interpretation of the Constitution, whereas those who hold that the Constitution authorizes nothing that is not spelled out specifically follow a "strict" interpretation.

6.   implied powers doctrine: The idea put forth by Hamilton in his argument in favor of the Bank, which held that the government has powers other than those enumerated in the Constitution. These "implied powers" rise from the government's right to select the means to exercise the powers given it and from the "necessary and proper" clause of the Constitution. Later this was stated even more directly by Chief Justice John Marshall: "Let the end . . . be within the scope of the constitution and all means which [are] appropriate . . . which are not prohibited . . . are constitutional."

7.   national system: A system of government (as opposed to a federal system) in which the central government is supreme and the local units (states) surrender most of their sovereignty to it.

8.   separation of powers: The division of governmental power among the various branches (legislative, executive, judicial) to prevent one branch from dominating the government.

Pertinent Questions

FRAMING A NEW GOVERNMENT (160-168)

1.   Who were the advocates of centralization, and why did they want to alter or abolish the Articles of Confederation?

2.   What did those who favored centralization see as the most serious problem of the Articles, and how would they have changed them? What had prevented any changes?

3.   What were the characteristics of the men who met at the Constitutional Convention in Philadelphia? Whose presence was essential to the meeting's success? Why?

4.   What were the two major points of view that divided the convention? What plans did each side propose to carry its view?

5.   How were the differences between the "large-state" and the "small-state" plans resolved? What other issues divided the convention, and how were they resolved?

6.   What was to be the role of the various branches of government under the new Constitution?

7.   Why did the supporters of the new Constitution call themselves "Federalists"? Were they actually Federalists, or did their philosophy of government reveal them to be something else? If so, what?

8.   What methods did the Federalists employ to get their views across to the people? What were their arguments, and how did the "Antifederalists" respond?

9.   What was the process by which the Constitution was finally ratified? Which states supported it, by what margins, and which states did not? What objections were raised by the states?

10.   What was the process by which the new government set up operations? What were the initial matters discussed, and how were they resolved?

11.   In what way did Congress continue the work of the Constitutional Convention? What "gaps" in the Constitution did Congress fill?

12.   Who were the men Washington selected for his cabinet, and why did he pick these men?

FEDERALISTS AND REPUBLICANS (168-171)

13. How did the divisions of the 1790s reflect the differences in philosophy that were at the heart of debate over the Constitution?

14. What was the view of society and politics held by Hamilton? Who did he feel should govern, and why? Which country's political system did Hamilton most admire?

15. What was Hamilton's plan for paying the nation's debts and restoring credit on a sound basis? To which social-economic-political group would this have appealed?

16. How did Hamilton propose to enact his programs? Who opposed him, and to what degree was he successful?

17. How did political parties rise as a result of Hamilton's programs?

18. What was the political philosophy of Jefferson and Madison? How did it differ from that of Hamilton?

19. How did the French Revolution highlight the differences between the Federalists and the Republicans?

ESTABLISHING NATIONAL SOVEREIGNTY (171-174)

20. How did Washington's reaction to the Whiskey Rebellion underscore the difference between the Constitution and the Articles of Confederation?

21. How did the government under the Constitution guarantee that people on the frontier would be loyal to it? What was the impact on Native Americans?

22. What diplomatic problem did the French Revolution and the war that followed pose for the United States? How did Washington and Congress deal with this problem?

23. What was the French reaction to the policy in question 22, and what resulted from this?

24. What were the circumstances that sent John Jay to England, and what were the results of his mission?

25. How did Jay's Treaty affect American relations with Spain?

THE DOWNFALL OF THE FEDERALISTS (174-178)

26. Why was John Adams selected as the Federalist candidate in 1796?

27. What circumstances led to an administration with a Federalist president and a Republican vice president?

28. What caused the "quasi war" with France during the Adams administration? What was the result of this struggle?

29. How did the Federalists attempt to silence those who opposed the undeclared war, and what groups did these attempts most affect?

30. What gave rise to the Virginia and Kentucky Resolutions, and what attitude toward the nature of the federal government did these resolutions reveal?

31. What were the issues in the election of 1800, and what strategy did each party employ to get elected?

32. What was the outcome of the election of 1800, and what were the reactions of the losers and the victors?

WHERE HISTORIANS DISAGREE (164-165)

33.   Explain the ongoing debate between historians over the motives of the men who framed the American Constitution.

34.   How has the debate over the origins of the Constitution mirrored the debate over the causes of the American Revolution?

Identification

Identify each of the following, and explain why it is important within the context of the chapter.

1.   Society of the Cincinnati
2.   the "Indian menace"
3.   Annapolis Conference
4.   Virginia Plan
5.   New Jersey Plan
6.   "Great Compromise"
7.   three-fifths formula
8.   Antifederalists
9.   The Federalist Papers
10.   Bill of Rights
11.   Tenth Amendment
12.   Judiciary Act of 1789
13.   Assumption Bill
14.   Hamilton's "Report on Manufacturers"
15.   Hamilton's bank bill
16.   Whiskey Rebellion
17.   a "nation within a nation"
18.   Citizen Genet
19.   Jay's Treaty
20.   Pinckney's Treaty
21.   Washington's "Farewell Address"
22.   XYZ Affair
23.   Alien and Sedition Acts
24.   Virginia and Kentucky Resolutions
25.   Aaron Burr
26.   Judiciary Act of 1801
27.   "midnight appointments"

Document 1

The series of essays known as The Federalist Papers was published anonymously, over the pen name Publius. In fact, they were the work of three men: Alexander Hamilton, James Madison, and John Jay. The Federalist No. 1, written by Hamilton, summarizes the purposes of the papers to come. How does this excerpt reflect not only what the Federalists wanted to promote, but also how they wanted to head off objections to the Constitution that were already beginning to surface? From your readings in the text, what were these objections?

After an unequivocal experience of the inefficacy of the subsisting federal government, you are called upon to deliberate on a new Constitution for the United States of America. The subject speaks its own importance; comprehending in its consequences nothing less than the existence of the UNION, the safety and welfare of the parts of which it is composed, the fate of an empire in many respects the most interesting in the world. It has been frequently remarked that it seems to have been reserved to the people of this country, by their conduct and example, to decide the important question, whether societies of men are really capable or not of establishing good government from reflection and choice, or whether they are forever destined to depend for their political constitutions on accident and force. If there be any truth in the remark, the crisis at which we are arrived may with propriety be regarded as the era in which that decision is to be made; and a wrong election of the part we shall act may, in this view, deserve to be considered as the general misfortune of mankind. . . .

I propose, in a series of papers, to discuss the following interesting particulars:--The utility of the UNION to your political prosperity--The insufficiency of the present Confederation to preserve that Union--The necessity of a government at least equally energetic with the one proposed, to the attainment of this object--The conformity of the proposed Constitution to the true principles of republican government--Its analogy to your own State constitution--and lastly, The additional security which its adoption will afford to the preservation of that species of government, to liberty, and to property.

In the progress of this discussion I shall endeavor to give a satisfactory answer to all the objections which shall have made their appearance, that may seem to have any claim to your attention. . . .

PUBLIUS

Document 2

The document to be studied is the Constitution of the United States and its first twelve amendments. First, read the Constitution in the Appendices to your text; then, consider the following.

1. How does the organization and election of the House and the Senate reflect attitudes that existed in 1787? Why is impeachment held in the House and the trial in the Senate? What does this tell you about the Founding Fathers' attitude toward "popular" government?

2. Why are all revenue bills required to originate in the House of Representatives?

3. Examine the powers given Congress in Article I, Section 8. How does this section make the Constitution different from the Articles?

4. Outline how the president was elected before the ratification of the Twelfth Amendment. What role did the popular vote play in this process? Why was it designed this way?

5. List the specific powers given the president, and be prepared to follow the evolution of these powers.

6. Why are Supreme Court justices (and judges on inferior courts) appointed rather than elected, and why do they hold office during good behavior? Look at the terms of office for the other branches. What does this reveal about what the people can, and cannot, do regarding changes in their government? Why was it done this way?

7. How does the amendment process under the Constitution differ from that under the Articles? Why was this change made?

8. Reread the second paragraph of Article VI. According to this article, is the Constitution creating a national or a federal government?

Now read the first ten amendments to the Constitution—the Bill of Rights—and consider the following.

1. Look carefully at Amendments I through V, and consider the relations between Great Britain and its colonies from 1700 to 1776. It has been contended that these amendments were insisted on to make sure that the abuses experienced at the hands of the mother country would not be repeated. What evidence of this do you find?

2. Examine Amendments VI through VIII. What fears do these amendments reflect, and how were these fears resolved?

3. What seems to have been the purpose of Amendments IX and X? How do these amendments reflect concerns felt by opponents of the Constitution?

Compare and contrast the provisions in Amendment XII for electing the president with those in Article II, Section 1. What circumstances gave rise to this change?

Document 3

Once the Constitution was ratified, the debate over the Bank of the United States moved to center stage, and some historians have suggested that it was this issue that divided the Jeffersonians and the Hamiltonians into "parties." Below is an excerpt from Alexander Hamilton's view on the constitutionality of the Bank.

It is conceded that implied powers are to be considered as delegated equally with express ones. Then it follows, that as a power of erecting a corporation may as well be implied as any other thing, it may as well be employed as an instrument or mean of carrying into execution any of the specified powers, as any other instrument or mean whatever. . . .

It is objected that none but necessary and proper means are to be employed; and the Secretary of State maintains that no means are to be considered as necessary but those without which the grant of the power would be nugatory. . . .

It is certain that neither the grammatical nor popular sense of the term requires that construction. According to both, necessary often means no more than needful, requisite, incidental, useful, or conducive to. . . .

If the end be clearly comprehended within any of the specified powers, and if the measure have an obvious relation to that end, and is not forbidden by any particular provision of the Constitution, it may safely be deemed to come within the compass of the national authority. . . .

A bank has a natural relation to the power of collecting taxes—to that of regulating trade—to that of providing for the common defence. . . . [Therefore] the incorporation of a bank is a constitutional measure. . . .

Here is Thomas Jefferson's opinion of the constitutionality of the Bank. On what did Hamilton and Jefferson differ? Was there room for compromise? What interests in the nation supported each side? What does this suggest about the supporters of the two emerging political parties?

The incorporation of a bank, and the powers assumed by this bill, have not, in my opinion, been delegated to the United States by the Constitution.

I. They are not among the powers specially enumerated. . . .

II. Nor are they within either of the general phrases, which are the two following:

1. To lay taxes to provide for the general welfare of the United States. . . . They [Congress] are not to do anything they please, to provide for the general welfare, but only to lay taxes for that purpose. . . . It was intended to lace them up straitly within the enumerated powers, and those without which, as means, these powers could not be carried into effect. . . .

2. The second general phrase is, "to make all laws necessary and proper for carrying into execution the enumerate powers." But they can all be carried into execution without a bank. A bank, therefore, is not necessary, and consequently not authorized by this phrase.

It has been much urged that a bank will give great facility or convenience in the collection of taxes. Suppose this were true; yet the Constitution allows only the means which are "necessary," not those which are merely "convenient," for effecting the enumerated powers.

Map Exercise

Fill in or identify the following on the blank map provided. Use the maps in the text as your sources and consult maps in your library as needed.

1. Original thirteen states.
2. States admitted to the Union between the Revolution and 1800.
3. Ohio, Mississippi, Tennessee, and Missouri Rivers.
4. Territory held or claimed by Spain.
5. New Orleans, Mobile, and Pittsburgh.
6. The Appalachian Mountains.

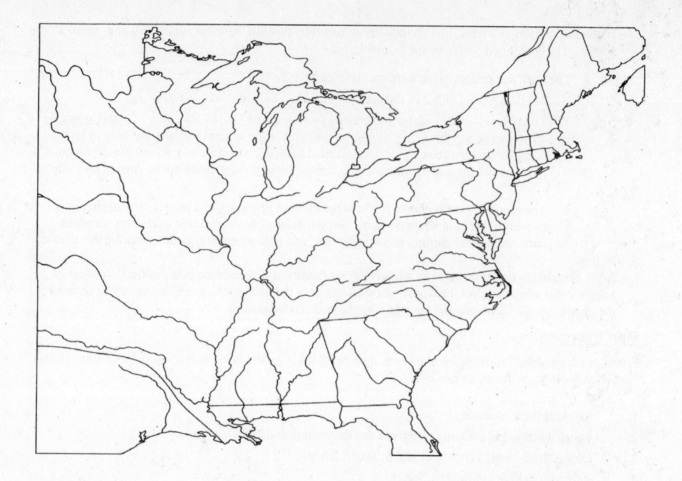

Interpretative Questions

Based on what you have filled in, answer the following. On some of the questions you will need to consult the narrative in your text for information or explanation.

1. Thomas Jefferson "believed that farmers were God's chosen people and that an ideal republic would consist of sturdy citizens, each tilling his own soil." Furthermore, he advocated policies designed to make this republican ideal a reality. Which groups would have been most likely to support Jefferson because of this? Where were they located?

2. Which groups were most likely to oppose Jefferson? Where were they located? Why were members of this opposition less inclined to support the admission of new states?

3. Why did farmers in western Pennsylvania challenge federal authority in 1794? What does their location, and the nature of their economy, have to do with this?

4. What Indian problems did the new nation experience? What role did the Spanish play in this? How were these problems solved?

5. Identify the settlements and areas of the United States affected by Jay's Treaty. Why did some regions oppose this treaty?

6. Identify the areas of the United States affected by Pinckney's Treaty. How did this treaty solve (for the time being) one of the major problems facing western expansion?

Summary

The period between 1785 and 1800 was one of the most politically productive in American history. During these fifteen years, the nation, guided by some of the most talented men in history, reorganized itself under a new framework of government and then struggled to define (for itself as well as for others) just what had been created. It was a period marked by the rise of a party that called itself Federalist, although the philosophy it espoused was, as its opponents were quick to point out, more "nationalist" in emphasis. Arguing that to prosper, the United States had best follow the economic and political example of Great Britain, these Federalists, led by Hamilton, interjected foreign policy into domestic differences and set the stage for one of the earliest and most serious government assaults on individual civil liberties. Seeing their less elitist, proagriculture, Republican opponents as supporters of France in an undeclared conflict between that nation and the United States, the Federalists set out to suppress dissent and those who promoted it. This assault brought a swift response and so heightened tensions that many feared that the nation could not survive. It was against this background that a shift of power occurred, and by the end of the decade, the Federalists, who had been the moving force for so many years, were clearly losing ground to the Republicans. This meant that if wounds were to be healed and divisions mended, it would have to be done by the man many believed to be the personification of all that separated the two groups— Thomas Jefferson.

Review Questions

These questions are to be answered with essays. This will allow you to explore relationships between individuals, events, and attitudes of the period under review.

1. Explain Hamilton's motives for proposing his plans for taxation, assumption, and currency regulation. What was it in his motives that so upset Jefferson and Madison?

2. The Bill of Rights is generally recognized as protecting the citizens of the United States from their government, but what safeguards are contained in the Constitution to protect the states from violations of their rights? What additional safeguards were proposed by Jefferson and Madison in the Virginia and Kentucky Resolutions, and what were the implications of these resolutions with regard to the growth of the central government?

3. Compare and contrast the political, economic, and social philosophies of Thomas Jefferson and Alexander Hamilton. Explain the sort of nation each wished created. (The documents provided in the Study Guide should be consulted in answering this question.)

4. During the period we have just studied, two opposing political parties arose. Both had their roots in the era governed under the Articles, but unlike competing groups during that period, both factions claimed to support the Constitution. If both felt that the Constitution created the best form of government, what was the basis for their disagreement? Compare and contrast the two parties—their goals, methods, and philosophies.

5. During the "Federalist era," events in other countries did much to shape political-party growth and domestic policy. Look at American relations with England, Spain, and France; analyze how these relations affected the two political parties that emerged during this period; and explain the way the government responded to this foreign influence on the parties.

Chapter Self Test

After you have read the chapter in the text and done the exercises in the Study Guide, take the following self test to see if you understand the material you have covered. Answers appear at the end of the Study Guide.

MULTIPLE-CHOICE QUESTIONS

Circle the letter of the response which best answers the question or completes the statement.

1. By 1786, even defenders of the Articles of Confederation accepted the fact that which of the following needed to be strengthened?
   a. The power to tax.
   b. The executive.
   c. The court system.
   d. The army.

2. By the mid-1780s, advocates of a stronger central government included:
   a. military veterans disgruntled by the refusal of Congress to fund their pensions.
   b. American manufacturers upset with the imposition of high national tariffs.
   c. creditors who demanded an inflation of the nation's money supply.
   d. investors who wanted Confederation debts repudiated.

3. Which of the following was not a characteristic of the men who attended the Constitutional Convention in 1787?
   a. They represented the great property interests.
   b. They were relatively young.
   c. They believed in democracy.
   d. They were well educated.

4. The most significant division in the Constitutional Convention was between:
   a. slave and free states.
   b. large and small states.
   c. eastern and western interests.
   d. agricultural and manufacturing interests.

5. James Madison's Virginia Plan proposed:
   a. revision and strengthening of the Articles of Confederation.
   b. larger influence within a new national government for the richer and more populous states.
   c. a unicameral national legislature with equal representation for the states.
   d. a bicameral national legislature with state representatives in both houses chosen by popular vote.

6. The most important issue left unaddressed when the Constitutional Convention adjourned was:
   a. the question of counting slaves for representation.
   b. whether to have an executive or not.
   c. the absence of a list of individual rights.
   d. the question of the power of the national government to tax.

7. The Constitution's most distinctive feature was its:
   a. "separation of powers" with "checks and balances."
   b. system for the direct election of the executive.
   c. lack of a national judicial system.
   d. single house legislature.

8. Which of the following was not addressed by the first Congress under the new Constitution?

   a. A Bill of Rights.

   b. A federal court system.

   c. An executive department.

   d. The role of political parties in the election of a president.

9. To prevent an "excess of democracy" and the tyranny of mob rule, the Constitution restricted direct popular election to:

   a. the president.

   b. federal judges.

   c. senators.

   d. representatives.

10. Which of the following was not a belief of Alexander Hamilton?

    a. The best leaders are those democratically elected.

    b. A stable and effective government required an elite ruling class.

    c. The new government needed the support of the wealthy and powerful.

    d. A permanent national debt was desirable.

11. Small farmers, who comprised the majority of the population, opposed Hamilton's plan on the grounds that it:

    a. taxed them excessively.

    b. favored a small, wealthy elite.

    c. created too many government offices.

    d. put power in the hands of slaveholders.

    e. achieved both a. and b.

    f. achieved both c. and d.

12. President Washington helped stabilize the western frontier by:

    a. putting down the Whiskey Rebellion.

    b. allowing existing states to incorporate additional land claims.

    c. refusing to bargain with Indian resistance leaders.

    d. relieving General "Mad Anthony" Wayne of his command.

13. Jefferson and his followers believed the Federalists were creating a political party because they were:

    a. using their offices to reward supporters and win allies.

    b. forming local associations to strengthen their stand in local communities.

    c. working to establish a national network of influence.

    d. doing all of the above.

14. Which of the following was not a belief held by Jefferson and his followers?

    a. The ordinary farmer-citizen could, if properly educated, be trusted to govern through elected representatives.

    b. Urban people posed a danger to a republic, because they could easily become a lawless mob.

    c. The best citizen was one who tilled his own soil.

    d. Commercial activity was a danger to the republic.

15. Under the Constitution, the status of the western Indian tribes was:
    a. not clearly defined.
    b. that of independent nations.
    c. that of conquered nations.
    d. the same as states.

16. Although the treaty between England and the United States that John Jay negotiated in 1794 fell short of his instructions, it did:
    a. little to improve commercial relations with England.
    b. give America undisputed sovereignty over the entire Northwest.
    c. end the impressment of American soldiers.
    d. indicate that the United States and France were not going to war.

17. In the election of 1796:
    a. Thomas Jefferson was the choice of southern Federalists.
    b. the Federalist Party united behind Adams.
    c. George Washington took an active role.
    d. the Federalist Party divided when southern Federalists refused to support Adams.

18. Republicans pinned their hopes for a reversal of the Alien and Sedition Acts on the:
    a. Supreme Court.
    b. state legislatures.
    c. House of Representatives.
    d. Army of the United States.

19. Which of the following is not true of the campaign and election of 1800?
    a. It was probably the ugliest in American history.
    b. Parties and party organization played an important role.
    c. It underscored problems in the method of electing a president.
    d. It resulted in a clear victory for the winning candidate.

20. The Federalists made a last gasp attempt to maintain power by:
    a. repealing the Alien and Sedition Acts.
    b. supporting Aaron Burr for President.
    c. creating new federal courts and judges.
    d. plotting a revolution to prevent the election of Jefferson.

TRUE-FALSE QUESTIONS

Read each statement carefully. Mark true statements "T" and false statements "F."

1. The adoption of the Constitution completed the creation of the republic.
2. The most resourceful advocate of a centralized government was Alexander Hamilton.
3. The intellectual leader of the Constitutional Convention was James Madison.
4. The "Great Compromise" was important because it solved the problem of representation.
5. The Constitution did not resolve the question of which law—state or national—would be the supreme law of the land.

6. Abiding by the rules set up under the Articles of Confederation, the Constitution could not go into effect until it was ratified by all the states in the union.

7. The Constitution was attacked because it did not contain a list of individual rights protected under the national government.

8. The essays, known collectively as <u>The Federalist Papers,</u> called for the ratification of the Constitution.

9. The Constitution had little chance of success unless it was ratified by Virginia and New York.

10. Supporters of the Constitution had the advantage of being better organized than their opponents.

11. After the Constitution was ratified, Americans agreed that the government should strive to create a highly commercial, urban nation.

12. The Federalist vision for America included government by a wealthy, enlightened ruling class.

13. Virginia agreed to support Hamilton's assumption bill in return for locating the national capital in the South.

14. Most of the framers of the Constitution believed organized political parties were evil and should be avoided.

15. The "Republican Party" that opposed the Federalists is the same Republican Party that exists today.

16. The national government's response to the Whiskey Rebellion was to win allegiance through intimidation.

17. In 1796, Thomas Jefferson ran for vice-president on the Federalist ticket.

18. President Washington welcomed Citizen Genet to America in hopes of an alliance with France.

19. Aaron Burr's role in the election of 1800 was not very significant.

20. After the election of 1800, Federalists tried to hold on to power through the federal judiciary.

CHAPTER SEVEN
THE JEFFERSONIAN ERA

Objectives

A thorough study of Chapter Seven should enable the student to understand:

1. Thomas Jefferson's views on education and the role of education in the concept of a "virtuous and enlightened citizenry."

2. The indications of American cultural nationalism that were beginning to emerge during the first two decades of the nineteenth century.

3. The effects of the Revolutionary era on religion, and the changing religious patterns that helped bring on the Second Great Awakening.

4. The evidence noticeable in the first two decades that the nation was not destined to remain the simple, agrarian republic envisioned by the Jeffersonians.

5. The political philosophy of Jefferson, and the extent to which he was able to adhere to his philosophy while president.

6. The Jeffersonian-Federalist struggle over the judiciary—its causes, the main points of conflict, and the importance of the outcome for the future of the nation.

7. President Jefferson's constitutional reservations concerning the Louisiana Purchase, and the significance of his decision to accept the bargain.

8. The reasons for President Jefferson's sponsorship of the Lewis and Clark expedition, and the importance of that exploration.

9. The many problems involved in attempting to achieve an understanding of Aaron Burr and his "conspiracy."

10. What Thomas Jefferson and James Madison were attempting to accomplish by "peaceable coercion," and why their efforts were not successful.

11. The numerous explanations of the causes of the War of 1812, and why there is so much disagreement among historians.

12. The problems caused by Tecumseh's attempts at confederation and by the Spanish presence in Florida as Americans surged westward.

13. The state of the nation in 1812, and how the Madison administration waged war against the world's foremost naval power.

14. The extent of the opposition to the American war effort, and the ways in which the New England Federalists attempted to show their objections.

15. The ways in which the skill of the American peace commissioners and the international problems faced by England contributed to a satisfactory—for Americans—peace settlement.

16. The effects of the War of 1812 on banking, shipping, farming, industry, and transportation.

17. How the industrial revolution in the United States was largely a product of rapid changes in Great Britain and the impact this revolution had on American society.

Main Themes

1. How Americans expressed their cultural independence..

2. The impact of industrialism on the United States and its people.

3. The role that Thomas Jefferson played in shaping the American character.

4. How the American people and their political system responded to the nation's physical expansion.

5. How American ambitions and attitudes came into conflict with British policies and led to the War of 1812.

6. How Americans were able to "win" the war, and the peace that followed.

Glossary

1. <u>Jeffersonian democracy:</u> Not actually a democrat, in the classic sense of the word, Jefferson believed that the masses were capable of selecting their own representatives and, if properly educated and informed, would select the best and the wisest to govern. Once these were chosen, however, this "natural aristocracy" should be allowed to govern without interference from those who selected them. Only when they stood again for election would these representatives be called on to explain their actions.

2. <u>patronage:</u> The control of political appointments assumed by the victors in an election—the "spoils" of victory, which the victors hand out as rewards to their followers; hence the practice became known as the "spoils system."

3. <u>judicial review:</u> The power of a court to review a law, compare it with the Constitution, and rule on whether it does or does not conform to the principles of the Constitution—whether it is constitutional or unconstitutional.

4. <u>impeachment:</u> The bringing of charges against a governmental official by the House of Representatives. Removal from office cannot come from impeachment alone. A trial must be held in the Senate, and on conviction there, the offender may be removed from his or her post.

5. <u>embargo:</u> An act that prohibits ships from entering or leaving a nation's ports.

Pertinent Questions

THE RISE OF CULTURAL NATIONALISM (182-188)

1. Why was education "central to the Republican vision of America"?

2. What effect did Republican ideology have on education in the United States?

3. Explain the "cultural independence" that Jeffersonian Americans sought. What means of expression did this "independence" find?

4. What were the obstacles faced by Americans who aspired to create a more elevated national literary life? What efforts were made to overcome these obstacles?

5. What sort of works by America authors were most influential? Why?

6. How did the American Revolution affect traditional forms of religious practice? What challenges to religious traditionalism arose during this period?

7. What caused the Second Great Awakening?

8. Why were the Methodists, the Baptists, and the Presbyterians so successful on the frontier?

9. What was the "message" and the impact of the Second Great Awakening? What impact did it have on women? On African Americans? On Native Americans?

STIRRINGS OF INDUSTRIALISM (188-194)

10. What was the industrial revolution? Where and why did it begin?

11. Explain the initial American ambivalence toward British industrialism. What technological advances helped change this attitude?

12. Explain the role that Eli Whitney played in America's industrial revolution. What impact did his inventions have on the South? on the North?

13. What effect did America's transportation system have on industrialization?

14. What were the characteristics of American population growth and expansion in the years between 1790 and 1800?

JEFFERSON THE PRESIDENT (194-200)

15. How and why did Jefferson attempt to minimize the differences between the two political parties?

16. How was it that "at times Jefferson seemed to outdo the Federalists at their own work?"

17. How was the relative "unimportance of the federal government" during the Jefferson administration symbolized by the character of the national capital?

18. What were the characteristics of the "spirit of democratic simplicity" that was the style set by Jefferson for his administration?

19. How did Jefferson combine his duties as president and as party leader in his efforts to govern the country?

20. How did the Republican administration move toward dismantling the structure of federal power that the Federalists had erected?

21. Why did Jefferson, despite his views on government spending, go to "war" with the Pasha of Tripoli? What was the outcome?

22. What were the roots of Jefferson's conflict with the federal court system, and how did the case of Marbury v. Madison fit into the controversy? What is the significance of Marbury v. Madison?

23. What method did Jefferson employ to bring the judiciary under Republican control, and what were the results?

DOUBLING THE NATIONAL DOMAIN (200-204)

24. How did France come into possession of Louisiana?

25. Why was New Orleans "the one single spot" that made its possessor the "natural enemy" of the United States?

26. Which group in America was most concerned with the French possession of New Orleans, and how did this concern threaten Jefferson politically?

27. How were the negotiations for the Louisiana Purchase conducted, and what were the terms agreed on?

28. What were the reasons behind Jefferson's reservations over the purchase of Louisiana, and how was he able to reason these doubts away?

29. What was the purpose of the Lewis and Clark expedition, and what did the expedition accomplish?

30. What was the reaction of the New England Federalists to the Louisiana Purchase, and what was their plan to overcome its effects?

31. What were the circumstances that led to the duel between Hamilton and Burr?

32. What was the "Burr conspiracy," and what was its outcome?

EXPANSION AND WAR (204-208)

33. Why was America important to both sides in the conflict between England and France, and what role did the Americans hope to play in the struggle?

34. How did each belligerent nation attempt to prevent America from trading with the other, why was one more successful than the other, and what was the American response?

35. What was Jefferson's response to the <u>Chesapeake-Leopard</u> affair, and why did he take this action?

36. What was the major issue standing between a compromise between Britain and America, and why was this issue so crucial to both sides?

37. Which areas of the nation supported the Embargo of 1807, and which opposed it? Why?

38. How did the Embargo affect the election of 1808, and what was the response of the new president to diplomatic problems that the Embargo had addressed?

39. How did conditions in the West heighten the tension between the United States and Britain?

40. What was Tecumseh's attitude toward the treaties previously negotiated between the United States and various Indian tribes? How did he plan to prevent the expansion of white settlements?

41. What role did Native American religious leaders play in the events leading to the War of 1812?

42. Why did Americans want to gain control of Florida from the Spanish? What attempts were made to do this before 1812? Which attempts were successful, and which failed?

THE WAR OF 1812 (208-213)

43. What were the relative successes and failures of the American military during the first year of the war?

44. How did America's fortunes of war change during 1813 and early 1814, and what were the results of this change?

45. Why did Britain feel confident in launching an invasion of the United States in 1814, and what was the plan and purpose of that invasion? What was the result?

46. Why did New England oppose the War of 1812? Prior to 1814, what did the New England states do to hinder the war effort?

47. What caused the leaders of New England to regard the War of 1812 as a threat to their future as a meaningful force in the United States? What did they propose to remedy this situation?

48. What effect did the Hartford Convention have on the Federalist Party?

49. What was the background to the peace negotiations at Ghent? What did both sides initially demand, and why did they finally agree on the terms they did?

PATTERNS OF POPULAR CULTURE (194-195)

50. Why was horse racing a "natural" leisure activity for early Americans?

51. How was this pastime "bounded by lines of class and race?"

AMERICA IN THE WORLD (190-191)

52. How did the industrial revolution in Great Britain lead to and influence the industrial revolution in the United States?

53. How did the industrial revolution change societies in the United States and in the world?

Identification

Identify each of the following, and explain why it is important within the context of the chapter.

1. "republican mother"
2. Benjamin Rush
3. <u>American Spelling Book</u>
4. Hartford Wits

5.   deism
6.   Unitarianism
7.   Handsome Lake
8.   James Watt
9.   Oliver Evans
10. Robert Fulton
11. Pierre L'Enfant
12. Albert Gallatin
13. Charles C. Pinckney
14. William Marbury
15. Barbary states
16. John Marshall
17. Samuel Chase
18. Toussaint L'Ouverture
19. Robert Livingston
20. General James Wilkinson
21. Continental System
22. "peaceable coercion"
23. Non-Intercourse Act
24. Tecumseh
25. William Henry Harrison
26. Tenskwatawa
27. Battle of Tippecanoe
28. Henry Clay
29. Put-In Bay
30. Battle of Horseshoe Bend
31. Francis Scott Key
32. Battle of New Orleans
33. John Quincy Adams

Document 1

Manasseh Cutler was as diverse as the new United States. A teacher, doctor, lawyer, scientist, and land agent, he eventually turned to politics and in 1800 was elected to Congress as a Federalist from Massachusetts. Below is a selection taken from a letter to his daughter that describes his circumstances in Washington, the new national capital. With Cutler's letter is an excerpt from the writings of F. A. Michaux, a French botanist who traveled through the western areas of the nation. His description of the people of Kentucky stands in stark contrast to Cutler's description of Washington society and offers excellent proof of the variety that was America.

In both documents, religion played an important part. What do the religious differences reveal about the two ways of life? What can you gather about the relationship between religion and social class in America? What seems to be the main reason for the differences in attitude toward religion in the two areas? What attitudes toward religion do the two societies have in common? What does this reveal about religious toleration in the United States?

84

Notice the forms of entertainment enjoyed by the two groups. What do they tell you about the nature of the two societies and the people who made them up? Do these entertainments reveal any class divisions, or can they be explained by something else?

How do you think the two societies would respond to the question "To what degree should the people be allowed to govern themselves?" Why do you believe this? What evidence supports your conclusion? From these two documents, what can be told about the impact of the frontier on American life, culture, and values?

Read the description of Washington, D.C., found in the text. How does Cutler's letter compare with the account found there? What might account for the difference--note the date the letter was written, the month, and the year. Also note Cutler's political party.

Washington, Dec. 2, 1801

MY DEAR BETSY: . . . It shall be the subject of this letter to give you some account of my present situation and of occurrences since I left home.

The city of Washington, in point of situation, is much more delightful than I expected to find it. The ground, in general, is elevated, mostly cleared, and commands a pleasing prospect of the Potomac River. The buildings are brick, and erected in what are called large blocks, that is, from two to five or six houses joined together, and appear like one long building. . . . Mr. King, our landlord, occupies the south end, only one room in front, which is our parlor for receiving company and dining, and one room back, occupied by Mr. King's family, the kitchen is below. The four chambers are appropriate to the eight gentlemen who board in the family. In each chamber are two narrow field beds and field curtains, with every necessary convenience for the boarders. . . . Mr. King's family consists only of himself, his lady and one daughter, besides the servants, all of whom are black. Mr. King was an officer in the late American Army, much of a gentleman in his manner, social and very obliging. I have seen few women more agreeable than Mrs. King. . . . She was the daughter of Mr. Harper, a very respectable merchant in Baltimore; has been favored with an excellent education, has been much in the first circles of society in this part of the country, and is in nothing more remarkable than her perfect freedom from stiffness, vanity, or ostentation. Their only daughter, Miss Anna, is about seventeen, well formed, rather tall, small featured, but is considered very handsome. She has been educated at the best schools in Baltimore and Alexandria. She does not converse much, but is very modest and agreeable. She plays with great skill on the Forte Piano, which she always accompanies with a most delightful voice, and is frequently joined in the vocal part by her mother. Mr. King has an excellent Forte Piano, which is connected with an organ placed under it, which she fills and plays with her foot, while her fingers are employed upon the Forte Piano.

The gentlemen, generally, spend a part of two or three evenings in a week in Mr. King's room, where Miss Anna entertains us with delightful music. After we have been fatigued with the harangues of the Hall in the day, and conversing on politics, in different circles (for we talk about nothing else), in the evening, an hour of this music is truly delightful. On Sunday evenings, she constantly plays Psalm tunes, in which her mother, who is a woman of real piety, always joins. . . .

I can not conclude without giving you some description of our fellow-lodgers, with whom I enjoy a happiness which I by no means expected. . . . It is remarkable that all these gentlemen are professors of religion and members of the churches to which they respectively belong. An unbecoming word is never uttered by one of them, and the most perfect harmony and friendliness pervades the family.

William Parker Cutler and Julia Perkins Cutler, eds., Life, Journals and Correspondence of Rev. Manasseh Cutler (Cincinnati: Clarke, 1888), 2:50–53.

* * *

The inhabitants of Kentucky, are nearly all natives of Virginia, and particularly the remotest parts of that state; and exclusive of the gentlemen of the law, physicians, and a small number of citizens who have received an education suitable to their professions in the Atlantic states, they have preserved the manners of the Virginians. With them the passion for gaming and spirituous liquors is carried to excess, which frequently terminates in quarrels degrading to human nature. The public-houses are always crowded, more especially during the sittings of the courts of justice. Horses and law-suits comprise the usual topic of their conversation. If a traveller happens to pass by, his horse is appreciated; if he stops, he is presented with a glass of whiskey, and then asked a thousand questions

. . . their only object being the gratification of that curiosity so natural to people who live isolated in the woods, and seldom see a stranger. They are never dictated by mistrust; for from whatever part of the globe a person comes, he may visit all the ports and principal towns of the United States, stay there as long as he pleases, and travel in any part of the country without ever being interrogated by a public officer.

Among the various sects that exist in Kentucky, those of the Methodists and Anabaptists are the most numerous. The spirit of religion has acquired a fresh degree of strength within these seven or eight years among the country inhabitants, since, independent of Sundays, which are scrupulously observed, they assemble, during the summer, in the course of the week, to hear sermons. These meetings, which frequently consist of two or three thousand persons who come from all parts of the country within fifteen or twenty miles, take place in the woods, and continue for several days. Each brings his provisions, and spends the night round a fire. The clergymen are very vehement in their discourses. Often in the midst of the sermons the heads are lifted up, the imaginations exalted, and the inspired all backwards, exclaiming, "Glory! glory!" This species of infatuation happens chiefly among the women, who are carried out of the crowd, and put under a tree, where they lie a long time extended, heaving the most lamentable sighs.

There have been instances of two or three hundred of the congregation being thus affected during the performance of divine service; so that one-third of the hearers were engaged in recovering the rest. Whilst I was at Lexington I was present at one of these meetings. The better informed people do not share the opinion of the multitude with regard to this state of ecstacy, and on this account they are branded with the appellation of <u>bad folks.</u> Except during the continuance of this preaching, religion is very seldom the topic of conversation. Although divided into several sects, they live in the greatest harmony; and whenever there is an alliance between the families, the difference of religion is never considered as an obstacle; the husband and wife pursue whatever kind of worship they like best, and their children, when they grow up, do just the same, without the interference of their parents.

F. A. Michaux, "Travels West of the Allegheny Mountains," in Reuben Gold Thwaites, ed., <u>Early Western Travels, 1748–1846</u> (Cleveland: Clark, 1904), 3:246–250.

Document 2

Few inaugural addresses have had the lasting impact of Thomas Jefferson's first inaugural address, which he delivered in early 1801. Some historians have suggested that it was addressed not to his supporters, but to his political enemies. What evidence is there in the excerpt below to suggest that this is true? What evidence is there that this was in keeping with the principles that Jefferson had endorsed as long as he had been in public office? How do the principles espoused here relate to those in the Declaration of Independence? in the Virginia Statue of Religious Liberty?

We are all Republicans, we are all Federalists. If there be any among us who would wish to dissolve this Union or to change its republican form, let them stand undisturbed as monuments of the safety with which error of opinion may be tolerated where reason is left free to combat it. I know, indeed, that some honest men fear that a republican government can not be strong, that this Government is not strong enough; but would the honest patriot, in the full tide of successful experiment, abandon a government which has so far kept us free and firm on the theoretic and visionary fear that this Government, the world's best hope, may by possibility want energy to preserve itself? I trust not. I believe this, on the contrary, the strongest Government on earth. I believe it the only one where every man, at the call of the law, would fly to the standard of the law, and would meet invasions of the public order as his own personal concern. Sometimes it is said that man can not be trusted with the government of himself. Can he, then, be trusted with the government of others? Or have we found angels in the forms of kings to govern him? Let history answer this question.

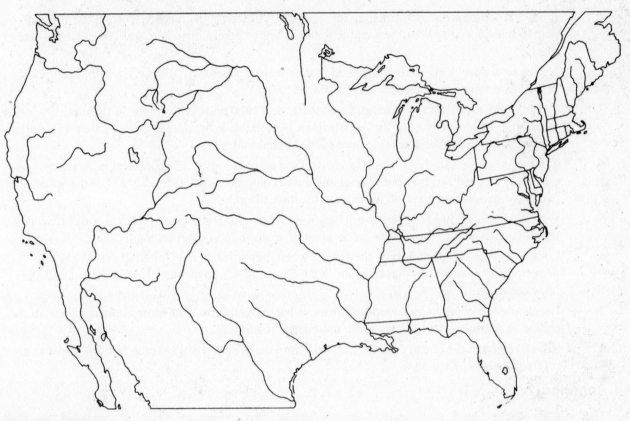

Map Exercise

Fill in or identify the following on the blank map provided. Use the map in the text as your source.

1. Settled areas (non-Indian).
2. States in the Union in 1800.
3. Cities, settlements, and other outposts founded in the eighteenth century, and the dates they were established.
4. Forts founded in the eighteenth century and their dates.
5. Other pre-eighteenth-century cities identified on the map.
6. Oregon country, British America, and the Spanish possessions.
7. United States and territories belonging to the United States.
8. British America and its principal towns.
9. Spanish Florida and its principal towns.
10. Principal ports on the Atlantic coast.

11. Routes of troop movements.

12. Battle sites and dates, indicating the victor.

13. Extent of the British blockade.

Interpretative Questions

Based on what you have filled in, answer the following. On some of the questions you will need to consult the narrative in your text for information or explanation.

1. Study the settled areas on the map in this chapter of the text and compare these to the physical map in the Appendix. What geographic features helped determine where settlement would take place?

2. Notice how many forts were established in the nineteenth century. What geographic features helped determine where these would be placed?

3. Consider the population of America's major cities in 1800 and compare this to the rural population—east and west of the Appalachian Mountains. What does this population distribution suggest about the cultural development of the United States?

4. The period you are studying was one of significant technological advancement in America—especially in trade and transportation. How did developments in technology help Americans overcome geographic barriers? Where did this take place?

5. Why did northern and southern frontiersmen want to expand into Canada and Florida? How did foreign occupation of these areas hinder western expansion in other regions?

6. Locate the major routes taken by the British when they invaded the United States. What geographic considerations played a part in the choice of where to attack? What made these sites important?

7. Locate the routes taken by American forces. What geographic considerations played a part in the choice of where to attack? What made these sites important?

8. Which region of the country gained the most from the War of 1812? Which felt that it lost as a result of the war? Explain.

Summary

The period just covered was marked by definition and expansion. Having achieved political independence, Americans struggled to achieve cultural independence as well, and this search for self-identity touched almost every phase of the nation's life. "American" tastes in music, literature, and art developed, encouraged by a growing recognition that we were different from other countries and that the difference was worth calling attention to. Religious bodies with ties to the old, colonial ways declined as the Second Great Awakening swept America; technology, unrestrained by mercantile rules and regulations, expanded to solve problems that were particularly American; American politics began to take on characteristics and respond to needs that found little precedent in European systems. At the center of this activity, at times leading it and at times being led, was Thomas Jefferson, a president whose versatility seemed to mirror the diversity of the nation. An aristocrat with democratic sentiments, a strict constructionist who bought half a continent, Jefferson was as contradictory as the American people; but like those people, his ultimate goal was the freedom of individuals to pursue their interests, to expand their talents to the fullest. In that sense, Jefferson, although a pragmatic politician, was also a committed idealist—one who deserves to be the symbol of the age that bears his name. The War of 1812 did more than test the army and navy of the United States—it tested the nation's ability to survive deep internal divisions that threatened America's independence as surely as did the forces of Great Britain. Hoping to keep his nation out of war, Jefferson followed a policy that kept the peace but raised fears among his political enemies. Those opponents, their power and influence declining, saw the government's policies as much directed against themselves as the British and opposed the conflict. Most other Americans rallied to Jefferson and to his successor, James Madison. The consensus Jefferson had forged held, and the United States survived this test.

Review Questions

These questions are to be answered with essays. This will allow you to explore relationships between individuals, events, and attitudes of the period under review.

1. Considering the variety of movements covered in the section of your text entitled "The Rising Glory of America," how did American cultural life in the early nineteenth century reflect the Republican vision of the nation's future?

2. Jefferson and the Republicans championed the rights of the states and advocated a strict adherence to the Constitution, but once in office, they found new situations that demanded governmental actions that, in some cases, went beyond what the Federalists had done. What caused Jefferson and his party to change their approach to governing, what reservations did they have about what they were doing, and how were they able to rationalize this apparent change in program and philosophy?

3. How did the Federalists respond to Republican programs? If the Federalists favored a loose interpretation of the Constitution, why did they protest when Jefferson used a loose interpretation as well? What was it in the Republican program that the Federalists saw as a threat, and how did they respond?

4. Many historians view the War of 1812 as the "second American war for independence," but is this an accurate characterization? In what way did British policies prior to 1812 threaten our independence? Had the United States not fought the war, what might the results have been? Assess these questions, and determine if we were indeed fighting for "independence."

5. What happened to the Federalists? For the first decade under the Constitution, the Federalist Party held the nation together, started the government working on a day-to-day basis, and set precedents that are still held valid. Twenty years later, they had all but ceased to exist as a party. Why? Examine the events and issues that accompanied the decline of the Federalists, and determine what caused this powerful party to fall.

Chapter Self Test

After you have read the chapter in the text and done the exercises in the Study Guide, take the following self test to see if you understand the material you have covered. Answers appear at the end of the Study Guide.

MULTIPLE-CHOICE QUESTIONS

Circle the letter of the response which best answers the question or completes the statement.

1. In the Republican vision of America, education was essential because:
    a. schools were the best place to teach children to be good party members.
    b. an ignorant electorate could not be trusted to preserve democracy.
    c. business leaders needed to be educated.
    d. schools were where religious values were taught.

2. Early in the eighteenth century, religious traditionalists were alarmed over:

    a. a decline in religious education.

    b. the popularity of immoral literature.

    c. demands of separate church and state.

    d. the rise of "rational" religious doctrines.

3. The Second Great Awakening:

    a. combined a more active piety with a belief in a God whose grace could be attained through faith and good works.

    b. turned back the doctrine of predestination.

    c. drew many converts to Unitarianism and Universalism.

    d. had no impact on women and slaves.

4. The work of Eli Whitney:

    a. improved transportation in the South.

    b. led to the expansion of the cotton culture and slavery.

    c. made the South a major textile-producing region.

    d. led to the decline of slavery, for fewer workers were needed to process the cotton.

5. During his administration, Thomas Jefferson:

    a. used the Alien and Sedition Acts against the Federalists.

    b. cut the national debt almost in half.

    c. showed little interest in westward expansion.

    d. made peace with Aaron Burr.

6. In the case of <u>Marbury</u> v. <u>Madison,</u> the Supreme Court:

    a. affirmed its power to nullify an act of Congress.

    b. upheld Adams' right to make "midnight appointments."

    c. confirmed the power of Congress to expand judicial authority.

    d. ordered Madison to deliver Marbury's commission.

7. The greatest accomplishment of Chief Justice John Marshall was that he:

    a. stopped the growth of Republican power.

    b. prevented a Federalist revival in New England.

    c. refused to expand the power of the judiciary.

    d. made the judiciary a coequal branch of government.

8. What possibility concerned Jefferson when he said, "we must marry ourselves to the British fleet and nation"?

    a. An Indian uprising in the Ohio Valley.

    b. The French occupation of New Orleans.

    c. Increased Spanish strength in the Gulf of Mexico.

    d. A war between England, France, and Spain.

9. Jefferson had reservations about buying Louisiana because:

    a. he doubted his constitutional power to do so.

    b. he feared it would upset western Indian tribes.

    c. New Orleans had few Americans living there.

    d. the Spanish claimed the territory as theirs.

10. Federalists were upset by the Louisiana Purchase because they believed:
    a. it was unconstitutional.
    b. more slave states would come into the Union.
    c. western states would be Republican states.
    d. the British were behind it.

11. The Essex Junto was:
    a. a Federalist organization created to support Jefferson.
    b. the anti-Burr coalition in New York.
    c. a literary club in New England.
    d. a group of radical Federalists who wanted to take New England out of the Union.

12. The apparent goal of the "Burr conspiracy" was to:
    a. make Burr "king" of the American Southwest.
    b. invade Mexico and take it from the Spanish.
    c. return Louisiana to France.
    d. force Jefferson to accept Burr back into the Republican Party.

13. Early in the nineteenth century, the American merchant marine could be described as:
    a. weak and ineffective.
    b. one of the most important in the world.
    c. unable to compete with Britain in the West Indian trade.
    d. of little consequence in the American economy.

14. Jefferson refused to ask for war after the <u>Chesapeake-Leopard</u> incident because he:
    a. believed "peaceable coercion" would work.
    b. felt the British were within their rights.
    c. did not want the Federalists to make it an issue.
    d. was against war in general.

15. The Embargo act hurt which of the following most?
    a. England.
    b. France.
    c. New England.
    d. The South.

16. Jefferson told the Indians of the Northwest they could:
    a. convert themselves to farmers.
    b. move to the West.
    c. continue to live as they always had.
    d. do both a. and b.
    e. do none of the above.

17. The Prophet, Tenskwatawa, was significant because he:
    a. brought Indians to the Christian faith.
    b. inspired an Indian religious revival that helped unite the tribes.
    c. advocated a religious war with southern tribes.
    d. convinced the Indians to accept Jefferson's policies.

18. Tecumseh was important because he:
    a. advocated Indian unity to stop white expansion.
    b. allied the northwestern Indians with the British in Canada.
    c. was able to defeat the Americans at Tippecanoe.
    d. helped his brother, the Prophet, in his religious work.

19. The congressional election of 1810 was important because it:
    a. added a number of young, western, anti-British representatives to the House.
    b. greatly increased the Republican part.
    c. brought in a number of peace advocates.
    d. gave rise to a new political party.

20. Apart from the British, the real losers in the War of 1812 were the:
    a. Spanish in Florida and Mexico.
    b. Canadians.
    c. Indian tribes in the Southwest and the Great Lakes region.
    d. Republicans in the West.

21. The Hartford Convention was held in an effort to:
    a. force Republicans to address the grievances New England Federalists had against the Madison administration.
    b. forge an alliance between the Northeast and the West.
    c. convince Republicans in New England that the region should secede from the union.
    d. reorganize the Federalist party and pick a candidate for the election of 1816.

TRUE-FALSE QUESTIONS

Read each statement carefully. Mark true statements "T" and false statements "F."

1. In the Jeffersonian Era, schooling was primarily the responsibility of private institutions.

2. An argument for the education of women was that they could not be good "republican mothers" unless they were educated themselves.

3. Once Americans won political independence from England, they had little interest in cultural independence.

4. Early in the nineteenth century, most Americans abandoned traditional religious doctrines.

5. In the early nineteenth century industrialization in the United States was hampered by an inadequate transportation system.

6. Thomas Jefferson refused to use political office to reward loyal supporters.

7. Jefferson wanted to reduce internal taxes, not abolish them.

8. Napoleon's plans for an American empire were blocked by a British invasion of Belgium.

9. Reports from explorer Zebulon Pike convinced Americans that land between the Missouri River and the Rockies was good for agriculture.

10. Federalists in New York tried to get Aaron Burr to join them in an anti-Jefferson coalition, but he refused.

11. The Burr conspiracy was a plot by a desperate man, acting alone.

12. Both Jefferson and Marshall wanted Burr convicted for treason.

13. Americans agreed that the British should be free to search for deserters who might be serving in the American marine.

14. Americans had little problem with French violations of our neutral rights.

15. After the <u>Chesapeake-Leopard</u> affair, Britain renounced its policy of impressment.

16. The Harrison Land Law of 1800 made it possible for white settlers to acquire farms from the public domain on easier terms than before.

17. Under Jefferson's Indian policy the tribes were granted their tribal lands forever.

18. The Indians in the West would not have risen against the United States if the British in Canada had not told them to do so.

19. White southerners wanted Florida because it blocked river access to the Gulf of Mexico.

20. As a result of the Battle of New Orleans the United States was able to force Britain to sign the Treaty of Ghent.

CHAPTER EIGHT
VARIETIES OF AMERICAN NATIONALISM

Objectives

A thorough study of Chapter Eight should enable the student to understand:

1. The effects of the War of 1812 on banking, shipping, farming, industry, and transportation.
2. The "era of good feelings" as a transitional period.
3. The causes of the Panic of 1819, and the effects of the subsequent depression on politics and the economy.
4. The arguments advanced by North and South during the debates over the admission of Missouri, and how they were to influence sectional attitudes.
5. The ways in which the status of the federal judiciary was changed by the Marshall Court, and how the Court's decisions altered the relationships between the federal government and the states and the federal government and business.
6. The reasons why President James Monroe announced his "doctrine" in 1823, and its impact on international relations at the time.
7. Presidental politics in the "era of good feelings," and how they altered the political system.
8. The frustrations experienced by John Quincy Adams during his term as president.
9. The reasons why Andrew Jackson was elected in 1828, and the significance of his victory.

Main Themes

1. How postwar expansion shaped the nation during the "era of good feelings."
2. How it was that sectionalism and nationalism could exist at the same time and in the same country.
3. How the "era of good feelings" came to an end and a new two-party system emerged.

Glossary

1. internal improvements: The building of canals and roads, the improvement of harbors, and the clearing of rivers to improve transportation and stimulate commerce. To be done with the help of the national government, this was a major part of the postwar nationalistic program. The concept was opposed by those who felt it was too expensive or was an unconstitutional assumption of the rights and responsibilities of the states.

2. wildcat bank: Usually defined as a state bank in the West, organized with little capital resources, free with credit, and generally unsound. These banks were responsible for much of the land speculation in the West, and when the bank of the United States began to tighten credit restrictions, they were among the first to fail. This had much to do with the West's dislike for the Bank.

3. diplomacy: The conducting of negotiations between nations and the drawing up of treaties. The act of concluding an alliance to national advantage.

4. American nationalism: Between 1820 and 1840, many American politicians advocated programs that stressed the supremacy of the central government over the states, called for direct federal involvement to aid the growth of commerce, and in general advocated an aggressive course of action designed to make America a nation without equal. Much of their program, embodied in

Henry Clay's American System, resembled Hamiltonian federalism, but with a significant difference. These nationalists, unlike their Federalist counterparts, decided not to oppose the rising tide of democracy, but chose to present their programs in such a way as to appeal to the common man.

5. American System: The plan, advanced by Henry Clay, that was designed to foster commercial growth and economic stability. Its basic components consisted of a tariff to protect "infant industries" and to secure American jobs (thus making it appealing to labor), a national bank into which the money from the tariff (and other taxes) would be deposited, and an internal-improvements program paid for by the federal government. As conceived, money raised from taxes would pay for the roads, canals, and the like designed to improve transportation and thus stimulate more commerce, which would produce more jobs and revenue. To keep this growing economy stable would be the function of the bank, which would issue notes and make loans for business development and expansion. Therefore, all three elements were linked in a cycle of taxing, banking, and spending that made it difficult to oppose one without opposing them all.

6. contract clause: The clause in the Constitution (Article I, Section 10) that prohibits the government (national or state) and individuals from impairing the obligation of contract.

7. commerce clause: The clause in the Constitution (Article I, Section 8) that gives the national government the power to regulate foreign commerce as well as commerce between the states (interstate commerce).

8. necessary-and-proper clause: The clause in the Constitution (Article I, Section 8) that authorizes Congress to make "all laws" necessary and proper to carry out its powers; also called the "elastic" or "implied powers" clause.

Pertinent Questions

A GROWING ECONOMY (218-221)

1. Who were the leading exponents of the "national" over the "local" or "sectional" point of view that rose after the war? What factors contributed to the growth and development of this attitude?

2. What were the programs proposed by the "nationalists" to deal with problems of currency and credit, "infant industries," and transportation? How were these separate programs linked together into a cohesive plan to develop America?

3. What was the "internal improvements bill"? How did it fit into the nationalists' program, and what happened to it?

EXPANDING WESTWARD (221-225)

4. What were the general characteristics of the westward movement after the War of 1812, and what geographical factors affected the decisions of where to settle?

5. How did the advance of the southern frontier differ from the advance of settlement in the North?

6. Describe the trade that developed between the western regions of North America and the United States early in the nineteenth century.

THE "ERA OF GOOD FEELINGS" (225-227)

7. Why were the leaders of New England disturbed at the nomination and election of James Monroe for president, and what did Monroe do to calm these fears?

8.   Why did the United States want to annex Florida? How did the Adams-Onís negotiations resolve the issue?

9.   What were the causes of the Panic of 1819? What political and economic issues did the Panic raise?

SECTIONALISM AND NATIONALISM (227-231))

10.   What were the major elements of disagreement in the debate over the admission of Missouri into the Union?

11.   What was the Missouri Compromise? Why did nationalists regard it as a "happy resolution of a danger to the Union"? Why were others less optimistic?

12.   What was the net effect of the opinions delivered by the Marshall Court? How did these opinions reflect John Marshall's philosophy of government?

13.   Who led the opposition to the Marshall Court, and what was the position they took in denouncing it?

14.   How did the case of Cohens v. Virginia answer these critics?

15.   What was the long-range significance of the case of Gibbons v. Ogden? Of immediate importance, how did this case help to blunt criticism of the Court?

16.   How were the nationalist inclinations of the Marshall Court visible in its decisions concerning the legal status of Indian tribes within the United States?

17.   How was it that the United States' proclamation of neutrality in the wars between Spain and its colonies actually aided the colonies? Why did the United States do this?

18.   What was the Monroe Doctrine? Why was it announced and what was its significance?

THE REVIVAL OF OPPOSITION (231-233)

19.   Why was the caucus system viewed with such disdain before the election of 1824?

20.   Who were the candidates in the election of 1824? What was the "platform" of each?

21.   What was the outcome of the election in 1824? How was that result arrived at, and what part did Henry Clay play in it?

22.   What was the "corrupt bargain," and why did it take place?

23.   What did John Quincy Adams plan to accomplish during his presidency? What role was the federal government to play in these plans? Was he successful? Why?

24.   What problems brought on the tariff debates of 1827 and 1828? In what way did the South respond to northeastern demands for a higher tariff, and on what did the antitariff forces base their stand?

25.   What was the outcome of these tariff debates, and why was it that few were pleased with these results?

26.   How had Andrew Jackson's supporters prepared for the election of 1828? What were the issues in the campaign, and what was the outcome?

27.   Who were the National Republicans? Who were their leaders? What programs did they support, and from what areas did they draw their strength?

Identification

Identify each of the following, and explain why it is important within the context of the chapter.

1. Second Bank of the United States
2. "infant industries"
3. Francis C. Lowell
4. National Road
5. Black Belt
6. William Becknell
7. Rocky Mountain Fur Company
8. Jedediah S. Smith
9. "Great American Desert"
10. "Presidential Jubilee"
11. Tallmadge Amendment
12. Thomas Amendment
13. Fletcher v. Peck
14. Dartmouth College v. Woodward
15. McCulloch v. Maryland
16. Gibbons v. Ogden
17. Johnson v. McIntosh
18. Worcester v. Georgia
19. "King Caucus"
20. The American System
21. "tariff of abominations"
22. "coffin handbill"

Document

One of the issues that led to the revival of the two-party system was the protective tariff. Henry Clay emerged as a champion of the tariff and made it a critical part of his American System. Below is an excerpt from an 1824 speech by Clay. How does he appeal to the nationalistic sentiments of the period to draw support for his cause? How does he answer the criticism that a protective tariff helps some at the expense of others? In what way does he attempt to neutralize southern opposition to the plan? Do you think the South will accept his argument?

Having called the attention of the committee to the present adverse state of our country, and endeavored to point out the causes which have led to it; having shewn that similar causes, wherever they exist in other countries, lead to the same adversity in their condition; and having shewn that, wherever we find opposite causes prevailing, a high and animating state of national prosperity exists, the committee will agree with me in thinking that it is the solemn duty of government to apply a remedy to the evils which afflict our country, if it can apply one. Is there no remedy within the reach of the government? Are we doomed to behold our industry languish and decay yet more and more? But there is a remedy, and that remedy consists in modifying our foreign policy, and in adopting a genuine American System. We must naturalize the arts in our country, and we must naturalize them by the only means which the wisdom of nations has yet discovered to be effectual—by adequate protection against the otherwise overwhelming influence of foreigners. This is only to be accomplished by the establishment of a tariff, to the consideration of which I am now brought.

And what is this tariff? It seems to have been regarded as a sort of monster, huge and deformed; a wild beast, endowed with tremendous powers of destruction, about to be let loose among our people, if not to devour them, at least to consume their substance. But let us calm our passions, and deliberately survey this alarming, this terrific being. The sole object of the tariff is to tax the produce of foreign industry, with the view of promoting American industry. The tax is exclusively levelled at foreign industry. That is the avowed and the direct purpose of the tariff. If it subjects any part of American industry to burthens, that is an effect not intended, but is altogether incidental and perfectly voluntary.

It has been treated as an imposition of burthens upon one part of the community by design for the benefit of another; as if, in fact, money were taken from the pockets of one portion of the people and put into the pockets of another. But, is that a fair representation of it? No man pays the duty assessed on the foreign article by compulsion, but voluntarily; and this voluntary duty, if paid, goes into the common exchequer, for the common benefit of all. Consumption has four objects of choice. 1. It may abstain from the use of the foreign article, and thus avoid the payment of tax. 2. It may employ the rival American fabric. 3. It may engage in the business of manufacturing, which this bill is designed to foster. 4. Or it may supply itself from the household manufactures. But, it is said by the honorable gentleman from Virginia, that the South, owing to the character of a certain portion of its population, cannot engage in the business of manufacturing. Now, I do not agree in that opinion to the extent in which it is asserted. The circumstance alluded to may disqualify the South from engaging in every branch of manufacture as largely as other quarters of the Union, but to some branches of it that part of our population is well adapted. It indisputably affords great facility in the household or domestic line.

But, if the gentleman's premises were true, could his conclusion be admitted? According to him, a certain part of our population, happily much the smallest, is peculiarly situated. The circumstance of its degradation unfits it for the manufacturing arts. The well being of the other, and the larger part of our population, requires the introduction of those arts. What is to be done in this conflict? The gentleman would have us abstain from adopting a policy called for by the interests of the greater and freer part of our population. But is that reasonable? Can it be expected that the interests of the greater part should be made to bend to the condition of the servile part of our population? That, in effect, would be to make us the slaves of slaves. I went, with great pleasure, along with my Southern friends, and I am ready again to unite with them in protesting against the exercise of any legislative power, on the part of Congress, over that delicate subject, because it was my solemn conviction, that Congress was interdicted, or at least not authorized, by the constitution, to exercise any such legislative power. And I am sure, that the patriotism of the South may be exclusively relied upon to reject a policy which should be dictated by considerations altogether connected with that degraded class, to the prejudice of the residue of our population.

Annals of Congress, 12th Cong., 1st sess., December 9, 10, and 16, 1811.

Map Exercise

Fill in or identify the following on the blank map provided. Use the map in the text as your source.

1. Free states and territories in 1820.
2. Slave states and territories in 1820.
3. Missouri Compromise line.
4. Dates that states entered the Union.
5. Territory closed to slavery by the Missouri Compromise.
6. Territory open to slavery by the Missouri Compromise.
7. Mexico, British America, and Oregon.

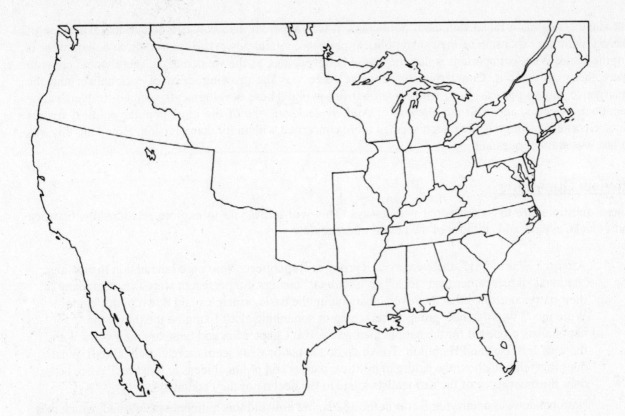

Interpretative Questions

Based on what you have filled in, answer the following. On some of the questions you will need to consult the narrative in your text for information or explanation.

1. Study America's expansion into Florida. What impact did the War of 1812 have on this?

2. What migration and settlement patterns helped determine that Missouri would want to enter the Union as a slave state?

3. What impact did the manner in which states were previously admitted to the Union have on the reaction to the admission of Missouri?

4. Why would the South accept the Missouri Compromise? What does this tell you about the nature of the plantation system and attitudes toward the institution of slavery and its ability to expand?

5. What potential existed (as a result of the Missouri Compromise) for an eventual upsetting of the balance between slave and free states? Which section seemed to gain the most from this?

6. How did the Missouri Compromise reflect the tensions between political parties at the time, especially tensions that were the result of the expansion of the nation?

Summary

After the War of 1812 a new spirit of nationalism and expansion emerged, and the nation, led by a president determined to heal old wounds, embarked on an "era of good feelings"—party and sectional divisions forgotten. That attitude was soon challenged. The 1820s and 1830s were highlighted by two forces, one divisive and the other unifying. The first appeared during the Missouri debates, which, despite overtones that resembled the earlier Federalist-Republican clashes, brought the issue of slavery and its expansion to the forefront. The immediate question—which section would control the Senate—was dealt with through the Missouri Compromise, but the underlying problem was more difficult to resolve. What the debates revealed was that some in the nation saw the addition of slave states (not just western states, but slave states) as a threat. Southern politicians, it was apparent, had come to equate the expansion of slavery with the expansion of their own political philosophy (and power). How true these beliefs were is not the issue. What is important is that they were believed, and, as the years passed, more would come to share these convictions. Countering this divisive force was the growing spirit of nationalism and the emergence of two parties—both with a national following. These developments seemed to overshadow sectional concerns, and with the election of Andrew Jackson, one of the most popular political figures since George Washington, the nation seemed more concerned with unity than division. How long this was to last was another question.

Review Questions

These questions are to be answered with essays. This will allow you to explore relationships between individuals, events, and attitudes of the period under review.

1.	After the War of 1812, there emerged a group of Republicans who urged the nation to consider "national" issues rather than "local" or "sectional" matters. So persistent were they that many of their party contended that they were abandoning the basic principles laid down by Jefferson. Were they? Was this new group Jeffersonian or something else? Examine the things the nationalists proposed for the nation, then go back to Chapter Six and compare their plans with those of Jefferson and Hamilton. To which do the nationalists seem more closely allied? What does this tell you about the nature of political parties and political ideas at this time? Also, how does the emergence of the nationalists relate to the decline of the Federalists?

2.	Nationalism was a unifying factor in the 1820s, but how did this nationalistic attitude, which was so evident in domestic affairs, influence foreign policy? What were the effects of nationalism on American foreign policy during this period, and what forces, if any, tended to negate its influence?

3.	Although they were dead as a national party, the Federalists, and their political philosophy, continued to influence American politics. Explain how the Federalists were able to continue to make their presence known, what they hoped to accomplish, and how the ideas of Hamilton reappeared, in slightly altered form, under the national Republican banner.

4.	How did the career of John Marshall contribute to the rise of nationalism during this era? In what specific areas did he increase the power of the national government? Of the two political parties, which was more likely to support Marshall? Why?

5.	The War of 1812, although fought for free seas and sailors' rights, was opposed by the group most directly interested in seagoing commerce, the New England merchants. Why? Why did these people not see a threat to their independence in the policies of Great Britain, yet see the policies of Jefferson and Madison as just that? Put yourself in the place of those merchants, and, from their point of view, explain (and justify) the position they took.

Chapter Self Test

After you have read the chapter in the text and done the exercises in the Study Guide, take the following self test to see if you understand the material you have covered. Answers appear at the end of the Study Guide.

MULTIPLE-CHOICE QUESTIONS

Circle the letter of the response which best answers the question or completes the statement.

1. Which of the following did <u>not</u> occur after the War of 1812?
   a. Commerce revived and expanded.
   b. An economic boom was followed by a disastrous bust.
   c. All banking was left to the states.
   d. Westward expansion accelerated dramatically.

2. After peace was restored, "infant industries" that prospered during the war:
   a. were strong enough to withstand British competition.
   b. expanded into foreign markets.
   c. were competitive with foreign markets.
   d. demanded that the government protect them from foreign competition.

3. After the war, the nation's most pressing economic need was:
   a. access to foreign markets that were not open to our commerce.
   b. a trained labor force to work in complex industries.
   c. a transportation system that would provide manufacturers access to raw materials and markets.
   d. a system by which worn-out soil could be reclaimed.

4. The second Bank of the United States could deal with the nation's currency problem by:
   a. prohibiting state banks from issuing notes.
   b. using its size and power to compel state banks to issue sound notes or go out of business.
   c. using only gold and silver as currency.
   d. dealing only with major land speculators.

5. According to "nationalists" in the government, "internal improvements" should be financed by:
   a. a series of local, internal improvement taxes.
   b. the national government.
   c. the states in which the "improvements" are made.
   d. private investments.

6. The administration of President James Monroe was called the "Era of Good Feelings" because:
   a. it was a time of few factional disputes and partisan divisions.
   b. there were no economic depressions.
   c. most Americans were content to remain where they were.
   d. the national bank successfully managed the economy.

7. Which of the following was <u>not</u> a reason for the "great migration" westward?
   a. An increased population.
   b. The end of Indian opposition to expansion.
   c. The government "factor" system.
   d. A shift from farming to industry in the West.

8. The Black Belt was:
   a. the area where most were settled.
   b. an area of dark, rotted limestone soil that was excellent for cotton.
   c. a burned-over region in upstate New York.
   d. the dark swamps of southern Georgia and northern Florida.

9. In the American mind of the 1820s the far west was seen as:
   a. a great desert.
   b. a wooded region like the Northeast.
   c. a paradise on earth.
   d. rich farmland ready to be settled.

10. The Panic of 1819:
   a. brought a halt to western expansion for decades.
   b. convinced the West that the national bank was a sound institution.
   c. did little to change American attitudes toward growth and expansion.
   d. removed the national bank as a political issue.

11. The Missouri crisis, which was settled by a compromise in 1820, was significant because it was a sign of sectional crisis and because it:
   a. revealed how strong pro-slavery attitudes were.
   b. revealed how deep anti-slavery attitudes were.
   c. stood in such sharp contrast to the rising American nationalism of the 1820s.
   d. involved most of the major politicians of the day.

12. John Marshall's influence on the Supreme Court was so great that he:
   a. was able to get whomever he wanted appointed to the bench.
   b. more than anyone other than the farmers themselves, molded the development of the Constitution.
   c. was able to ignore the other justices.
   d. could singlehandedly overturn acts of Congress.

13. The lasting significance of Gibbons v. Ogden was that it:
   a. opened the way for steamboat travel on the Mississippi.
   b. confirmed the state's right to regulate commerce.
   c. made peace between the court and the Adams administration.
   d. freed transportation systems from restraints by the states.

14. The decisions of the Marshall Court:
   a. established the primacy of the federal government in regulating the economy.
   b. gave strength to the doctrine of state rights.
   c. destroyed what was left of Hamiltonian federalism.
   d. opened the way for an increased federal role in promoting economic growth.
   e. achieved a. and d.
   f. achieved b. and c.

15. In its rulings concerning the Indian tribes, the Marshall Court held that:
    a. the national government, not the states, had authority.
    b. Indians were citizens like everyone else.
    c. Indians had the same status as slaves.
    d. tribal lands belong to the states.

16. The charge of a "corrupt bargain" was raised when:
    a. Clay supported Adams for the presidency and was appointed secretary of state.
    b. Jackson promised to reward his supporters if he won.
    c. Adams won with the support of southern planters.
    d. the Republican caucus threw its support to Adams.

17. Adams's nationalistic program, which was a lot like Clay's American System, was not funded because:
    a. the nation could not afford it.
    b. business opposed it.
    c. western interests opposed it.
    d. Jackson's supporters in Congress voted against it.

18. In his victory in 1828, Jackson drew his greatest support from the:
    a. South and the West.
    b. New England region and the Southeast.
    c. Middle Atlantic states and the Old Northwest.
    d. South and the Middle Atlantic states.

TRUE-FALSE QUESTIONS

Read each statement carefully. Mark true statements "T" and false statements "F."

1. Difficulties in financing the War of 1812 underlined the need for a national bank.
2. Tariffs were generally favored by manufacturing interests but opposed by those who made their living from agriculture.
3. One reason for the growing interest in internal improvements was the sudden and dramatic surge in westward expansion in the years following the War of 1812.
4. The second Bank of the United States was essentially the same institution Hamilton founded.
5. Because Jefferson had opposed Hamilton's plans, his administration did little to meet the nation's internal improvement needs.
6. The advance of the southern frontier meant the spread not just of cotton but also of slavery.
7. Andrew Jackson took Florida, and the Adams-Onís Treaty made it legal.
8. For America's rapidly growing population the Southwest offered the best opportunity for land on which to farm.
9. During this period Americans had little interest in the far West, so there was little trade with that region.
10. In McCulloch v. Maryland the Supreme Court declared the national bank unconstitutional.
11. The decision in Gibbon v. Ogden was popular because it was a stand against monopoly power.
12. The Marshall Court's rulings concerning the Indian tribes were among its most popular decisions.

13. The Monroe Doctrine was passed by Congress and immediately became an important part of our foreign policy.

14. The political divisions that appeared in the late 1820s were in no way related to the divisions of the 1790s.

15. Henry Clay's "American System" included a national bank, a protective tariff, and federally funded internal improvements.

16. The Panic of 1819 convinced many Americans that a national bank was a bad idea.

17. Thomas Jefferson was convinced that the Missouri Compromise had solved the question of the expansion of slavery.

18. The decisions of the Marshall Court established the primacy of the federal government over the states in regulating the economy.

19. In 1828, Andrew Jackson lost the presidential election because he was too closely identified with an "economic aristocracy" that his enemies claimed controlled him.

20. John Quincy Adams opposed Georgia's efforts to gain control of Creek Indians' land within the state.

GENERAL DISCUSSION QUESTIONS FOR CHAPTERS FIVE–EIGHT

These questions are designed to help you bring together ideas from several chapters and see how the chapters relate to one another.

1. Review the sections entitled "Where Historians Disagree," as well as the "schools" of historical interpretation found in Chapter Five of the study guide. With these in mind, read Chapters Five and Six of the text, and then write an essay in which you explain which interpretation (or combination thereof) best explains to you the period under consideration. Which interpretation does the text seem to follow? Why do you think so?

2. How were American Revolutionary ideals translated into political realities? Examine the programs of the Hamiltonian Federalists and of the Jeffersonian Republicans, and then write an essay explaining which you feel better caught the spirit of the American Revolution.

3. During the period being studied here, a number of strong individuals emerged to shape the course taken by the United States. Select the four persons you feel most influenced America between 1775 and 1820, and then write an essay in which you explain your choices.

4. It was during this period that the "West" emerged as a major force in the nation's political and economic development. Just what influence did this section have? Consider the growth of American political institutions and attitudes, along with the expansion of the national economy between 1783 and 1820 from the standpoint of the West, and from this exercise determine just how that section shaped, or tried to shape, what took place. Also examine how the Northeast and the Southeast reacted to the growth of the western regions.

5. During the period just covered, the status of women in America changed. Some of these changes were positive; others were not. Write an essay in which you discuss these changes and the impact they had on women in the United States.

6. What were the cadastral systems used by the English in America? What were the advantages and disadvantages of each?

7. Review the conditions which existed under the Articles of Confederation. How did the Land Ordinance of 1785 fit into this context? What problems did the Ordinance seek to address? Was it successful?

8. What was the environmental effect of the 1785 Ordinance?

CHAPTER NINE
JACKSONIAN AMERICA

Objectives

A thorough study of Chapter Nine should enable the student to understand:

1. Andrew Jackson's philosophy of government and his impact on the office of the presidency.

2. The debate among historians about the meaning of "Jacksonian Democracy," and Andrew Jackson's relationship to it.

3. The nullification theory of John C. Calhoun, and President Jackson's reaction to the attempt to put nullification into action.

4. The supplanting of John C. Calhoun by Martin Van Buren as successor to Jackson, and the significance of the change.

5. The reasons why the eastern Indians were removed to the West and the impact this had on the tribes.

6. The reasons for the Jacksonian war on the Bank of the United States, and the effects of Jackson's veto on the powers of the president and on the American financial system.

7. The causes of the Panic of 1837, and the effect of the panic on the presidency of Van Buren.

8. The differences in party philosophy between the Democrats and the Whigs, the reasons for the Whig victory in 1840, and the effect of the election on political campaigning.

9. The negotiations that led to the Webster-Ashburton Treaty, and the importance of the treaty in Anglo-American relations.

10. The reasons why John C. Calhoun, Henry Clay, and Daniel Webster were never able to reach their goal—the White House.

Main Themes

1. How mass participation became the hallmark of the American political system.
2. The growing tension between nationalism and states' rights.
3. The rise of the Whig Party as an alternative to Andrew Jackson and the Democrats.

Glossary

1. political machine: A well-organized local political group that can turn out voters on specific issues. In return for delivering these votes, the machine is allowed to dispense patronage in its particular area.

2. party boss: The politician in charge of the machine, usually the ranking elected official in a political unit (state, county, city, and so on); the person responsible for getting out the vote and for dispensing patronage.

3. "Jacksonian Democracy:" A term that more accurately describes the spirit of the age than a movement led by Andrew Jackson. During this period (1820–1850), more offices became elective, voter restrictions were reduced or eliminated (for white male adults), and popular participation in politics increased. The Democratic Party, led by Jackson, appealed to this growing body of voters by stressing its belief in rotation in office, economy in government, governmental response to popular demands, and decentralization of power.

4. states' rights: The belief that the United States was formed as a compact of sovereign states and that the national government was violating that sovereignty. The theory rests on the conviction that the states did not surrender their sovereignty to the central government by adopting the Constitution and that when their rights are violated, they can act in their own defense. (See the discussion of nullification in the text and interposition below.)

5. interposition: The idea that a state, having retained its sovereignty in a federal system, can interpose its authority between the central government and an individual, to protect its citizens from illegal or unconstitutional action. (See the discussion of nullification in the text and states' rights above.)

6. Marxism: The theory that history has been characterized by a struggle between the working classes and their masters, the middle-class capitalists. The outcome of struggle is to be an uprising of the oppressed and the overthrow of capitalism. In part, this belief was shared by John C. Calhoun, who feared that the growth of industrial capitalism in America would lead to just such a class struggle.

7. soft money: Paper money. Easily produced, this currency increased the amount of money in circulation, made credit easier, and made prices higher. Generally favored by speculators, by agricultural interests, and by debtors.

8. hard money: Specie, coin with a fixed value, which could not be cheaply manufactured to flood the market. Its use made money scarce and credit expensive and difficult, and it discouraged speculation. It also kept wages low and reduced commercial activity. Its advocates were known as "sound money" men.

9. land-poor: The condition in which many speculators found themselves during the Panic of 1837 (and in 1819, as well). Having bought land on credit, they were unable to pay their debts when the land did not sell. Hence, they had a lot of land, but no money, and the result was bankruptcy.

Pertinent Questions

THE RISE OF MASS POLITICS (236-240)

1. What were the general characteristics of "Jacksonian Democracy," its philosophy, and its practice?

2. How did the spoils system fit into Jackson's "democratic" plans? What other means did he use to bring more people into the political process?

3. What role did social rank and occupation play in the growing democratization of American politics?

4. What was the reaction in New York and Rhode Island to these democratic trends?

5. What groups were excluded from this widening of political opportunity? Why?

6. What was the effect of this growth of democracy? How did it change, or not change, the American political system? What is its significance?

"OUR FEDERAL UNION" (240-244)

7. What was the dilemma faced by John C. Calhoun, and what factors gave rise to it?

8. How did Calhoun attempt to resolve this dilemma? What arguments did he use, and on which sources did he draw?

9. What did Calhoun really hope this theory of nullification would accomplish?

10. How did Martin Van Buren's and John C. Calhoun's backgrounds and rise to prominence differ?

11. What was the Kitchen Cabinet? Who were its members? Why did it come into existence?

12. What were the origins of the Calhoun-Jackson split? How did the Eaton affair contribute to the division? What effect did it have on the Jackson administration?

13. How did the Webster-Hayne debate fit into the controversy between Jackson and Calhoun? What brought about the debate, what was the major point of disagreement between the two, and what were the arguments advanced?

14. How did Calhoun and South Carolina propose to test the theory of nullification? What factors contributed to their decision?

15. What was Jackson's reaction to South Carolina's attempt at nullification? How did his action in this case correspond to his action in the case of the Cherokee removal? What accounts for this?

16. What was the outcome of the nullification crisis? What, if anything, did the antagonists learn from the confrontation?

THE REMOVAL OF THE INDIANS (244-248)

17. What were the whites' attitudes toward the tribes and how did they contribute to the decision in favor of removal?

18. What was the program (inherited by Jackson) designed to deal with the Indians who lived east of the Mississippi? What happened when this program was applied to the Cherokee in Georgia?

19. Explain the Supreme Court's decisions regarding the Indian tribes and Jackson's response.

20. How did Jackson's action in the matter of the Cherokee removal correspond to his views on the role of the president and on the issue of states' rights?

21. How were Jackson's views concerning the Indians "little different" from those of most white Americans?

22. What was "the meaning of removal"?

JACKSON AND THE BANK WAR (248-251)

23. What was Jackson's opinion on the Bank of the United States? On what did he base his views? What other factors contributed to his stand?

24. What was Nicholas Biddle's initial attitude toward the Bank's involvement in politics? What caused him to change his mind, what steps did he take, and who were his supporters?

25. How did Jackson respond to the efforts to recharter the Bank? What reasons did he give for his action, and what effect did the election of 1832 have on his Bank policy?

26. How did the supporters of the Bank respond to Jackson's action? What did Biddle do? What were the results?

27. How did the Supreme Court under Roger B. Taney differ from the court under Marshall? What groups profited from Taney's decisions?

THE CHANGING FACE OF AMERICAN POLITICS (251-258)

28. How did the "party philosophy" of the Whigs differ from that of the Democrats?

29. Who were the Whig leaders? How do they reflect the variety of political opinions found in the Whig Party?

30. What was the Whig strategy in the election of 1836? Who was the Democratic candidate? Why was he selected? What was the result?

31. What was the general condition of the American economy in 1836? What factors contributed to this? What was the most pressing problem that Congress and the administration faced between 1835 and 1837, and how did they propose to solve it?

32. What was the effect of the government's decision to lend surplus money to state banks? What action did Jackson take to ease that effect, and what was the result?

33. What caused the Panic of 1837? What effect did it have on the nation? on the Democratic Party?

34. What programs did Martin Van Buren propose to ease the depression? Why did he act in this way?

35. What other programs did Van Buren propose? How did these proposals reflect the balance of power in the Democratic Party?

36. Why did the Whigs select William Henry Harrison as their candidate in 1840? How did his campaign set a new pattern for presidential contests?

37. What did the selection of John Tyler as Harrison's vice-presidential candidate reveal about the composition of the Whig Party?

38. What was the legislative program that Clay and the leading Whigs hoped to institute under Tyler? On what parts did Tyler agree? disagree?

39. What was the origin of the split between Tyler and Clay? What effect did it have on the administration? on the Whig Party? What was the result?

40. What were the accomplishments of Whig diplomacy?

WHERE HISTORIANS DISAGREE (238-239)

41. How have historians differed over the nature of Jacksonian Democracy?

42. Explain how these different opinions reflect divisions over what historians feel was the role Andrew Jackson played in the era named for him.

PATTERNS OF POPULAR CULTURE (256-257)

43. How did the advent of the penny press reflect the social, technological, and cultural changes taking place in America during the 1820s and 1830s?

44. How did the penny press capture the spirit of the Age of Jackson?

Identification

Identify each of the following, and explain why it is important within the context of the chapter.

1. "The reign of King 'Mob' "
2. James Kent
3. Dorr Rebellion
4. Albany Regency
5. William L. Marcy
6. Tariff of Abominations
7. Peggy Eaton
8. Robert Y. Hayne
9. Webster's Second Reply to Hayne
10. Democrats' Jefferson banquet
11. force bill
12. Black Hawk War
13. Five Civilized Tribes
14. Indian Removal Act
15. Worcester v. Georgia
16. Trail of Tears
17. "soft money"/"hard money"

18.   "pet banks"

19.   Locofocos

20.   Anti-Mason Party

21.   the Great Triumvirate

22.   specie circular

23.   independent treasury

24.   "log cabin" campaign

25.   Caroline affair

26.   "Aroostook war"

27.   Creole

28.   Webster-Ashburton Treaty

Document 1

Below is an excerpt from Daniel Webster's reply to Robert Y. Hayne's defense of the theory of nullification. What does Webster see as the danger inherent in Calhoun's doctrine? How is this speech in keeping with Webster's political views—especially his view of the nature of the Union and the role of the national government?

> I have not allowed myself, Sir, to look beyond the Union, to see what might lie hidden in the dark recess behind. I have not coolly weighed the changes of preserving liberty when the bonds that unite us together shall be broken asunder. I have not accustomed myself to hang over the precipice of disunion, to see whether, with my short sight, I can fathom the depth of the abyss below; nor could I regard him as a safe counsellor in the affairs of this government, whose thoughts should be mainly bent on considering, not how the Union may be best preserved, but how tolerable might be the condition of the people when it should be broken up and destroyed. While the Union lasts, we have high, exciting, gratifying prospects spread out before us, for us and our children. Beyond that I seek not to penetrate the veil. God grant that in my day, at least, that curtain may not rise! God grant that on my vision never may be opened what lies behind! When my eyes shall be turned to behold for the last time the sun in heaven, may I not see him shining on the broken and dishonored fragments of a once glorious Union; on States dissevered, discordant, and belligerent; on a land rent with civil feuds, or drenched, it may be, in fraternal blood! Let their last feeble and lingering glance rather behold the gorgeous ensign of the republic, now known and honored throughout the earth, still full high advanced, its arms and trophies steaming in their original lustre, not a stripe erased or polluted, nor a single star obscured, bearing for its motto, no such miserable interrogatory as "What is all this worth?" nor those other words of delusion and folly, "Liberty first and Union afterwards"; but everywhere, spread all over in characters of living light, blazing on all its ample folds, as they float over the sea and over the land, and in every wind under the whole heavens, that other sentiment, dear or every true American heart,—Liberty <u>and</u> Union, now and for ever, one and inseparable!

Daniel Webster, <u>The Writings and Speeches of Daniel Webster,</u> National Edition (Boston, 1903), 6:75.

Document 2

Joseph G. Baldwin's <u>Flush Times of Alabama and Mississippi</u> caught the spirit and unmasked the pretensions of the age of Jackson. With unerring aim, his satire hit its mark, and future generations were left with a delightful portrait of the period. But Baldwin, like most good satirists, was serious about his subject, and his insights into the era may tell us more than a hundred political speeches on the same subject.

What is the author describing here? What gave rise to the economic conditions he pictures, and what is his opinion of what was taking place? What does Baldwin feel to be the main problem highlighted by these activities? On whom does he place the blame?

Who was the "Jupiter Tonans of the White House" to whom the author calls attention? What action did this individual take to stop the abuses, and what resulted? From the way it was described, what was the author's opinion of the action taken by this Jupiter Tonans, and, considering what you have read in your text, would the author have been a Whig or a Democrat? In either case, what element (or branch or faction) of that party does he seem to support? What was the result of the action taken by Jupiter Tonans?

Historian Bray Hammond, in his study of American banking, described the Jacksonian program as "one of enterpriser against capitalist, of banker against regulation." How does the account by Baldwin correspond with Hammond's theory? How might it be possible that the Jacksonian program both created and ended the situation described here?

In the fulness of time the new era had set in—the era of the second great experiment of independence: the experiment, namely, of credit without capital, and enterprise without honesty. . . .

This country was just settling up. Marvellous accounts had gone forth of the fertility of its virgin lands; and the productions of the soil were commanding a price remunerating to slave labor as it had never been remunerated before. Emigrants came flocking in from all quarters of the Union, especially from the slaveholding States. The new country seemed to be a reservoir, and every road leading to it a vagrant stream of enterprise and adventure. Money, or what passed for money, was the only cheap thing to be had. Every cross road and every avocation presented an opening--through which a fortune was seen by the adventurer in near perspective. Credit was a thing of course. To refuse it—if the thing was ever done--were an insult for which a bowie knife were not a too summary or exemplary a means of redress. The State banks were issuing their bills by the sheet, like a patent steam printing-press its issues; and no other showing was asked of the applicant for the loan than an authentication of his great distress for money. Finance, even in its most exclusive quarter, had thus already got, in this wonderful revolution, to work upon the principles of the charity hospital. . . .

Under this stimulating process prices rose like smoke. Lots in obscure villages were held at city prices; lands, bought at the minimum cost of government, were sold at from thirty to forty dollars per acre, and considered dirt cheap at that. . . .

The old rules of business and the calculations of prudence were alike disregarded, and profligacy, in all the departments of the <u>crimen falso,</u> held riotous carnival. Larceny grew not only respectable, but genteel, and ruffled it in all the pomp of purple and fine linen. . . .

"Commerce was king"—and Rags, Tag and Bobtail his cabinet council. Rags were treasurer. Banks, chartered on a specie basis, did a very flourishing business on the promissory notes of the individual stockholders ingeniously substituted in lieu of cash. They issued ten for one, the one being fictitious. They generously loaned all the directors could not use themselves. . . .

The Jupiter Tonans of the White House saw the monster of a free credit prowling about like a beast of apocalyptic vision, and marked him for his prey. Gathering all his bolts in his sinewy grasp, and standing back on his heels, and waving his wiry arm, he let them all fly, hard and swift upon all the hydra's heads. . . .

To get down from the clouds to level ground, the Specie Circular was issued without warning, and the splendid lie of a false credit burst into fragments. . . . he did some very pretty fairy work, in converting the bank bills back again from rags and oak-leaves. Men worth a million were insolvent for two millions: promising young cities marched back again into the wilderness. The ambitious town plat was re-annexed to the plantation, like a country girl taken home from the city. The frolic was ended, and what headaches, and feverish limbs the next morning! The retreat from Moscow was performed over again, and "Devil take the hindmost" was the tune to which the soldiers of fortune marched. The only question was as to the means of escape, and the nearest and best route to Texas. . . .

Joseph G. Baldwin, <u>The Flush Times of Alabama and Mississippi</u> (New York: Appleton, 1853), pp. 80–91.

Map Exercise

Fill in or identify the following on the blank map provided. Use the map in the text as your source.

1. Tribal lands and the states and territories in which they were located.
2. Other states in the region.
3. Removal routes (including the towns and forts along the way).
4. Reservations and the forts within them.

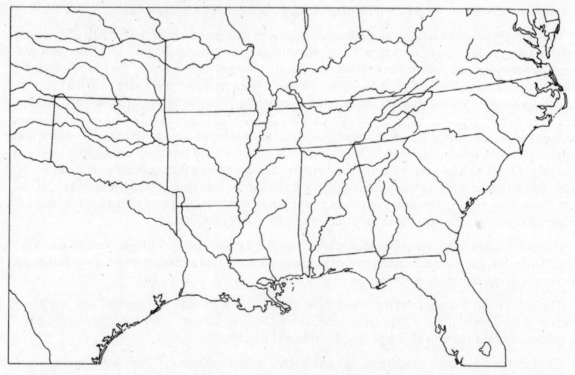

Interpretative Questions

Based on what you have filled in, answer the following. On some of the questions you will need to consult the narrative in your text for information or explanation.

1. Why did the states involved want the Indians removed? Look at the location of the tribal lands, and explain why their continued occupation by the Indians represented not only the loss to the state of valuable territory but might also have threatened the westward movement itself.

2. How did the land to which the Indians were removed differ from that on which they had lived? Were whites aware of the significance of the difference? What does this suggest about white attitudes toward the Indians?

3. Note the removal routes. What geographic features were considered in determining where the Indians would travel? Do you feel this made the trek easier or more difficult?

4. What geographic features made it possible for the Seminoles (and some Cherokees) to resist removal?

5. Note the location of the forts in or near the Indian Territory. Why were they placed as they were? What does this indicate about American Indian policy?

Summary

At first glance, Andrew Jackson seems a study in contradictions: an advocate of states' rights who forced South Carolina to back down in the nullification controversy; a champion of the West who removed the Indians from land east of the Mississippi River and who issued the specie circular, which brought the region's "flush times" to a disastrous halt; a nationalist who allowed Georgia to ignore the Supreme Court; and a defender of majority rule who vetoed the Bank after the majority's representatives, the Congress, had passed it. Perhaps he was, as his enemies argued, simply out for himself. But in the end, few would argue that Andrew Jackson was a popular president, if not so much for what he did as for what he was. Jackson symbolized what Americans perceived (or wished) themselves to be—defiant, bold, independent. He was someone with whom they could identify. So what if the image was a bit contrived, it was still a meaningful image. Thus Jackson was reelected by an overwhelming majority and was able to transfer that loyalty to his successor, a man who hardly lived up to the image. But all this left a curious question unanswered. Was this new democracy voting for leaders whose programs they favored or, rather, for images that could be altered and manipulated almost at will? The answer was essential for the future of American politics, and the election of 1840 gave the nation a clue.

Review Questions

These questions are to be answered with essays. This will allow you to explore relationships between individuals, events, and attitudes of the period under review.

1. Historian Lee Benson has contended that the democratic movement in America during this period was much broader than the Democratic Party and that this should be called the age of egalitarianism rather than the age of Jackson. Having read the text chapter (paying attention to "Where Historians Disagree") and completed this unit in the guide, what evidence have you found to support Benson? What have you found to contradict his assertion? Write an essay evaluating both sides.

2. Andrew Jackson thought of himself as the "president of the people." Was he? What can you find in the career of Jackson that would support his assertion, and what can you find to deny it?

3. How were Andrew Jackson's attitudes toward the Indian tribes "little different from those of most other white Americans"? How did eastern Indians attempt to live in harmony with whites, and how did attitudes like Jackson's make that impossible?

4. Why the split between Calhoun and Jackson? The Eaton affair is generally seen as a symptom, not a cause, which would indicate the real division between the two men was much deeper. Assess the causes of the split, and speculate on the significance of the split for the South and for the Democrats.

5. How did William Henry Harrison win in 1840? What were the issues that worked against him, and how did his party exploit them? Furthermore, how was this candidate presented to the people? What image were his managers trying to create, and what does this image tell you about the American electorate?

6. How did Calhoun (and South Carolina) justify and explain the theory of nullification? On what points did Webster (and Jackson) oppose this theory? Be sure to read your documents in the text.

7. Analyze the presidency of John Tyler. On which programs can he be considered successful, and on which did he fail? What does his elevation to the presidency and the problems he experienced tell you about the nature of the Whig Party?

Chapter Self Test

After you have read the chapter in the text and done the exercises in the Study Guide, take the following self test to see if you understand the material you have covered. Answers appear at the end of the Study Guide.

MULTIPLE-CHOICE QUESTIONS

Circle the letter of the response which best answers the question or completes the statement.

1. The goal of the Jacksonians was to:
   a. redistribute the wealth of the nation.
   b. reduce the influence of southern planters.
   c. ensure that people could rise to prominence on the basis of their own talents and energies.
   d. put as many of their own people in office as possible.

2. During the Jacksonian era, the number of voters:
   a. increased at a more rapid pace that did the population as a whole.
   b. increased at a slower pace than in the previous decade.
   c. actually decreased as a percentage of the population.
   d. remained stable.

3. The most significant change regarding "party" to take place in the Jacksonian era was the:
   a. recognition of the value of "third parties".
   b. view that institutionalized parties were a desirable part of the political process.
   c. view that party leaders should be presidential candidates.
   d. emergence of a hard core of party loyalists who picked all candidates for national office.

4. Which of the following did Jackson and the Jacksonians not attack?
   a. A "class" of permanent officeholders.
   b. The system by which presidential candidates were selected.
   c. The "spoils system."
   d. The party caucus.

5. Which of the following was not a democratic reform of the age of Jackson?
   a. Adoption of the national nominating convention for the selection of presidential candidates.
   b. Adoption of the secret ballot.
   c. Popular election of presidential electors in most states.
   d. Removal by most states of property and taxation requirements for voting.

6. The South Carolina Exposition and Protest condemned as unconstitutional the:
   a. recharter of the national bank.
   b. Maysville Road Bill.
   c. Indian Removal Act.
   d. "tariff of abominations."

7. John C. Calhoun advanced the theory of nullification as:
   a. a moderate alternative to secession.
   b. a means of making the national government secondary to the states.
   c. a concession to western interests.
   d. a way to force Congress to pass a protective tariff.

8. The most significant result of the Eaton affair was that:
   a. John C. Calhoun became the leader of the Kitchen Cabinet.
   b. it led to the Webster-Hayne debate.
   c. Martin Van Buren emerged as Jackson's choice to succeed him.
   d. John Eaton became Jackson's secretary of state.

9. Robert Y. Hayne supported the continued sale of western lands in an effort to:
   a. aid the expansion of slavery.
   b. help finance internal improvements.
   c. add to the deposits in the National Bank.
   d. get western support for efforts to reduce the tariff.

10. Daniel Webster's "Second Reply to Hayne" was made in an attempt to:
    a. refute Calhoun's theory of nullification.
    b. affirm the integrity of nullification.
    c. support the sale of western lands.
    d. a. and b.
    e. b. and c.

11. The "force bill" of 1832:
    a. authorized the president to use force to see that acts of Congress were obeyed.
    b. forced Jackson to stand up to Calhoun.
    c. forced the president to consult Congress if he planned to use troops against South Carolina.
    d. made it impossible for other southern states to nullify laws.

12. The "Five Civilized Tribes" were the:
    a. Cherokee, Creek, Seminole, Chickasaw, and Choctaw.
    b. Cherokee, Cahaba, Iroquios, Mohawk, and Pequot.
    c. Cherokee, Creek, Miami, Mowa, and Iroquios.
    d. Creek, Seminole, Choctaw, Cahaba, and Pequot.

13. The Cherokees were supported in their unsuccessful battle for removal by:
    a. President Jackson.
    b. the Supreme Court.
    c. Congress.
    d. the state of Georgia.

14. When the Indian removal was completed:
    a. every Indian west of the Mississippi River was gone.
    b. only elements of the Seminoles and Cherokees remained.
    c. the Indians were relocated in reservations much like the tribal lands they left.
    d. the Indians were far enough removed from whites where they would not face further encroachments.

15. Under Nicholas Biddle, the national bank:
    a. withheld credit from new businesses.
    b. restrained less well managed state banks.
    c. did little general banking business.
    d. operated solely from its Philadelphia headquarters.

16. The national bank was supported by:
    a. "hard-money" advocates.
    b. "soft-money" advocates.
    c. western farmers.
    d. eastern business interests.

17. Determined to reduce the Bank's power even before its charter expired, Jackson:
    a. fired most of its officials, including Biddle.
    b. removed government deposits from the Bank.
    c. removed government deposits from state banks.
    d. exposed the high officials who had been borrowing from the Bank.

18. After the Panic of 1837 the Democrats' efforts to produce a new financial system resulted in the creation of:
    a. a third national bank.
    b. the "independent treasury" or "subtreasury" system.
    c. a system without state banks.
    d. a system where only gold was used as currency.

19. Roger B. Taney's tenure as chief justice:
    a. marked a sharp break with the Marshall Court in constitutional interpretation.
    b. was little more than an extension of the Marshall Court.
    c. helped modify Marshall's vigorous nationalism.
    d. was greatly influenced by the views of John C. Calhoun.
20. The Whig Party:
    a. favored expanding the power of the federal government.
    b. encouraged industrial and commercial development.
    c. advocated knitting the country together into a consolidated economic system.
    d. did all of the above.
    e. did none of the above.

TRUE-FALSE QUESTIONS

Read each statement carefully. Mark true statements "T" and false statements "F."

1. If the Jacksonians were consistent in nothing else, they were consistent Democrats.
2. During the age of Jackson, politics became open to virtually all of the nation's white male citizens.
3. Jackson wanted to weaken the functions of the federal government and give the states more power.
4. Jackson opposed the "spoils system" because it was undemocratic.
5. Calhoun wanted his nullification theory to be put to the test as soon as possible.
6. Andrew Jackson's "Kitchen Cabinet" was a group of men the president wanted to have as little to do with as possible.
7. Daniel Webster believed that the Union was essential to liberty.
8. When South Carolina nullified the tariffs of 1828 and 1832, Jackson had no choice but to go along.
9. If Calhoun and his allies learned nothing else from the nullification crisis, they learned that, alone, no state could defy the federal government.
10. During the first decades of the nineteenth century the American view of Indians as "noble savages" changed to a view of them simply as "savages."
11. Indian removal was a purely Jacksonian idea.
12. President Jackson vigorously supported (and even actively encouraged) Georgia's efforts to remove the Cherokees before the Supreme Court could rule on the legality of removal.
13. Jackson believed the national bank was a citadel of privilege, and he was determined to destroy it.
14. Clay was able to use Jackson's veto of the bank to defeat him for the presidency.
15. When the Bank of the United States died in 1836, the country was left with a fragmented and chronically unstable banking system.
16. The Democratic Party looked with suspicion on government efforts to stimulate commercial and industrial growth.
17. The Whig vision of America was one of a nation embracing the industrial future and rising to world greatness as a commercial and manufacturing power.
18. The Van Buren presidency was successful because he was able to quickly bring the nation out of the Panic of 1837.

19. The 1840 presidential campaign illustrated how getting elected had become as important as governing.

20. Though Harrison died soon after he took office, John Tyler pushed ahead with Whig programs.

CHAPTER TEN
AMERICA'S ECONOMIC REVOLUTION

Objectives

A thorough study of Chapter Ten should enable the student to understand:

1.   The changes that were taking place within the nation in terms of population growth, population movement, urbanization, and the impact of immigration.

2.   The importance of the Erie Canal for the development of the West and of New York City.

3.   The changes that were taking place in transportation, business, industry, labor, and commerce as the full impact of the industrial revolution was felt in the United States.

4.   The reasons why the Northeast and Northwest tended to become more dependent on each other, while the South became isolated from the rest of the nation in the 1840s and 1850s.

5.   The vast changes taking place in the Northeast as agriculture declined while urbanization and industrialization progressed at a rapid rate.

6.   The characteristics of the greatly increased immigration of the 1840s and 1850s, and the immigrants' effects on the development of the free states.

7.   The reasons for the appearance of the nativist movement in the 1850s.

8.   The living and working conditions of both men and women in the northern factory towns and on the northwestern farms.

Main Themes

1.   How the American population changed between 1820 and 1840, and the effect this had on the nation's economic, social, and political systems.

2.   How the dramatic economic growth of the 1820s and 1830s was accomplished.

3.   How the rapid development of the economy and society of the North influenced the rest of the nation.

Glossary

1.   packet line: A shipping line that carried mail, passengers, and goods on a regular schedule.

2.   technology: Industrial science. The study of how to improve industries through better machines, work schedules, factory organization.

3.   division of labor: The assigning of various duties to various workers rather than having one worker do an entire project. As a result, the worker becomes more specialized, more competent, and more productive.

4.   merchant capitalist: One who invests capital in the buying, selling, and shipping of goods, but not in their production.

5.   industrial capitalist: One who invests capital in manufacturing.

Pertinent Questions

THE CHANGING AMERICAN POPULATION (262-267)

1.   What were the reasons for and the effect of the rapid increase in population between 1820 and 1840?

2. What were the major immigrant groups that came to the United States and where did they settle? What population shifts took place between 1820 and 1840, and how did they affect political divisions?

3. Why was the rise of New York City so phenomenal? What forces combined to make it America's leading city?

4. How did the foreign-born population become a major factor in American political life between 1820 and 1850. What elements considered this an "alien menace," and what was their response?

TRANSPORTATION, COMMUNICATIONS, AND TECHNOLOGY (268-275)

5. Why did Americans continue to use, whenever possible, water routes for transportation and travel? What advantages did water have over land?

6. Why were natural means of carrying commerce (lakes and rivers) unsatisfactory to most Americans?

7. How did Americans propose to overcome the geographical limitations on water travel? What role was the federal government forced to play in this? Why?

8. Which area took the lead in canal development? What was the effect of these canals on that section of the country? How did other sections respond to this example?

9. What were the general characteristics of early railroad development in the United States? What innovations aided the progress of railroads, and what advantages did railroads have over other forms of transportation?

10. How did innovations in communications and journalism draw communities together? How did these innovations help divide the sections?

COMMERCE AND INDUSTRY (275-278)

11. In the broadening of business described here, what shifts in manufacturing took place, what business innovations occurred, and what effect did this have on the general distribution of goods in America?

12. What influence did technology have on the growth of American industry?

13. What forces contributed to the rise of the factory in the Northeast and how did this promote industrial development?

14. What role did American inventors and industrial ingenuity play in the growth of American industry?

MEN AND WOMEN AT WORK (278-283)

15. How did the textile mills recruit and use labor? What was the general response to the Lowell method, by worker and by observer? What caused the breakdown of this system?

16. What was the "lot of working women" in Lowell and other factory towns? How did this differ from conditions in Europe? What problems did these women have in adjusting to factory and factory-town life?

17. With the growth of industry came the growth of labor, but how did the rise of American labor organizations differ from the usual patterns of union growth? What groups organized first, and why?

18. What was the "factory system," and what impact did it have on the American artisan tradition?

19. What was the general condition of workers in northeastern factories?

20. What attempts were made to better conditions in northeastern factories? What role did unions play in these attempts, and what was accomplished?

PATTERNS OF INDUSTRIAL SOCIETY (283-292)

21.   Why was the increasing wealth of America not widely or equitably distributed? What effect did this pattern of distribution have on mobility?

22.   How did middle-class life in the years before the Civil War establish itself as the most influential cultural form of urban America?

23.   What "profound change in the nature and function of the family" took place during this era? What caused this change?

24.   What conditions put women in a "separate sphere," and what were the characteristics of the "distinctive female culture" women developed?

25.   What was the "cult of domesticity," and what costs and benefits did it bring to middle-class women? working-class women?

26.   Explain the "culture of public leisure" that existed in the mid-nineteenth century. What were its elements and who took part?

THE AGRICULTURAL NORTH (292-295)

27.   What caused the decline of farming in the Northeast? What did farmers in the Northeast do to overcome this decline, and what new patterns in agriculture resulted?

28.   What industries were found in the Northwest? How did industrial growth in the area compare with that in the rest of the nation?

29.   What was the basis of the economy in the Northwest? What goods were produced there?

30.   Where were most of the goods produced in the Northwest marketed? What role did this play in the pre-1860 sectional alignment?

31.   What factors contributed to the growth and expansion of the Northwest's economy? Who were the men responsible for this?

32.   Why was the Northwest considered the most democratic of the three sections?

33.   What were the elements that defined rural life in America at mid-nineteenth century?

THE AMERICAN ENVIRONMENT (270-271)

34.   Explain how "water was the catalyst that made trade and settlement possible" during the first half of the nineteenth century.

35.   What were "water power towns" and how did they relate to the streams that served them?

PATTERNS OF POPULAR CULTURE (290-291)

36.   Explain how the popularity of the theater, and especially the works of Shakespeare, reflected the society of Jacksonian America.

37.   How does the theater fit into the "culture of public leisure" discussed in this chapter?

Identification

Identify each of the following, and explain why it is important within the context of the chapter.

1.   Native American Association
2.   Erie Canal
3.   Mohawk and Hudson Railroad
4.   Samuel F. B. Morse
5.   "corporations"
6.   interchangeable parts

7.   Lowell or Waltham system
8.   Factory Girls Association
9.   "express contract"
10.   Central Park
11.   "safety valve"
12.   Oberlin College
13.   "domestic virtues"
14.   Sarah Hale
15.   P. T. Barnum
16.   Cyrus H. Mccormick

Document 1

Few places better reflected the growth and diversity of the United States than the city of New York. With the opening of the Erie Canal, New York City became the gateway to the West, and its size grew with its importance. The following account of the city was written by James Silk Buckingham, an Englishman who visited America between 1837 and 1840. What impressed him most about the city? How did his English experience seem to shape these impressions? What evidence did Buckingham find of social customs and distinctions being different from those of Europe? What do you feel accounted for this?

What accounted for New York's growth and diversity? What forces combined to make it America's principal city? Considering the nationalistic spirit of the age, how would Americans have responded to Buckingham's description? Assuming that his assessment was accurate, would they have pointed with pride to the city? Why?

The hotels are generally on a larger scale than in England. The great Astor House, which overlooks the Park from the west side of Broadway, is much larger in area than the largest hotels in London or Paris; it makes up 600 beds, and has a proportionate establishment to suit the scale of its general operations. It is built wholly of granite, is chaste in its style of architecture, and is called after the rich John Jacob Astor. . . .

Of places of public amusement there are a great number, including six theatres, which are well filled every night, though the majority of what would be called the more respectable classes of society, the most opulent, and the most religious members of the community do not generally patronize or approve of theatrical exhibitions under the present management.

The private dwellings contain, as must be the case in all large cities, a great variety of kinds and descriptions. The older houses are small, and mostly built of wood, painted yellow or white. These are now confined to the residences of the poorer classes, and are fast disappearing in every quarter, their places being occupied by substantial buildings of brick, though here and there are a few with granite fronts. The style of decoration, in the steps of ascent, the area of railings, and the doors, is more florid and ornamental than in the best parts of London, and the interior of the principal houses may be described as spacious, handsome, and luxurious, with lofty passages, good staircases, large rooms, and costly and gorgeous furniture. There are many individual houses of much greater splendour in London than any to be seen in New York, especially in the mansions of the English nobility; but, on the whole, the number of large, commodious, and elegantly furnished private dwellings in New York is much greater in proportion to the whole population than those in London, and approaches nearer to the ratio of Edinburgh or Paris.

The streets are very unequal in their proportions and conditions. The great avenue of Broadway is striking from its continuous and unbroken length of three miles in a straight line; but its breadth, about eighty feet, is not sufficiently ample for the due proportion of its length. It is, moreover, wretchedly paved, both in the centre and on the sides. Large holes and deep pits are frequently seen in the former; and in the latter, while before some houses the slabs of stone are large, uniform, and level, there is often an immediate transition from these to broken masses of loose stones, that require the greatest caution to pass over, especially in wet or frosty weather. The lighting and cleansing of the streets are not nearly so good as in the large towns of England, the gas being scanty in quantity, the lamps too far removed from each other, and the body of scavengers both weak in numbers and deficient in organizations. Some of the smaller streets are almost impassable in times of rain and snow; and, when not incommoded by a profusion of mud or water, they are prolific in their supply of dust. Many of the streets have trees planted along the edge of the foot pavement on each side, which in summer affords an agreeable shade, but in autumn it has the disagreeable effect of strewing the path with falling leaves, and in winter it makes the aspect more dreary.

A custom prevails, in the principal streets for shops, of having wooden pillars planted along the outer edge of the pavement, with horizontal beams reaching from pillar to pillar, not unlike the stanchions and crosspieces of a ropewalk. . . .

Broadway, which is greatly disfigured by these, is therefore much inferior to Regent Street in London in the general air of cleanliness, neatness, light, spaciousness, good pavement, and fine shops, by which the latter is characterized; and although the number of beautiful and gayly dressed ladies, who make Broadway their morning promenade, uniting shopping, visiting, and walking at the same time, gives it a very animated appearance of a fine day, between twelve and two o'clock, yet the absence of handsome equipages and fine horses, and the fewness of well-dressed gentlemen who have leisure to devote to morning promenades of pleasure occasions Broadway to be inferior in the general effect of brilliance and elegance to the throng of Regent Street on a fine day in May, between three and four o'clock. . . .

The population of New York is estimated at present to be little short of 300,000. Of these perhaps there are 20,000 foreigners, including English and persons from Canada and the British possessions, and 30,000 strangers from other states of the Union, making therefore the fixed resident population 250,000 and the floating population about 50,000 more. The greatest number of these are engaged in commerce or trade, with a due admixture of professional men, as clergy, physicians, and lawyers. But among them all there are fewer than perhaps in any other community in the world who live without any ostensible avocation. The richest capitalists still take a part in the business proceedings of the day; and men who have professedly retired and have no counting-house or mercantile establishment still retain so much of the relish for profitable occupation that they mingle freely with the merchants, and are constantly found to be the buyers and sellers of stock, in funds, or shares in companies, canals, railroads, banks, et cetera.

The result of all this is to produce the busiest community that any man could desire to live in. In the streets all is hurry and bustle; the very carts, instead of being drawn by horses at a walking pace, are often met at a gallop, and always in a brisk trot.

J. S. Buckingham, America, Historical, Statistic, and Descriptive (New York: Harper and Brothers, 1841), pp. 42–46.

Document 2

The growth of American industry was one of the more remarkable aspects of the pre-Civil War era, and the town and factory of Lowell, Massachusetts, became known as the finest example of what American ingenuity could accomplish. One of those impressed by what he found at Lowell was the frontiersman and folk hero David Crockett, who left the following account. Before you read what Crockett describes, reread the section on Lowell and on northern industry in Chapter Nine and the section on the growth of commerce in the Northeast in this chapter.

What impressed Crockett most about the factory at Lowell? How did what he witnessed differ from the economy of the section from which he came? What did Crockett see as the general benefit of an operation such as the one at Lowell? With which political party did his views seem most closely associated?

What gave rise to the "prejudices against these manufactories" Crockett mentions as being held by the West and the South? What was taking place at the time this was written (1834) that would ease the prejudices in the former and heighten them in the latter?

Next morning I rose early, and started for Lowell in a fine carriage, with three gentlemen who had agreed to accompany me. I had heard so much of this place that I longed to see it not because I had heard of the "miles of gals;" no, I left that for the gallantry of the president, who is admitted, on that score, to be abler than myself: but I wanted to see the power of the machinery, wielded by the keenest calculations of human skill; I wanted to see how it was that these northerners could buy our cotton, and carry it home, manufacture it, bring it back, and sell it for half nothing; and, in the mean time, be well to live, and make money besides. . . .

There are about fourteen thousand inhabitants [in Lowell]. It contains nine meeting houses; appropriates seven thousand five hundred dollars for free schools; provides instruction for twelve hundred scholars, daily; and about three thousand annually partake of its benefits. It communicates with Boston by the Middlesex canal (the first ever made in the United States); and in a short time the railroad to Boston will be completed, affording every facility of intercourse to the seaboard.

This place has grown by, and must depend on its manufactures. Its location renders it important, not only to the owners, but to the nation. Its consumption not only employs the thousands of its own population, but many thousands far away from them. It is calculated not only to give individual happiness and prosperity, but to add to our national wealth and independence; and instead of depending on foreign countries, to have our own material worked up in our own country. . . .

I never witnessed such a combination of industry, and perhaps never will again. I saw the whole process, from the time they put in the raw material, until it came out completely finished. In fact, it almost came up to the old story of a fellow walking into a patent machine with a bundle of wood under his arm, and coming out at the other end with a new coat on.

Nothing can be more agreeable that the attention that is paid by every one connected with these establishments. Nothing appears to be kept secret--every process is shown and with great cheerfulness. I regret that more of our southern and western men do not go there, as it would help much to do away with their prejudices against these manufactories.

David Crockett, Life of David Crockett, The Original Humorist and Irrepressible Backwoodsman (Philadelphia: Potter, 1865), pp. 213–317.

Document 3

In spite of what Crockett implied, there were also northerners who had a "prejudice" against the industrial expansion of the United States. Even the railroad, the lifeline of the northern economy, was not free from criticism, as this excerpt from Walden, by Henry David Thoreau, indicates. Why did Thoreau object to the railroad? Consider Thoreau's social philosophy--how did he think that the railroad would alter society, and what effect would that have? What did Thoreau see as the ultimate outcome of the growth of the railroad?

Men think that it is essential that the <u>Nation</u> have commerce, and export ice, and talk through a telegraph, and ride thirty miles an hour, without a doubt, whether <u>they</u> do or not; but whether we should live like baboons or like men, is a little uncertain. If we do not get our sleepers, and forge rails, and devote days and nights to the work, but go to tinkering upon our <u>lives</u> to improve <u>them,</u> who will build railroads? And if railroads are not built, how shall we get to heaven in season? But if we stay at home and mind our business, who will want railroads? We do not ride on the railroad; it rides upon us. Did you ever think what those sleepers are that underlie the railroad? Each one is a man, an Irishman, or a Yankee man. The rails are laid on them, and they are covered with sand, and the cars run smoothly over them. They are sound sleepers, I assure you. And every few years a new lot is laid down and run over; so that, if some have the pleasure of riding on a rail, others have the misfortune to be ridden upon. And when they run over a man that is walking in his sleep, a supernumerary sleeper in the wrong position, and wake him up, they suddenly stop the cars, and make a hue and cry about it, as if this were an exception. I am glad to know that it takes a gang of men for every five miles to keep the sleepers down and level in their beds as it is, for this is a sign that they may sometime get up again.

Henry David Thoreau, <u>Walden</u> (Boston: Houghton Mifflin, 1893), pp. 145–146.

Map Exercise

Fill in or identify the following on the blank map provided. Use the map in the text as your source.

1. Principal rivers.
2. Principal canals.
3. Railroad routes in 1850.
4. Principal cities on the 1850 routes.
5. Railroad routes in 1860.
6. Principal cities on the 1860 routes.
7. Main East-West lines.

Interpretative Questions

Based on what you have filled in, answer the following. On some of the questions you will need to consult the narrative in your text for information or explanation.

1. Note the relationship between canals and railroads. Why did railroads better meet the nation's transportation needs?

2. Compare and contrast the 1850 and 1860 maps. Where did most of the railroad construction take place? How did this construction change earlier transportation patterns?

3. Where railroads went, industry followed (and vice versa). What does the growth of railroads between 1850 and 1860 suggest about the industrial development of the nation?

4. Compare the principal cities in 1850 to those in 1860. Where were most of the rising urban centers located? What does this indicate about the economy and way of life of the North and the South?

5. Identify the railroad lines that linked North to South in 1850. In 1860. What does this suggest about how this transportation network united or divided the nation?

Summary

During this period a combination of a rapid growth in population, the expansion of communication and transportation systems, and the development of an agricultural system sufficient to feed an urban population gave rise to the American industrial revolution. The two sections of the nation most affected by this were the Northeast and the Northwest, which were drawn closer together as a result. Canals, railroads, and the telegraph made it easier to move goods and information. Business expanded as corporations began to shape the world of trade and commerce. Technological innovations helped expand industries, and soon the factory system began to replace the artisan tradition. In the Northwest, agriculture also expanded to meet the increasing demand for farm products. All of this had profound implications for American men and women, both in the way they worked and in their family lives.

Review Questions

These questions are to be answered with essays. This will allow you to explore relationships between individuals, events, and attitudes of the period under review.

1. Examine the development of the system of railroads and canals during this period. What geographical factors contributed to this? What sections did this transportation system link together, and what effect did this have on the economy of each? How might this transportation network have influenced political alliances?

2. What were the reasons behind the increase in population during this period? What impact did this have on the nation's economic, social, and political system?

3. It has been said that the most conspicuous changes in American life in the 1840s and 1850s took place in the Northeast. What were these changes, and what impact did they have on the northwestern section of the nation?

4. What effect did the economic changes of this era have on the American family and especially on the lives of American women in the Northeast? the Northwest?

5. What were the major technological inventions and innovations of this period? How did they both unify and divide the nation?

Chapter Self Test

After you have read the chapter in the text and done the exercises in the Study Guide, take the following self test to see if you understand the material you have covered. Answers appear at the end of the Study Guide.

MULTIPLE-CHOICE QUESTIONS

Circle the letter of the response which best answers the question or completes the statement.

1. The rise of New York City in the first half of the nineteenth century was the result of all of the following except:

a. a superior natural harbor.

b. liberal state laws that made the city attractive for both foreign and domestic commerce.

c. an absence of "nativist" sentiment.

d. unrivaled access to the interior.

2. At the time it was completed, the Erie Canal was:

a. already obsolete.

b. beginning to fill with silt from the Great Lakes.

c. the greatest construction project Americans had ever undertaken.

d. cited as an example of how not to construct a canal.

3. Which of the following helped enlarge the urban population in this era?

a. Immigrants from Europe.

b. Northeast farmers.

c. The growth of the population as a whole.

d. All of the above.

e. Both a. and c.

4. The nativist movement wanted to:

a. return all land to Native Americans.

b. enact more restrictive naturalization laws.

c. increase aid to education so voters would be literate.

d. make immigrants feel this was their home.

5. One of the immediate results of the new transportation routes constructed during the "canal age" was:

a. an increased white settlement in the Northwest.

b. an increased white settlement in the Southwest.

c. the renewed cooperation between states and the national environment on internal improvement projects.

d. the conviction that the national government should be responsible for all internal improvements.

6. During the 1820s and 1830s, railroads:

a. played only a secondary role in the nation's transportation system.

b. replaced canals as the most important means of transportation.

c. generated little interest among American businessmen.

d. consisted of a few long lines, which were not connected to water routes.

7. The most profound economic development in mid-nineteenth-century America was the:

a. development of a national banking system.

b. creation of corporations.

c. decline of the small-town merchant and general store.

d. rise of the factory.

8. The great technical advances in American industry owed much to:

a. American inventors.

b. national research universities.

c. innovative businessmen.

    d. labor unions.

9. The beginnings of an industrial labor supply can be traced to:

    a. overcrowding in American cities.

    b. a dramatic increase in food production.

    c. the use of slaves in manufacturing industries.

    d. an increase in European immigration.

10. The Lowell or Waltham system of recruiting labor was to:

    a. enlist young women from farm families.

    b. recruit whole families from rural areas.

    c. recruit newly arrived immigrants.

    d. enlist young men from farm families.

11. The paternalistic factory system of Lowell and Waltham did not last long because:

    a. workers resented being watched over so carefully.

    b. in the highly competitive textile market, manufacturers were eager to cut labor costs.

    c. unions undermined the owners' authority.

    d. men found jobs in the factories, and they disliked the paternalistic system.

12. Most of the industrial growth experienced in the United States between 1840 and 1860 took place in the:

    a. South and Southwest

    b. Old Northwest.

    c. New England region and the mid-Atlantic states.

    d. Ohio Valley.

13. Which of the following was not a technological advance that sped the growth of industry during this period?

    a. Better machine tools.

    b. Interchangeable tools.

    c. Improved water-power generators.

    d. New steam engines.

14. The railroad network that developed during this period linked:

    a. the Northeast to the Northwest.

    b. the Northeast to the Gulf Coast.

    c. the East Coast to the West Coast.

    d. New York to New Orleans.

15. Crucial to the operation of railroads was:

    a. a system of federal railroad regulations.

    b. the invention of the telegraph.

    c. slave labor to build the lines.

    d. a canal and river system that supported the lines.

16. Which of the following did not inhibit the growth of effective labor resistance?

    a. Ethnic divisions between natives and immigrants.

    b. The availability of cheap labor.

c.   Slavery.

   d.   The strength of the industrial capitalists.

17.   Why did the unequal distribution of wealth not create more resentment?

   a.   The actual living standard of the workers was improving.

   b.   There was no social mobility, but people were content to stay where they were in the social system.

   c.   Geographic mobility was limited, so there were few other opportunities.

   d.   The political system offered few ways to express resentment.

18.   In the middle-class family during this era, the role of women changed from:

   a.   helpmate to workmate.

   b.   "republican mother" to "democratic female."

   c.   passive domestic to radical feminist.

   d.   income producer to income consumer.

19.   The growth of the agricultural economy of the Northwest affected the sectional alignment of the United States because:

   a.   northwestern goods were sold to residents of the Northeast.

   b.   northeastern industry sold its products to the Northeast.

   c.   northwestern grain was sold to the South, which allowed it to grow more cotton.

   d.   the Northwest was able to feed itself so it did not align with any other section.

   e.   of a. and b.

   f.   of a. and d.

TRUE-FALSE QUESTIONS

Read each statement carefully. Mark true statements "T" and false statements "F."

1.   During the first half of the nineteenth century the United States grew more rapidly in population than did Britain and Europe.

2.   During the first half of the nineteenth century the African-American population increased as fast or faster than did the white population.

3.   The city that gained the most from the new transportation routes built in this era was New York.

4.   Because it was agricultural, the Northwest experienced little urban growth during this era.

5.   Because we are a "nation of immigrants," the Know-Nothing movement had little success.

6.   Railroads had so many advantages over canals that, where free competition existed, they almost always prevailed.

7.   The consolidation of railroads affected the nature of sectional alignments.

8.   Credit mechanisms in the early nineteenth century were well designed and efficient.

9.   When compared to working conditions in European industries, the Lowell mills were a paradise for working women.

10.   Artisans, displaced by the factory system, formed the first American labor unions.

11.   The most conspicuous change in American life in the 1840s and 1850s was the rapid industrialization of the Northeast.

12.   During this period international trade became increasingly important for the national economy.

13.   The South was an important part of the national railroad network.

14. The majority of immigrants during this period came from Ireland and Russia.

15. Although conditions got worse in American factories, few workers tried to do anything about it.

16. Industrialization made no change in the nature and function of the American family.

17. Except for teaching and nursing, work by women outside the household gradually came to be seen as a lower-class preserve.

18. The typical white citizen of the Northwest was the owner of a reasonably prosperous family farm.

19. Although agriculture expanded in the Northwest, new agricultural techniques reduced the amount of labor needed to produce a crop.

20. The Northwest was the most self-consciously democratic section of the country.

CHAPTER ELEVEN
COTTON, SLAVERY, AND THE OLD SOUTH

Objectives

A thorough study of Chapter Eleven should enable the student to understand:

1.   The significance of the shift of economic power from the "upper South" to the "lower South."
2.   How cotton became "king," and the role it played in shaping the "southern way of life."
3.   How trade and industry functioned under the southern agricultural system.
4.   The structure of southern society, and the role of an enslaved people in that society.
5.   The place of the South, with its increasing reliance on King Cotton, in the nation's economy.
6.   The continuing historical debate over the South, its "peculiar institution," and the effects of enslavement on the blacks.

Main Themes

1.   How economic power shifted from the "upper" to the "lower" South, and the impact this had on southern social and political development.
2.   How society in the South developed both in myth and in reality.
3.   The nature of the South's "peculiar institution," and the effect it had on the southern way of life.

Glossary

1.   planter: A term used to identify one of those southerners whose combination of land and slaves was such that they stood out as the prominent staple producers in their area. A social as well as an economic designation, it was used to identify the agricultural elite in the South.
2.   manumission: The act of freeing a slave.

Pertinent Questions

THE COTTON ECONOMY (298-306)

1.   What was "the most important economic development in the South of the mid-nineteenth century"? What caused this, and what was its economic impact?
2.   What were the agricultural regions in the South, and what crops were grown in them?
3.   How did cotton become "king" in the South, and what did this mean for the development of the region?
4.   What role did the "business classes" of the South play in the region's economic development? What element was most important in this group? Why?
5.   What do the authors mean by the statement that the antebellum South had a "colonial" economy?
6.   What was the "cavalier" image, and how were southern planters able to create it?
7.   Though only a small minority of southern whites owned slaves, the region was seen—both by the outside world and by many southerners themselves—as a society dominated by great plantations and wealthy landowning planters. How did this happen?
8.   How did the idea of "honor" affect southern life in the years prior to the Civil War?

9. How was the role played by affluent southern white women like that of their northern counterparts? How was it different?

10. What accounted for the difference identified in question 9? Why did so few southern white women rebel against their role?

11. If "the typical white southerner was not a great planter," what was he? Describe and explain the way of life of the southern "plain folk."

12. Why did so few nonslaveholding whites oppose the slaveholding oligarchy? Where did these opponents live?

SLAVERY: THE "PECULIAR INSTITUTION" (306-313)

13. What were slave codes? What function did they serve? How were they applied, and what resulted from their violation?

14. How was slave life shaped by the slave's relationship with his or her owner?

15. Explain the "actual material condition of slavery" and the debate over it.

16. Were there "classes" among the slaves? What evidence is there to support this?

17. How did slavery in the cities differ from slavery on the plantation? What effect did urban slavery have on the "peculiar institution" and on the relationship between white and black?

18. How extensive was the practice of manumission in the South? What was the status of the freed slave in the South, and how did this compare with the status of freed people in the North?

19. Explain the characteristics of the foreign and domestic slave trade. On what grounds was this trade criticized, and how did the South answer this criticism?

20. How did the slave respond to slavery? What evidence exists to show that slaves did not accept their condition without protest and, in some cases, outright defiance?

21. What were the most widely recognized slave revolts? What did they accomplish?

THE CULTURE OF SLAVERY (313-316)

22. Explain how the process of adaptation helped slaves develop their own separate culture. How was this a form of resistance as well?

23. What role did language and music play in sustaining racial pride and unity for slaves?

24. What role did religion play in the life of slaves? What role did the slave family play?

WHERE HISTORIANS DISAGREE (309)

25. How have historical interpretations of the impact of slavery on the slaves evolved over the years?

26. What factors have shaped these historians' assessments?

PATTERNS OF POPULAR CULTURE (314)

27. How did music both shape and reflect the lives of African Americans on slave plantations?

Identification

Identify each of the following, and explain why it is important within the context of the chapter.

1. Long-staple cotton
2. Tredegar Iron Works
3. "factors"

Document 1

In the South, the plantation dominated the economy, much as industry did in the Northeast. Following is a description of and some observations on the plantation system and slave labor taken from the travel account of Frederick Law Olmsted. What similarities do you find between the regimentation of the factory workers at Lowell in the previous chapter and the status of the slaves? What differences exist? How might Thoreau have responded to what Olmsted described?

How did the objectives of the plantation owner differ from the objectives of those who owned the mills at Lowell? Might the plantation owner have argued that he offered his charges many of the same things as the factory? What analogy was the South fond of drawing between the factory and the plantation? What does this excerpt tell you about that analogy?

What evidence can you find to indicate classes among slaves? Read the section "Where Historians Disagree: The Character of Plantation Slavery," and consider how this excerpt relates to the theories advanced by Elkins, Fogel, and Engerman.

It is difficult to handle simply as property, a creature possessing human passions and human feelings, however debased and torpid the condition of that creature may be; while, on the other hand, the absolute necessity of dealing with property as a thing, greatly embarrassed a man in any attempt to treat it as a person. And it is the natural result of this complicated state of things, that the system of slave-management is irregular, ambiguous, and contradictory; that it is never either consistently humane or consistently economical.

As a general rule, the larger the body of negroes on a plantation or estate, the more completely are they treated as mere property, and in accordance with a policy calculated to insure the largest pecuniary returns. Hence, in part, the greater proportionate profit of such plantations, and the tendency which everywhere prevails in the planting districts to the absorption of small, and the augmentation of large estates. It may be true, that among the wealthier slave-owners there is oftener a humane disposition, a better judgment, and a greater ability to deal with their dependents indulgently and bountifully, but the effects of this disposition are chiefly felt, even on those plantations where the proprietor resides permanently, among the slaves employed about the house and stables, and perhaps a few old favourites in the quarters. It is more than balanced by the difficulty of acquiring a personal

134

interest in the units of a large body of slaves, and an acquaintance with the individual characteristics of each. The treatment of the mass must be reduced to a system, the ruling idea of which will be, to enable one man to force into the same channel of labour the muscles of a large number of men of various and often conflicting wills.

Frederick Law Olmsted, The Cotton Kingdom (London: Sampson Low, Son, 1862), p. 192.

Document 2

As the section "Where Historians Disagree" indicates, the South's "peculiar institution" has been debated for some time. Following is an excerpt from Joseph B. Cobb's Mississippi Scenes, published in 1851, that sheds some light on the question of the slave's response to slavery. Read it, and consider how it relates to the information and points of view presented in the text. From it determine, at least in this case, how slavery apparently changed blacks, and what elements of the system brought these changes about. In studying this question, reexamine Document 1. Would you call slavery a brutal system or, as many southerners (including Joseph B. Cobb) contended, a "positive good"?

The late Hon. William H. Crawford, so affectionately and proudly remembered by all Georgians, owned four native Africans, brought to this country among the last importations of those unfortunate wretches who could be sold within the time prescribed by the Federal Constitution. . . . In the same neighborhood, there happened to be residing another native African, rather more Americanized than the first, and these five old fellows, especially as some of them bore on their faces the strange scars inflicted for some unknown distinguishing purpose in their native country, were treated with marked respect by all the other negroes for miles and miles around. . . . Their illustrious owner himself always treated them with rather more kindness of manner and respect than his other slaves, and would never allow them to be subjected to the lash except in case of downright resistance to the authority of his overseer (and this was a fault with them occasionally), and even then with manifest reluctance, and only from imperative convictions of duty. Their habits and dispositions were as unlike those of our native negroes as it is possible to conceive, when it is considered that they are the same race. They had none of the merry-heartedness and vivacity which I have elsewhere pictured as a trait of our Southern negroes, and, though not decidedly morose, or fractious, they were yet exclusive, and somewhat unapproachable. They required far less whipping to coerce attention to their tasks; indeed, they worked with remarkable diligence, and it was only in case of a misunderstanding about some matter of business betwixt them and the overseer that they ever became refractory, or were brought under the lash. On the other hand, our Southern negroes rarely ever resist (though now and then they runaway when frightened by overseers freshly employed), but they are generally indolent and careless if they are allowed to think that whipping will not be resorted to. I never knew a native African to runaway from his master's plantation. They stand their ground doggedly, like the Roman or British soldier, regardless of consequences; and to carry out the simile, they often fight with the same determined courage, unhappily for them!

Joseph B. Cobb, Mississippi Scenes (Philadelphia: Hart, 1851), pp. 173–174.

Map Exercise

Fill in or identify the following on the blank map provided. Use the map in the text as your source.

1.   The slave states in 1820 and 1860.
2.   The distribution of slavery and cotton production in 1820 and 1860.

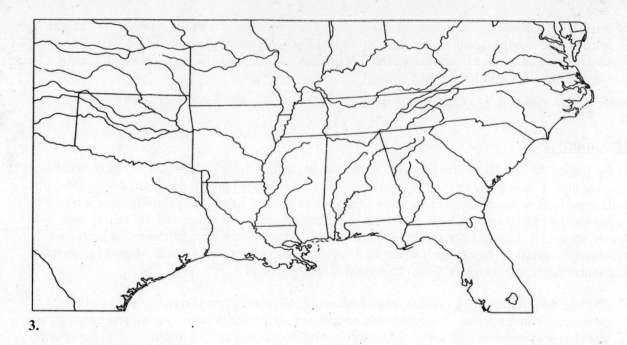

3.

Interpretative Questions

Based on what you have filled in, answer the following. On some of the questions you will need to consult the narrative in your text for information or explanation.

1. How did slavery relate to the growing of cotton? In what ways did slave labor serve the cotton economy, and how does this explain the relationship between the two?

2. In what non-cotton-growing areas did slavery exist? What economic role did slaves play in these areas?

3. Note the places where slavery did not exist. What was the economy of these areas? In what way did society in these areas differ from those areas where there was slavery?

Summary

In the 1830s and 1840s, as the societies of the North and South developed, the two diverged, and this had an impact on the growth of the nation. During the period both sections expanded physically and economically; but while the northern economy was characterized by industrial expansion, by the growth of transportation systems (especially railroads), and by an increasingly diverse population, the southern economy continued to rest on staple-crop agriculture and slave labor. This is not to say that the South did not experience many of the same changes felt in the North, but in comparison, the slave states' way of life seemed more rooted in the past than in the future. As the economic power of the region shifted from the "upper" South to the "lower," cotton became "king," and trade and business served this master. In a short period of time a planter class spread across the South, and though planters were a minority, they influenced society and politics far beyond their numbers. During this period the "cavalier" myth was born and the "Southern lady" made her appearance. Though most Southerners could be considered "plain folk," they supported the slaveholding elites and hoped someday to be part of it. All the while slaves worked, endured, resisted, and under the most trying of conditions created a culture that remains an important part of American life.

Review Questions

These questions are to be answered with essays. This will allow you to explore relationships between individuals, events, and attitudes of the period under review.

1. According to the text, "the most important economic development in the mid-nineteenth-century South was the shift of economic power from the 'upper South' . . . to the 'lower South.' Why was this so important?

2. What was "the southern way of life" for white southerners—the planter and his family, the plain folks?

3. What was "the southern way of life" for black southerners—men, women, house servants, field hands, rural and urban, slave and free?

4. If nothing else, slavery set the South apart, made it unique. But how did the institution function? Analyze the plantation system, its social and its economic functions. How did it control its labor? And what was the response of these workers?

5. Explain the "spirited debate" that has gone on among historians over the nature of American slavery. Where does your textbook fit into this debate?

Chapter Self Test

After you have read the chapter in the text and done the exercises in the Study Guide, take the following self test to see if you understand the material you have covered. Answers appear at the end of the Study Guide.

MULTIPLE-CHOICE QUESTIONS

Circle the letter of the response which best answers the question or completes the statement.

1. The southern failure to create a flourishing commercial or industrial economy was in part the result of:
    a. a lack of business talent in the South.
    b. an unwillingness on the part of the southerners to take risks.
    c. a set of values distinctive to the South that discouraged the growth of cities and industry.
    d. a slave labor force that could not work successfully in industry.

2. The most important economic development in the mid-nineteenth-century South was the:
    a. invention of the cotton gin.
    b. shift of economic power from the "upper South" to the "lower South."
    c. increased agricultural diversity of the region.
    d. decline in the price of slaves.

3. The expansion of southern agriculture from 1820 to 1860 was due to the expansion of the cultivation of:
    a. western rice.
    b. tobacco in Kentucky.
    c. Louisiana sugar.
    d. short-staple cotton in the Black Belt.

4. The South in 1860, in contrast to 1800, had become:
    a. a primarily rural and agricultural region.
    b. increasingly unlike the North and increasingly sensitive to criticism.
    c. a region where political power rested in the hands of small farmers.
    d. more urban and more industrialized.

5. A minority of southern whites owned slaves:
    a. and nonslaveholders dominated the political system in the region.
    b. but the slaveholding planters exercised power and influence far in excess of their numbers.
    c. so slavery was not very important in the lives of most whites.
    d. and most whites were happy with it that way.

6. The South had a "colonial" economy in that:
    a. most of its land was owned by outside interests.
    b. it employed slave labor.
    c. it produced raw materials and purchased finished products.
    d. had little political power.

7. According to the "cavalier" image, southern planters were:
    a. mostly horsebreeders.
    b. really a rough-and-tumble group of people.
    c. genteel aristocrats.
    d. successful agricultural businessmen.

8. Most southern white "ladies" were:
    a. less subordinate to men than in the North.
    b. relatively isolated from people outside their own families.
    c. better educated than their northern counterparts.
    d. more likely to engage in public activities or income-producing employment than their northern counterparts.

9. The typical white southerner was:
    a. a planter with many slaves and a lot of land.
    b. a small-town merchant or professional man.
    c. extremely poor.
    d. a modest yeoman farmer.

10. Although most whites did not own slaves, most supported the plantation system because:
    a. it controlled the slaves.
    b. they had economic ties to it.
    c. slaveholder and nonslaveholder were often related.
    d. of all of the above.

11. Which of the following was not a condition of slave life in the South?
    a. An adequate if rough diet.
    b. Hard work, even for women and children.
    c. The freedom to use the time after work as they wished to.
    d. Isolation and control.

12. The slave codes of the southern states:
   a. imposed a uniformly harsh and dismal regime for southern slaves.
   b. allowed slaves a great deal of flexibility and autonomy.
   c. created a paternal and benevolent relationship between master and slave.
   d. contained rigid provisions but were unevenly enforced.

13. Slaves seemed to prefer to live on larger plantations because:
   a. masters supervised workers personally and often worked alongside them.
   b. they had more opportunities for privacy and for a social world of their own.
   c. masters seemed more concerned with their health and welfare.
   d. the work was lighter and provisions were more abundant.

14. By 1860, which of the following states had the highest proportion of slaveholding to nonslaveholding white families?
   a. Virginia.
   b. Georgia.
   c. South Carolina.
   d. Arkansas.

15. If there was dangerous work to be done:
   a. masters generally hired slaves rather than use their own.
   b. free labor, often Irishmen, might be hired.
   c. it made no difference to masters, who used their slaves no matter what the conditions.
   d. only older slaves were used.

16. As southern cities grew, the number of slaves in them declined because:
   a. urban slaveholders, fearing rebellion, sold their slaves.
   b. diseases in cities killed them off.
   c. men outnumbered women, so there was no natural increase.
   d. slaves in the city ran away to the countryside.

17. The historical debate over the nature of plantation slavery demonstrates:
   a. the difficulty in researching a field in which few documents exist.
   b. the extent to which historians are influenced by the times in which they write.
   c. basic agreement that slavery was a brutal, savage institution that dehumanized all participants.
   d. that black slaves in the South were generally content and happy with their lot.

18. In The Black Family in Slavery and Freedom (1976), Herbert Gutman argued that:
   a. slave families were better treated and lived in greater comfort than did northern industrial workers.
   b. the black family survived slavery with impressive strength.
   c. slavery destroyed the significance of the father in the black family.
   d. slaves were unable to establish strong family ties.

19. The only slave insurrection in the nineteenth century South was led by:

    a. Gabriel Prosser.

    b. Denmark Vesey.

    c. Nat Turner.

    d. Frederick Douglass.

20. Black adaptation to slavery:

    a. revealed a passive contentment with bondage.

    b. produced a rich and complex culture in support of racial pride and unity.

    c. undermined black conversion to Christianity.

    d. resulted in the loss of all cultural elements of African life.

TRUE-FALSE QUESTIONS

Read each statement carefully. Mark true statements "T" and false statements "F."

1. The South, like the North, changed from an agricultural to an industrial economy during the period from 1820 to 1850.

2. The South had very few professional people.

3. According to De Bow's Review, the South had a "colonial" relationship with the North.

4. Planters in the South were just as much competitive capitalists as the industrialists in the North.

5. Most southern planters actually were "cavaliers."

6. Most nonslaveowning whites lived far from the planters and their plantations.

7. The South in mid-nineteenth century was the only area in the western world except for Brazil and Cuba where slavery still existed.

8. Under the code of "chivalry," women were to be protected, and in return they were expected to obey men.

9. When the foreign slave trade ended, the domestic slave trade declined as well.

10. The majority of the South's white population consisted of modest farmers largely excluded from the dominant plantation society.

11. Small farmers in the South were more committed to a traditional patriarchal family structure than were the planters.

12. As a group, slaves were as healthy as whites, and the black population increased more rapidly than the white.

13. More than half of the free blacks lived in Virginia and Maryland.

14. By the 1850s the domestic slave trade was no longer important to the growth and prosperity of the South.

15. Few slave families were actually broken apart by the slave trade.

16. African American religion reflected the influence of African customs and practices.

17. The dominant response of African Americans to slavery was a combination of adaptation and resistance.

18. Because of the pressures of bondage, slave marriages seldom lasted.

19. Masters used paternalism as a means of control.

20. According to Elizabeth Fox-Genovese, black and white women on plantations shared a common female identity born of their shared subordination to men.

CHAPTER TWELVE
ANTEBELLUM CULTURE AND REFORM

Objectives

A thorough study of Chapter Twelve should enable the student to understand:

1. The two basic impulses that were reflected in the reform movements, and examples of groups illustrating each impulse.

2. The contributions of a new group of literary figures (such as James Fenimore Cooper, Walt Whitman, and Edgar Allan Poe) to American cultural nationalism.

3. The transcendentalists and their place in American society.

4. The sources of American religious reform movements, why they originated where they did, their ultimate objectives, and what their leadership had in common.

5. The two distinct sources from which the philosophy of reform arose.

6. American educational reform in the antebellum period, and the contribution of education to the growth of nationalism.

7. The role of women in American society, and the attempts to alter their relationships with men.

8. The origins of the antislavery movement, the philosophy behind it, and the sources of its leadership.

9. The role of abolitionism in the antislavery movement, and the strengths and weaknesses of that part of the movement.

10. The role world opinion played in ending slavery.

Main Themes

1. How American intellectuals developed a national culture committed to the liberation of the human spirit.

2. How this commitment to the liberation of the human spirit led to and reinforced the reform impulse of the period.

3. How the crusade against slavery became the most powerful element in this reform movement.

Glossary

1. romanticism: The intellectual movement that replaced the Age of Reason (rationalism). Stressing imagination, emotion, and sentiment, the movement emphasized individual thought and action as well as human goodness and equality.

2. temperance: The use of moderation in one's indulgences. In the context of the reform movement, the abstinence from alcoholic drinks and ultimately the prohibition of these beverages.

3. socialism: A social, economic, and political theory based on collective ownership of the means of production and distribution. These means are directed by the people or their representatives for the good of society as a whole.

Pertinent Questions

THE ROMANTIC IMPULSE (320-326)

1. How was the work of James Fenimore Cooper the culmination of an effort to produce a truly American literature? What did his work suggest about the nation and its people?

2. Why was Whitman called the "poet of American democracy"?

3. Who were the transcendentalists? What was their philosophy, and how did they express it in literature?

4. How were the transcendentalists among the first Americans to anticipate the environmental movement of the twentieth-century?

5. How did the transcendentalists attempt to apply their beliefs to the problems of everyday life at Brook Farm? What was the result?

6. What other utopian schemes were put forth during this period, and how did they propose to reorder society to create a better way of life?

7. How did the utopian communities attempt to redefine the gender roles? Which communities were most active in this effort, and what did they accomplish?

8. Who were the Mormons? What were their origins, what did they believe, and why did they end up in Utah?

REMAKING SOCIETY (326-334)

9. The "philosophy of reform" that shaped this era rose from what two distinct sources?

10. What gave rise to the crusade against drunkenness? What successes and failures resulted from the movement's efforts?

11. What was the biggest problem facing American medicine during this period? What impact did this problem have on health care in the United States?

12. How did efforts to produce a system of universal public education reflect the spirit of the age?

13. What were the problems facing public education, and what types of institutions were created to deal with them?

14. How did the rise of feminism reflect not only the participation of women in social crusades, but also a basic change in the nature of the family?

15. How did feminists benefit from their association with other reform movements, most notably abolitionists, and at the same time suffer as a result?

THE CRUSADE AGAINST SLAVERY (334-341)

16. What was the antislavery philosophy of William Lloyd Garrison? How did he transform abolitionism into a new and "dramatically different phenomenon"?

17. What role did black abolitionists play in the movement? How did their philosophy compare with that of Garrison?

18. Why did many northern whites oppose the abolitionist movement? How did they show this opposition?

19. What divisions existed within the abolitionist movement itself? How did each faction express its position?

20. What efforts did abolitionists make to find political solutions to the question of slavery? How successful were they initially?

21. How did abolitionists attempt to arouse widespread public anger over slavery through the use of propaganda? What was the most significant work to emerge from this effort? Why did it have such an impact?

PATTERNS OF POPULAR CULTURE (338-339)

22. Explain how sentimental novels of this era "gave voice to both female hopes and female anxieties."

23. How did pressure of world opinion and Enlightenment ideals combine to end the slave trade and slavery in countries other than the United States?

24. How did world opinion and Enlightenment ideals influence the abolition movement in the United States and how, in turn, did American abolitionism help reinforce the movements abroad?

Identification

Identify each of the following, and explain why it is important within the context of the chapter.

1. Hudson River School
2. "Leatherstocking Tales"
3. Moby Dick
4. "The Raven"
5. "Oversoul"
6. "Resistance to Civil Government"
7. Nathaniel Hawthorne
8. "phalanxes"
9. "Owenites"
10. Oneida "Perfectionists"
11. Shakers
12. The Book of Mormon
13. Charles Grandison Finney
14. "burned-over district"
15. American Society for the Promotion of Temperance
16. Phrenology
17. Horace Mann
18. Dorothea Dix
19. asylums
20. Reservations
21. Sarah and Angelina Grimké
22. Seneca Falls convention
23. Emma Willard and Catharine Beecher
24. Amelia Bloomer
25. American Colonization Society
26. Monrovia
27. American Antislavery Society
28. Walker's Appeal . . . to the Colored Citizens
29. Frederick Douglass
30. Elijah Lovejoy
31. Prigg v. Pennsylvania
32. "personal liberty laws"
33. "free soil"
34. William Wilberforce

Document 1

If any man spoke for the new democratic age, it was Ralph Waldo Emerson. Here, in an excerpt from his essay "Self-Reliance," he exhorts his fellow citizens to have confidence in themselves and their potential—what is democratic about that? How does this selection reflect the force behind the reform movement in America? Read the section in your text on Emerson, and compare what you read in this document with the philosophy of transcendentalism. What similarities exist?

On the contrary, how might it be argued that Emerson is really saying nothing new, but is merely verbalizing what Americans already believed but had not put into words? Are the people Emerson is addressing once again being "forced to take with shame [their] own opinions from another"?

To believe your own thought, to believe that what is true for you in your private heart is true for all men,--that is genius. Speak your latent conviction, and it shall be the universal sense; for always the inmost becomes the outmost—and our first thought is rendered back to us by the trumpets of the Last Judgment. Familiar as the voice of the mind is to each, the highest merit we ascribe to Moses, Plato and Milton is that they set at naught books and traditions, and spoke not what men, but what they thought. A man should learn to detect and watch that gleam of light which flashes across his mind from within, more than the lustre of the firmament of bards and sages. Yet he dismisses without notice his thought, because it is his. In every work of genius we recognize our own rejected thoughts; they come back to us with a certain alienated majesty. Great works of art have no more affecting lesson for us than this. They teach us to abide by our spontaneous impression with good-humored inflexibility then most when the whole cry of voices is on the other side. Else to-morrow a stranger will say with masterly good sense precisely what we have thought and felt all the time, and we shall be forced to take with shame our own opinion from another.

Ralph Waldo Emerson, Essays (New York: Hurst, 1885), pp. 63–64.

Document 2

Most reformers agreed that for Americans to reach their full potential, education was essential, and most agreed that an area where much needed to be done was education for women. Mount Holyoke Seminary, founded in 1837, was one of the earliest and most successful attempts to meet this need. The following, taken from a letter written by one of America's greatest poets, Emily Dickinson, when she was a student there, describes the school and some of its activities. How does Mount Holyoke's general approach to education compare with that at your school? How does the curriculum reflect the general attitude toward education in the mid-nineteenth century? Look at the description of Dickinson's nonacademic activities. Does anything she did indicate that women were still being treated differently from men?

MY DEAR ABIAH,

I am really at Mt. Holyoke Seminary and this is to be my home for a long year. . . . I am now quite contented and am very much occupied now in reviewing the Junior studies, as I wish to enter the middle class. The school is very large, and though quite a number have left, on account of finding the examinations more difficult than they anticipated, yet there are nearly 300 now. Perhaps you know that Miss Lyon is raising her standard of scholarship a good deal, on account of the number of applicants this year and on account of that she makes the examinations more severe than usual. You cannot imagine how trying they are, because if we cannot go through them all in a specified time, we are sent home. I cannot be too thankful that I got through as soon as I did and I am sure that I never would endure the suspense which I endured during those three days again for all the treasures of the world. . . .

I will tell you my order of time for the day, as you were so kind as to give me your's. At 6 o'clock, we all rise. We breakfast at 7. Our study hours begin at 8. At 9 we all meet in Seminary Hall for devotions. At 10 1/4 I recite a review of Ancient history in connection with which we read Goldsmith and Grimshaw. At 11 I recite a lesson in "Pope's Essay on Man" which is merely transposition. At 12 I practice Calisthenics and at 12 1/4 read until dinner which is at 12 1/2. After dinner from 1 1/2 until 2 I sing in Seminary Hall. From 2 3/4 until 3 3/4 I practice upon the piano. At 3 3/4 I go to Section, where we give in all our accounts for the day, including Absence--Tardiness--Communications-- Breaking Silent Study hours--Receiving Company in our rooms and ten thousand other things which I will not take time or place to mention. At 4 1/2 we go into Seminary Hall and receive advice from Miss Lyon in the form of a lecture. We have supper at 6 and silent study hours from then until the retiring bell, which rings at 8 3/4 but the tardy bell does not ring until 9 3/4, so that we don't often obey the first warning to retire.

Unless we have a good and reasonable excuse for failure upon any of the items that I mentioned above, they are recorded and a <u>black mark</u> stands against our names. As you can easily imagine, we do not like very well to get "exceptions" as they are called scientifically here. My domestic work is not difficult and consists in carrying the knives from the 1st tier of tables at morning and noon, and at night washing and wiping the same quantity of knives. . . . You have probably heard many reports of the food here and if so I can tell you, that I have yet seen nothing corresponding to my ideas on that point, from what I have heard. Everything is wholesome and abundant and much nicer than I should imagine could be provided for almost 300 girls. We have also a great variety upon our tables and frequent changes. One thing is certain and that is, that Miss Lyon and all the teachers seem to consult our comfort and happiness in everything they do and you know that is pleasant. When I left home, I did not think I should find a companion or a dear friend in all the multitude. I expected to find rough and uncultivated manners, and to be sure I have found some of that stamp, but on the whole, there is an ease and a grace and a desire to make one another happy, which delights and at the same time surprises me very much. . . .

From your aff. EMILY, E.D.

Document 3

The influence of Harriet Beecher Stowe's book <u>Uncle Tom's Cabin</u> on the northern perception of the South's "peculiar institution" was such that Abraham Lincoln was said to have addressed her in 1862 as "the little woman who wrote the book who made this great war." Presented here is a selection from <u>Uncle Tom's Cabin,</u> which describes the arrival of Uncle Tom on the plantation of Simon Legree.

What was Stowe's purpose in writing this book? Notice that Legree is not a southerner, but is from New England. Why would she have created such a character? Also, what of the "two coloured men" who served Legree as his "principal hands"? What was the author trying to say about the effect of slavery on slaves? Reread the section "Where Historians Disagree" in Chapter Eleven of the text. With which of these historians would Stowe have agreed?

These two coloured men were the two principal hands on the plantation. Legree had trained them in savageness and brutality as systematically as he had his bull-dogs; and, by long practice in hardness and cruelty, brought their whole nature to about the same range of capacities. It is a common remark, and one that is thought to militate strongly against the character of the race, that the negro overseer is always more tyrannical and cruel than the white one. This is simply saying that the negro mind has been more crushed and debased than the white. It is not more true of this race than of every oppressed race, the world over. The slave is always a tyrant, if he can get a chance to be one. . . .

It was late in the evening when the weary occupants of the shanties came flocking home--men and women, in soiled and tattered garments, surly and uncomfortable, and in no mood to look pleasantly on newcomers. The small village was alive with no inviting sounds; hoarse, guttural voices contending at the hand-mills where their morsel of hard corn was yet to be ground into meal, to fit it for the cake that was to constitute their only supper. From the earliest dawn of the day, they had been

145

in the fields, pressed to work under the driving lash of the overseers; for it was now in the very heat and hurry of the season, and no means were left untried to press everyone up to the top of their capabilities. "True," says the negligent lounger; "picking cotton isn't hard work." Isn't it? And it isn't much inconvenience, either, to have one drop of water fall on your head; yet the worst torture of the Inquisition is produced by drop after drop, drop after drop, falling moment after moment, with monotonous succession, on the same spot; and work in itself not hard becomes so by being pressed, hour after hour, with unvarying, unrelenting sameness, with not even the consciousness of free-will to take from its tediousness. Tom looked in vain among the gang, as they poured along, for companionable faces. He saw only sullen, scowling, embruted men, and feeble, discouraged women, or women that were not women--the strong pushing away the weak--the gross, unrestricted animal selfishness of human beings, of whom nothing good was expected and desired; and who, treated in every way like brutes, had sunk as nearly to their level as it was possible for human beings to do.

Harriet Beecher Stowe, Uncle Tom's Cabin (London: Bentley, 1852), pp. 356–358.

Document 4

At the women's rights convention held at Seneca Falls, New York, in 1848, the delegates declared that "all men and women are created equal" and listed the "injuries and usurpations on the part of man toward woman." Then the convention adopted a series of resolutions for constructive action, among which were the following. What do these tell you about the goals of the early women's rights movement? What do they also tell you about the prejudices that women would have to overcome to gain the equality they sought?

Resolved, That the same amount of virtue, delicacy, and refinement of behavior that is required of woman in the social state, should also be required of man, and the same transgressions should be visited with equal severity on both man and woman.

Resolved, That the objection of indelicacy and impropriety, which is so often brought against women when she addresses a public audience, comes with a very ill grace from those who encourage, by their attendance, her appearance on the stage, in the concert, or in feats of the circus.

Resolved, That it is the duty of the women of this country to secure to themselves their sacred right to the elective franchise.

Resolved, That the equality of human rights results necessarily from the fact of the identity of the race in capabilities and responsibilities.

Resolved, That the speedy success of our cause depends upon the zealous and untiring efforts of both men and women, for the overthrow of the monopoly of the pulpit, and for the securing to women an equal participation in the various trades, professions, and commerce.

Map Exercise

Fill in or identify the following on the blank map provided. Use the maps you have filled in earlier, as well as maps in Chapter Thirteen of the text, as your sources, and consult the maps in your library as needed.

1. Major literary centers of the nation.
2. Location of the utopian experiments: Brook Farm, New Harmony, the Oneida Community, and the Amana Community.
3. Place where Mormonism began, and the key locations on its movement to Salt Lake City.
4. "Burned-over district."
5. States where public education and educational reform received the most support.
6. Seneca Falls, New York.

7. Major centers of abolitionist activity.

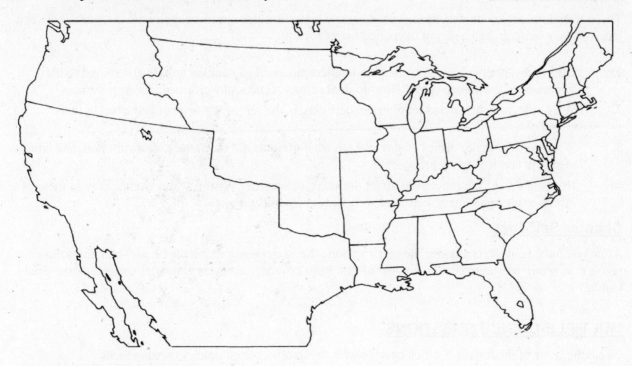

Interpretative Questions

Based on what you have filled in, answer the following. On some of the questions you will need to consult the narrative in your text for information or explanation.

1. Where was the "literary flowering" of America concentrated? What other regions had literary movements as well? How, and why, did these movements differ?

2. Where were most of the efforts to reform and improve education taking place? What connection might there be between this movement and the "literary flowering"?

3. Where were the major utopian communities located? What factors played a part in the choices of location?

4. What region of the country was less involved in the reform movement? What factors contributed to this?

Summary

By the 1820s, America was caught up in the spirit of a new age, and Americans, who had never been shy in proclaiming their nation's promise and potential, concluded that the time for action had come. Excited by the nation's technological advances and territorial expansions, many set as their goal the creation of a society worthy to be part of it all. What resulted was an outpouring of reform movements the like of which had not been seen before and have not been seen since. Unrestrained by entrenched conservative institutions and attitudes, these reformers attacked society's ills wherever they found them, producing in the process a list of evils so long that many were convinced that a complete reorganization of society was necessary. Most, however, were content to concentrate on their own particular cause, and thus, at least at first, the movements were many and varied. But in time, most reformers seemed to focus on one evil that stood out above the rest. The "peculiar institution," slavery, denied all they stood for—equality, opportunity, and, above all, freedom. Slavery became the supreme cause.

Review Questions

These questions are to be answered with essays. This will allow you to explore relationships between individuals, events, and attitudes of the period under review.

1. During this period, how did American intellectuals create a national culture committed to the liberation of the human spirit? How do their efforts relate to the efforts of social reformers?

2. What role did religion and religious leaders play in the reform movement described in this chapter?

3. Who were the major critics of slavery? On what grounds did they attack the institution, and what means to end it did they propose?

4. How did the reform movement affect the status of women? What role did women play in these efforts to change society, and what were they able to accomplish?

Chapter Self Test

After you have read the chapter in the text and done the exercises in the Study Guide, take the following self test to see if you understand the material you have covered. Answers appear at the end of the Study Guide.

MULTIPLE-CHOICE QUESTIONS

Circle the letter of the response which best answers the question or completes the statement.

1. The reform movements of the first half of the nineteenth century reflected which of the following impulses:
    a. an optimistic faith in human nature.
    b. a rational view of man and his ability.
    c. a desire for control and order.
    d. a. and c.

2. The first great American novelist was:
    a. Walt Whitman.
    b. James Fenimore Cooper.
    c. Herman Melville.
    d. Ralph Waldo Emerson.

3. Transcendentalists believed that:
    a. "understanding" was more important than "reason."
    b. man should repress instinct and strive for externally imposed learning.
    c. each individual should strive to "transcend" the limits of intellect and allow emotions to create an "original relation to the universe."
    d. individuals should avoid anything that would bring one too close to the natural world.

4. In his essay "Resistance to Civil Government," Henry David Thoreau claimed an individual should:
    a. not pay poll taxes.
    b. refuse to obey unjust laws.
    c. live in isolation and as simply as possible.
    d. reject the artificial constraints of government.

5. The Oneida Community:
    a. advocated "free love" to redefine gender roles.

b. called for celibacy and attracted members of conversion.

c. believed it liberated women from the demands of male "lust" and from traditional bonds of family.

d. was widely accepted and had almost no critics.

6. Like other experiments in social organization of this era, Mormonism reflected:

    a. a strong antislavery bias.

    b. a celebration of individual liberty.

    c. a desire to improve the status of women.

    d. a belief in human perfectibility.

7. Evangelical Protestantism added major strength to which of the following reforms:

    a. temperance.

    b. education and rehabilitation.

    c. women's rights.

    d. peace.

8. The emphasis on educational reform was consistent with the spirit of the age because it:

    a. focused on the unleashing of individual talents.

    b. stressed educational equality.

    c. focused on external learning.

    d. stressed the importance of community.

9. As women in various reform movements confronted the problems they faced in a male-dominated society, they responded by:

    a. withdrawing from the movements.

    b. accepting the notion that men and women were assigned separate "spheres" in society.

    c. focusing their attention on religious matters.

    d. setting in motion the first important feminist movement.

10. Which of the following groups was most involved in the feminist movement?

    a. Baptists.

    b. Quakers.

    c. Mormons.

    d. Shakers.

11. The "burned-over district" was a region of upstate New York prone to religious revivals because of:

    a. efficient transportation provided by the Erie Canal for traveling evangelists.

    b. the disorientation of residents caused by profound social and economic changes.

    c. the significant number of utopian communities in the vicinity.

    d. the location there of the headquarters for the Mormon Church.

12. Educational reformers intended public schools to perform all of the following roles <u>except</u> to:

    a. extend and protect democracy.

    b. raise questions and criticisms of authority.

    c. expand individual opportunities.

    d. inculcate values of thrift, order, discipline, and punctuality.

13. After 1830, which of the following reform movements began to overshadow the others:
    a. antislavery.
    b. women's rights.
    c. temperance.
    d. education.

14. The most noted black abolitionist of the day was:
    a. Ralph Waldo Emerson.
    b. William Lloyd Garrison.
    c. Frederick Douglass.
    d. Joseph Smith.

15. Opponents of abolitionism in the North believed:
    a. abolitionists were dangerous radicals.
    b. the movement would lead to a war between North and South.
    c. the movement would lead to a great influx of free blacks into the North.
    d. all the above.

16. "Immediate abolition gradually accomplished" was the slogan of:
    a. moderate antislavery forces.
    b. Garrison and his followers.
    c. southern antislavery planters.
    d. black abolitionists.

17. Personal liberty laws:
    a. allowed masters to claim slaves who ran away to the North.
    b. freed slaves who escaped to states in the Old Northwest.
    c. forbade state officials to assist in the capture and return of runaways.
    d. outlawed the interstate slave trade.

18. The movement that advocated keeping slavery out of the territories was known as the:
    a. "personal liberty" movement.
    b. "free-soil" movement.
    c. John Brown Brigade.
    d. Garrison solution.

19. Throughout the North, black Americans:
    a. enjoyed full access to education and most career opportunities.
    b. voted and held government jobs proportionate to their numbers.
    c. defended their freedom and responded eagerly to the cause of abolitionism.
    d. earned a decent standard of living.

20. The creation of "asylums" for social deviants was an effort to:
    a. punish the inmates.
    b. get the deviants out of society.
    c. reform and rehabilitate the inmates.
    d. cut down the cost of crime and punishment.

TRUE-FALSE QUESTIONS

Read each statement carefully. Mark true statements "T" and false statements "F."

1. American intellectuals were pleased with the high regard in which their culture was held by Europeans.

2. Thoreau believed that a government which required an individual to violate his or her own morality had no legitimate authority.

3. Unlike most writers of his era, Herman Melville believed that the human spirit was a troubled, often self-destructive, force.

4. Because transcendentalism was at heart an individualistic philosophy, its followers did not take part in communal living experiments.

5. The philosophy of reform in America drew heavily from Protestant revivalism.

6. Brooke Farm was the most successful of the utopian experiments.

7. The Shakers were able to prosper because of their high birth rate.

8. At the beginning of the Civil War, the United States had one of the highest literacy rates in the world.

9. The idea of asylums for social deviants was not simply an effort to curb the abuses of the old system, but also an attempt to reform and rehabilitate the inmates.

10. Early feminists made their point by drawing a parallel between the plight of women and the plight of slaves.

11. The American Colonization Society failed because it challenged both property rights and southern sensibilities.

12. The man who transformed the antislavery movement was Ralph Waldo Emerson.

13. Although there was opposition to abolitionism in the North, it was generally peaceful.

14. Radical abolitionists attacked slavery and the Constitution which seemed to sanction it.

15. Abolitionists were also pacifists and, therefore, did not advocate violence to free the slaves.

16. Antislavery and abolition were different words for the same thing.

17. Although it sold well, the novel Uncle Tom's Cabin had little impact on American antislavery attitudes.

18. Only a relatively small number of people before the Civil War ever accepted the abolitionist position that slavery must be entirely eliminated in a single stroke.

19. The women's rights movement patterned its "Declaration of Sentiments and Resolutions" after the Declaration of Independence.

20. "Free soil" was more popular than abolition in the North because it was a more moderate approach to the problem of slavery.

CHAPTER THIRTEEN
THE IMPENDING CRISIS

Objectives

A thorough study of Chapter Thirteen should enable the student to understand:

1. Manifest Destiny, and its influence on the nation in the 1840s.
2. The origin of the Republic of Texas, and the controversy concerning its annexation by the United States.
3. The reasons why the United States declared war on Mexico, and how the Mexican War was fought to a successful conclusion.
4. The impact of the Wilmot Proviso on the sectional controversy.
5. The methods used to enact the Compromise of 1850, and its reception by the American people.
6. The role of the major political parties in the widening sectional split.
7. The part played by Stephen A. Douglas in the enactment of the Kansas-Nebraska Act, and the effect of this act on his career and on the attitudes of the people in all sections.
8. The impact of the Dred Scott decision on sectional attitudes and on the prestige of the Supreme Court.
9. The reasons for Abraham Lincoln's victory in 1860, and the effect of his election on the sectional crisis.

Main Themes

1. How the idea of Manifest Destiny influenced America and Americans during the period.
2. How the question of the expansion of slavery deepened divisions between the North and the South.
3. How the issue of slavery reshaped the American political-party system.

Pertinent Questions

LOOKING WESTWARD (344-350)

1. What was Manifest Destiny? What forces created this concept?
2. What was the "empire of liberty"? How was it to be achieved, and what doubts were raised about its desirability?
3. How did Texas become available for annexation? What prevented its immediate annexation?
4. What was the history of American interest in Oregon?
5. What were the characteristics of western migrants? What problems did they face? How were these overcome?

EXPANSION AND WAR (350-355)

6. Why did Clay and Van Buren wish to avoid taking a stand on the question of the annexation of Texas? What effect did this have on their efforts to be nominated by their party?
7. How did Van Buren's position on Texas help the candidacy of James K. Polk? How did Polk's campaign catch the spirit of the time? What effect did Clay's position on Texas have on his campaign in the presidential election?

8.   What were the goals of President Polk? How did he resolve the Oregon question?

9.   What tensions emerged in the Southwest that threatened to lead the United States into war with Mexico?

10.   How did American interest in California develop?

11.   What were the origins of the Slidell mission? What was its goal, what did it accomplish, and what was Polk's reaction to it?

12.   On what grounds did Polk ask Congress to declare war on Mexico?

13.   On what grounds was Polk's call for war criticized?

14.   What was Polk's plan for the conduct of the war? How was it set in motion, and what was accomplished in the first offensive of the Mexican War?

15.   What were the objectives of the next two offensives in the war? What did they accomplish? What were the terms of the Treaty of Guadalupe Hidalgo?

THE SECTIONAL DEBATE (355-359)

16.   What was the Wilmot Proviso? What brought about its introduction, and what arguments were advanced in its favor?

17.   What were the South's arguments against the Wilmot Proviso? On what points did they differ from the arguments of the North?

18.   What compromises were proposed to settle the issues raised by the Wilmot Proviso?

19.   What part did the issue of slavery in the territories play in the election of 1848?

20.   What problems faced President Zachary Taylor when he took office? How did he propose to solve them, and what action did Congress initially take?

21.   How did the South react to President Taylor's program?

22.   What was the Compromise of 1850? How was it passed?

23.   Who were the "younger" politicians who emerged after 1850? How did they differ from the leaders they replaced?

24.   How did the Compromise of 1850 differ from the Missouri Compromise?

THE CRISES OF THE 1850s (359-367)

25.   How did the political parties react to the Compromise of 1850?

26.   How did the sections of the country react to the Compromise of 1850?

27.   What was the "Young America" movement? What national sentiment did it reflect? Who were its spokespersons? What did it accomplish?

28.   How was it that American foreign policy objectives in the 1850s began to reflect the growing sectional divisions in the country?

29.   How did the issue of a transcontinental railroad help to reopen the sectional controversy? Explain.

30.   How did the North react to the Kansas-Nebraska Act? the South? What effect did it have on the Whigs? the Democrats?

31.   Who were the Republicans? What caused their formation? Which groups comprised this party, and what was the party's platform?

32.   What problems were faced in the attempt to organize a legitimate government in Kansas? Why did these problems arise? How was it that Kansas became a battleground for the sectional controversy?

33.   Explain the maneuvering by proslavery and antislavery forces to gain control of the Kansas government. What did both sides come to believe that Kansas symbolized for the nation?

34. What were the "immediate, sweeping, and ominous consequences" of the Kansas-Nebraska Act?

35. What type of society did northerners wish to create? How did "free soil" and "free labor" fit into their plans? Why did they feel that the South was holding them back?

36. How did the "free-soil" ideology manifest itself in the Republican Party? What diverse views did it unite?

37. What were the elements of the South's proslavery response? Who were its major spokespersons?

38. What effect did the depression of 1857 have on political divisions in America? How did it increase the tension between the North and South? What did both sides see as the significance of this economic decline?

39. What were the origins of the Dred Scott case? What issues were involved, and what decision was handed down by the Court? How did the reaction to this case add to sectional tensions?

40. How did President James Buchanan respond to the Kansas question? What were his reasons, and what was the outcome? What does this tell you about the possibility of compromise on the issue of slavery in the territories?

41. Why did the Lincoln-Douglas debates take place, and why did they draw so much attention? How did Lincoln and Douglas differ on their solution to the question of slavery in the territories?

42. What were the goals of John Brown's raid, and why did it have such an impact on the South?

43. What caused the split between northern and southern Democrats in 1860, and what was the result of this division?

44. What was the Republican platform in 1860? To what specific political groups were the Republicans trying to appeal, and how did this platform propose to appeal to them?

PATTERNS OF POPULAR CULTURE (362)

45. What role did the Lyceum play in educating the American public, especially with regard to public controversies of the period?

46. What sort of people took part in the Lyceum movement?

Identification

Identify each of the following, and explain why it is important within the context of the chapter.

1. John L. O'Sullivan
2. "penny press"
3. Antonio de Santa Anna
4. San Jacinto
5. Oregon Trail
6. "re-occupation" and "re-annexation"
7. "Fifty-four forty or fight"
8. John C. Frémont
9. Zachary Taylor
10. Stephen W. Kearny
11. General Winfield Scott
12. Nicholas Trist
13. "All Mexico"
14. Lewis Cass
15. Free-Soil Party

16. forty-niners
17. William H. Seward
18. Millard Fillmore
19. "omnibus bill"
20. Franklin Pierce
21. Ostend Manifesto
22. Gadsden Purchase
23. Pottawatomie Massacre
24. "The Crime Against Kansas"
25. Preston Brooks
26. "slave power conspiracy"
27. "positive good" thesis
28. John C. Breckenridge
29. John Bell

Document 1

Below is an excerpt from a statement made in 1837 by John C. Calhoun that outlines his views on slavery. Note his comparison of the lot of slaves with that of European (and northern?) workers. How might William Lloyd Garrison have responded to this?

I hold that in the present state of civilization, where two races of different origin, and distinguished by color, and other physical differences, as well as intellectual, are brought together, the relation now existing in the slaveholding States between the two is, instead of an evil, a good--a positive good. I feel myself called upon to speak freely upon the subject where the honor and interests of those I represent are involved. I hold then, that there never has yet existed a wealthy and civilized society in which one portion of the community did not, in point of fact, live on the labor of the other. . . . I may say with truth that in few countries so much is left to the share of the laborer, and so little exacted from him, or where there is more kind attention paid to him in sickness or infirmities of age. Compare his condition with the tenants of the poor houses in the more civilized portions of Europe--look at the sick and the old and infirm slave, on one hand, in the midst of his family and friends, under the kind superintending care of his master and mistress, and compare it with the forlorn and wretched condition of the pauper in the poor house.

Document 2

One of the most outspoken critics of the Mexican War was the Massachusetts poet James Russell Lowell. Like so many of his fellow New Englanders, he believed that the conflict was part of an effort to advance the interests of the South, a view he set forth in The Bigelow Papers, a collection of observations that Lowell attributed to one Hosea Bigelow. In the following poem, Bigelow confronts a recruiting sergeant and explains, in Yankee vernacular, his opposition to the war.

What does Bigelow see as the main purpose of the war with Mexico? Whom does he blame, and why? What role does he see the North playing in the war, and what does he feel the results will be? Look at the final verse. What solution does he propose? Remember this when we get to 1860. With such sentiments being expressed in the North, why will the northern states be willing to fight to preserve the Union?

'T would n't suit them Southern fellers,

    They're a dreffle graspin' set,

We must ollers blow the bellers

    Wen they want their irons het;

May be it's all right ez preachin',

    By my narves it kind o' grates,

Wen I see the overreachin'

    O' them nigger-drivin' States.

They may talk o' Freedom's airy

    Tell they're pupple in the face,--

It's a grand gret cemetary

    Fer the barthrights of our race;

They jest want this Californy

    So's to lug new slave-states in

To abuse ye, an' to scorn ye,

    An' to plunder ye like sin.

Aint it cute to see a Yankee

    Take sech everlastin' pains

All to git the Devil's thankee,

    Helpin' on 'em weld their chains?

Wy, it's jest ez clear ez figgers,

    Clear ez one an' one make two,

Chaps thet make black slaves o' niggers

       Want to make wite slaves o' you.

Ef I'd <u>my</u> way I hed ruther

       We should go to work an' part,--

They take one way, we take t'other,--

       Guess it would n't break my heart;

Men hed ough' to put asunder

       Them thet God has noways jined;

An' I should n't gretly wonder

       Ef there's thousands o' my mind.

James Russell Lowell, <u>The Bigelow Papers</u> (London: Trubner, 1859), pp. 4–9.

Document 3

In 1846, President James K. Polk requested an appropriation of $2 million to pay expenses incurred in negotiations with Mexico. David Wilmot, a Pennsylvania Democrat, introduced an amendment to that bill and, in so doing, set off a new round of debate over the question of slavery in the territories. The following is a description of what took place.

Wilmot was a Democrat, and the Democratic Party depended on the South for much of its support. Why would he have introduced such an amendment? What does this tell you about divisions within the Democratic Party? What alternatives were offered, who offered them, and what resulted? What happened to the amendment in the House, where it was introduced? in the Senate? What does this tell you about the position of the South with regard to the rest of the nation? What would have been the future for the South had it become law?

On motion of Mr. McKay the committee proceeded under the resolution just adopted, limiting the time for debate of each member to ten minutes, to the consideration of the President's message, and of the following bill, introduced this morning by Mr. McKay:

<u>Be it enacted by the Senate and House of Representatives of the United States of America in Congress assembled.</u> That a sum of $2,000,000, in addition to the provision heretofore made, be, and the same is hereby, appropriated, for the purpose of defraying any extraordinary expenses which may be incurred in the intercourse between the United States and foreign nations, to be paid out of any money in the treasury not otherwise appropriated, and to be applied under the direction of the President of the United States, who shall cause an account of the expenditure thereof to be laid before Congress as soon as may be.

. . . Mr. Wilmot regretted that the President had not disclosed his views. He disliked to act in the dark on this or any subject. If this had been done, and it had been inexpedient to have received and deliberated upon it publicly, they might have gone into secret session. He would vote for this appropriation in case the amendment he intended to offer was adopted. He disagreed with some of his friends that this was an unnecessary war; he believed it a necessary and proper war. He believed it not to be a war of conquest; if so he was opposed to it now and hereafter. If this country was now to be forced into such a war, he pronounced it against the spirit of the age, against the holy precepts of our religion; he was opposed to it in every form and shape. But he trusted it was not to be a war of conquest. He trusted that the President was sincerely ready to negotiate for an honorable peace.

But the President asked for two millions of dollars for concessions which Mexico was to make. We claim the Rio Grande as our boundary--that was the main cause of the war. Are we now to purchase what we claim as a matter of right? Certainly she was not to be paid for the debt she owes our citizens.

Mr. W. took it, therefore, that the President looked to the acquisition of territory in that quarter. To this he had no objection, provided it were done on proper conditions. On the contrary, he was most earnestly desirous that a portion of territory on the Pacific, including the bay of San Francisco, should come into our possession by fair and honorable means, by purchase or negotiation--not by conquest.

But whatever territory might be acquired, he declared himself opposed, now and forever, to the extension of this "peculiar institution" that belongs to the South. He referred to the annexation of Texas, and to his affirmative vote on the proposition connected with it at this session; he was for taking it as it was: slavery had already been established there. But if free territory comes in, God forbid that he should be the means of planting this institution upon it.

He concluded by offering the amendment . . . providing against the establishment of slavery, or involuntary servitude, in any territory which may be acquired.

Provided, That, as an express and fundamental condition to the acquisition of any territory from the Republic of Mexico by the United States, by virtue of any treaty which may be negotiated between them, and to the use by the Executive of the moneys herein appropriated, neither slavery nor involuntary servitude shall ever exist in any part of said territory, except for crime, whereof the party shall first be duly convicted.

The first section of the bill was still under consideration, and, after some conversation, the amendment of Mr. WILMOT was received as an amendment to this section.

Mr. DOBBIN rose to a point of order. He contended that the amendment of the gentleman from Pennsylvania [Mr. WILMOT] was not in order, the subject of slavery having no connexion with the bill.

The CHAIRMAN overruled the point of order. The bill (he stated) appropriated a certain sum of money to be put at the disposal of the President. It was certainly competent on the part of the House to adopt a provision limiting the application of the money, and providing that it should be applied only on certain conditions.

Mr. DOBBIN appealed from the decision.

The question on the appeal was taken by tellers, and the decision of the Chairman was sustained-- ayes 92, noes 37.

Thus the amendment was decided in order.

Mr. WICK moved to amend the amendment by inserting therein after the word "territory," the words "north of 36°30' north latitude."

The amendment to the amendment was disagreed to--ayes 54, noes 89.

The question recurring on the original amendment of Mr. WILMOT, tellers were asked and ordered; and, the question begin taken, it was decided in the affirmative--ayes, 83, noes 64.

So the amendment was adopted.

Congressional Globe, 29th Cong., 1st sess., 1213–1217.

Document 4

Many people believed (and many more hoped) that the Compromise of 1850 would save the Union. But as the excerpts that follow show, the divisions were deep and healing would be difficult. The first excerpt is from John C. Calhoun's last speech. What stand did he take regarding compromise? Calhoun's views are followed by those of William H. Seward, a senator from New York who became a leading Republican and secretary of state in the Lincoln administration. What is his position? Is there room for compromise?

It is time, Senators, that there should be an open and manly avowal on all sides, as to what is intended to be done. If the question is not now settled, it is uncertain whether it ever can hereafter be; and we, as the representatives of the States of this Union, regarded as governments, should come to a distinct understanding as to our respective views, in order to ascertain whether the great questions at issue can be settled or not. If you, who represent the stronger portion, cannot agree to settle them on the broad principle of justice and duty, say so; and let the States we both represent agree to separate and part in peace, tell us so; and we shall know what to do, when you reduce the question to submission or resistance. If you remain silent, you will compel us to infer by your acts what you intend.

* * *

I am opposed to any such compromise, in any and all the forms in which it has been proposed. Because, while admitting the purity and the patriotism of all from whom it is my misfortune to differ, I think all legislative compromises radically wrong and essentially vicious. They involve the surrender of the exercise of judgment and conscience on distinct and separate questions, at distinct and separate times, with the indispensable advantages it affords for ascertaining truth. They involve a relinquishment of the right to reconsider in future the decisions of the present, on questions prematurely anticipated. And they are a usurpation as to future questions of the province of future legislators.

Document 5

The Republicans' 1860 platform was hardly the radical pronouncement that southern fire-eaters expected, for its primary purpose was to show potential supporters in the North that it was the party of moderation and progress. Still, among its declarations were statements that made it clear where the Republicans stood on the issues most crucial to the South. What follows is an excerpt from that platform. Note declaration 3. Does this give you any indication why the Republicans were willing to fight to preserve the Union? How would the South have reacted to this?

What was declaration 4 designed to do? What effects did the Republicans hope it would have on the South? How does declaration 7 relate to 4? To whom was it designed to appeal? What is the purpose of declarations 12 and 15? What do they reveal about the composition of the Republican Party? Again, what would the South's reaction have been?

Resolved, That we, the delegated representatives of the Republican electors of the United States in convention assembled, in discharge of the duty we owe to our constituents and our country, unite in the following declarations: . . .

3. That to the union of the States this nation owes its unprecedented increase in population, its surprising development of material resources, its rapid augmentation of wealth, its happiness at home, and its honor abroad; and we hold in abhorrence all schemes for disunion, come from whatever source they may: . . . and we denounce those threats of disunion, in case of a popular overthrow of their ascendancy, as denying the vital principles of a free government, and as an avowal of contemplated treason, which it is the imperative duty of an indignant people sternly to rebuke and forever silence.

4. That the maintenance inviolate of the rights of the States, and especially the right of each State to order and control its own domestic institutions according to its own judgment exclusively, is essential to that balance of powers on which the perfection and endurance of our potential fabric depends; and we denounce the lawless invasion by armed force of the soil of any State or Territory, no matter under what pretext, as among the gravest of crimes. . . .

7. That the new dogma that the Constitution, of its own force, carries slavery into any or all of the Territories of the United States, is a dangerous political heresy, at variance with the explicit provisions of that instrument itself. . . .

12. That, while providing revenue for the support of the general government by duties upon imports, sound policy requires such an adjustment of these imposts as to encourage the development of the industrial interests of the whole country. . . .

15. That appropriations by Congress for river and harbor improvements of a national character, required for the accommodation and security of our existing commerce, are authorized by the Constitution, and justified by the obligations of government to protect the lives and property of its citizens.

New York Times, 18 May 1860.

Map Exercise

Fill in or identify the following on the blank map provided. Use the map in the text as your source.

1. Free states and territories.
2. Slave states and territories (with slave percentages of total population).
3. Areas where the decision on slavery was left to the territories.
4. Missouri Compromise line.
5. District of Columbia.

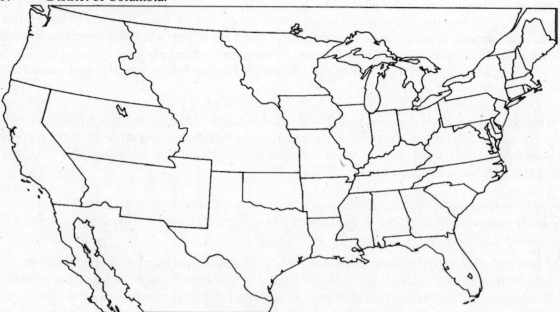

Interpretative Questions

Based on what you have filled in, answer the following. On some of the questions you will need to consult the narrative in your text for information or explanation.

1.   Note the western boundary of Texas today and compare it to the map of "American Expansion into the Southwest, 1845-1853." How does the change in the western boundary reflect northern fears that may have resulted from the agreement under which Texas was annexed?

2.   Study the areas that remain open to slavery. As far as the expansion of the institution is concerned, did the South gain or lose from the Compromise of 1850?

3.   After studying the map, what evidence do you find to support John C. Calhoun's fear that the South would be relegated to permanent minority status?

4.   How had the knowledge of land west of the Mississippi River changed since the early 1800s, and what impact did this have on settlement patterns? In the light of these changes, how would the population be expected to expand in the next few decades and what impact would this have on the balance between slave and free states in the Senate?

5.   What changes did the Kansas-Nebraska Act make in the agreements reached in the Missouri Compromise and the Compromise of 1850?

Summary

Between 1845 and 1860, critical events and issues seemed to come in a rush, giving Americans little time to analyze what was happening and reflect on long-range solutions. Emotion seemed to replace reason as the debate grew increasingly repetitive and loud. The question, or so it seemed, was the expansion of slavery into the territories gained during the Polk administration. But something far more fundamental was at stake—the future of the nation. Northerners had become convinced that the expansion of slavery threatened the democratic foundations of the United States and that expansion would give the South control of the government that would lead to economic stagnation, unemployment, and financial ruin--all the effect of the depression of 1837, but magnified. From this point of view, the South, and its "peculiar institution," threatened the nation's growth and progress and had to be overcome. The South, however, convinced of the legality of its position and the validity of its institutions, fought back, and with remarkable success. By combining the power in the Democratic Party (which gave it extraordinary influence in Congress and with the president) with its supporters on the Supreme Court, the slave states seemed secure. But still they were fearful. Convinced that they had given up all they could in earlier compromises, they feared future gains by those they considered to be enemies; and those they feared most were the Republicans.

Review Questions

These questions are to be answered with essays. This will allow you to explore relationships between individuals, events, and attitudes of the period under review.

1.   Why did the South perceive the Wilmot Proviso as such a threat? What did the proviso indicate about the North's attitude toward slavery? Was the abolition of slavery the issue, or was it something else? Examine the proviso, its implications, and the Southern response.

2.   Your text states that eventually the majority of northerners came to believe "that the existence of slavery was dangerous not because of what it did to blacks but because of what it threatened to do to whites." How did this feeling shape the northern attack on slavery, and how did southerners attempt to defend their institution?

161

3. As your text states, Kansas became a symbol for both the North and the South—but a symbol of what? What did both sides find in the controversy over Kansas to support their charges against their adversaries? What did Kansas come to mean to the nation? Assess Kansas as a symbol of the positions and problems that characterized the divisions in the United States.

4. One historian has claimed that a lack of leadership contributed to the inability of the nation to overcome its divisions. This argument contends that a "blundering generation" of politicians who failed to understand the nature of the divisions offered solutions that resolved issues but did not deal with the real problems. Look at the concerns expressed by both the North and the South, and look at the proposals advanced to ease these concerns. From this assessment, do you feel that the "blundering generation" theory has merit, or were these deeper, fundamental questions that even the most capable leaders could not have resolved? In short, had the conflict between North and South become "irrepressible"?

Chapter Self Test

After you have read the chapter in the text and done the exercises in the Study Guide, take the following self test to see if you understand the material you have covered. Answers appear at the end of the Study Guide.

MULTIPLE-CHOICE QUESTIONS

Circle the letter of the response which best answers the question or completes the statement.

1. The idea that God and history had selected America to expand its boundaries over the continent of North America was known as:
   a. Manifest Destiny.
   b. divine right.
   c. white supremacy.
   d. nativism.

2. When the new republic of Texas requested annexation by the United States:
   a. the American government quickly agreed.
   b. Americans in the North opposed acquiring a large new slave territory.
   c. Southerners, led by President Jackson, pushed for annexation.
   d. Mexico gave up all claims to Texas.

3. American immigrants into Oregon:
   a. did not outnumber the British until after the Civil War.
   b. had little impact on the few Native Americans there.
   c. outnumbered the British by 1850.
   d. were mostly fur trappers.

4. Immigrants going west on the great overland trails faced the least danger from:
   a. hostile Indians.
   b. diseases.
   c. mountain and desert terrain.
   d. hunger.

5. Which of the following was <u>not</u> part of President Polk's policy regarding New Mexico and California?

    a. Sending troops to the Nueces River in Texas.

    b. Informing Americans in California that the United States would respond sympathetically to a revolt against Mexico.

    c. Instructing the Pacific naval commander to seize California ports if Mexico declared war.

    d. Ceasing all diplomatic contact with Mexico.

6. By combining the Oregon and the Texas issue in 1844, Democrats hoped to:

    a. start a war with Mexico and Great Britain.

    b. attract John Tyler to the Democratic Party.

    c. divert attention from the slavery issue.

    d. appeal to both northern and southern expansionists.

7. The war with Mexico was criticized:

    a. by southerners who believed Polk deliberately maneuvered the country into the conflict on behalf of northern interests.

    b. by northerners who believed it was part of a slaveholders' plot to bring in more slave states.

    c. by businessmen who believed it would hurt commerce with England and Mexico.

    d. by Democrats from all sections of the nation.

8. The Wilmot Proviso:

    a. went into law without the president's signature.

    b. passed the House but not the Senate.

    c. was a compromise acceptable to the South and the North but not the West.

    d. drew very little attention outside of Congress.

9. The man on whose land the gold that led to the California gold rush was discovered was:

    a. John C. Frémont.

    b. John A. Sutter.

    c. Nicholas Trist.

    d. Lewis Cass.

10. The Compromise of 1850 included all of the following <u>except:</u>

    a. California would come in as a free state.

    b. in the rest of the lands acquired from Mexico, territorial governments would be formed without restrictions on slavery.

    c. the national government would not pay the Texas debt.

    d. the slave trade, but not slavery, would be abolished in the District of Columbia.

11. Which of the following <u>did not</u> support the Compromise of 1850?

    a. Henry Clay.

    b. Zachary Taylor.

    c. John C. Calhoun.

    d. Daniel Webster.

12. The new leaders emerging in Congress after the Compromise of 1850 were:
   a. less able politicians.
   b. more concerned with narrow interest of self-promotion.
   c. as skilled at compromise as the older leaders.
   d. interested in broad national issues.

13. The question of statehood for Kansas and Nebraska became a critical issue because:
   a. of the question of whether they would be slave or free states.
   b. of southern fear that a transcontinental railroad would be built through them.
   c. of northern concern over new wheat states and depressed grain prices.
   d. many believed that they could never support a population sufficient to justify statehood.

14. Northerners who accepted the concepts of "free soil" and "free labor" believed:
   a. slavery was dangerous not because of what it did to blacks but because of what it did to whites.
   b. slavery opened the door to economic opportunity for whites.
   c. slavery was what made the South a glorious civilization and one that should be admired.
   d. slave labor would work in northern factories and should be allowed to expand.

15. Through personal liberty laws northern states attempted to:
   a. use state authority to interfere with the deportation of fugitive slaves.
   b. force industries to recognize labor unions.
   c. allow women to own property.
   d. extend the right to vote to all tax-paying adults.

16. Southerners who believed in the "positive-good" theory argued:
   a. slavery was good for blacks.
   b. slavery was maintained, even though it was not profitable for whites.
   c. northern factory workers were better off than slaves, but they deserved to be because they were white.
   d. blacks were not biologically inferior, they just needed time to catch up culturally.

17. American efforts to buy or seize Cuba failed because:
   a. international pressure was put on President Pierce.
   b. there was little nationalism in the nation by the 1850s.
   c. antislavery forces in the North opposed it.
   d. it was believed we had more territory than we could use.

18. The Dred Scott decision:
   a. affirmed the South's argument that the Constitution guaranteed the existence of slavery.
   b. was a victory for the antislavery movement.
   c. declared Scott a free man.
   d. outlawed the interstate slave trade.

19. Abraham Lincoln:
    a. believed slavery was morally wrong but was not an abolitionist.
    b. had been a Democrat before he became a Republican.
    c. believed the expansion of slavery would hurt the spread of free labor.
    d. tried to avoid the slavery issue in his debates with Douglas.
    e. a. and c.
    f. a. and d.

20. The single event that did the most to convince white southerners they could not live safely in the Union was:
    a. the election of Lincoln.
    b. the Pottawatomie Massacre.
    c. John Brown's raid.
    d. the Dred Scott decision.

TRUE-FALSE QUESTIONS

Read each statement carefully. Mark true statements "T" and false statements "F."

1. The "penny press" was important because it exposed a significant proportion of the population to the rhetoric of nationalistic politicians.

2. Texas was not able to get any European nation to recognize it as an independent nation.

3. Missionary efforts in Oregon converted large numbers of Indians to Christianity.

4. Most travelers on the Oregon Trail went as individuals, even if they joined a wagon train.

5. Though a "dark horse" candidate, James K. Polk was not an obscure politician.

6. The Oregon question was finally settled by Britain surrendering claims below the 54th parallel.

7. President Polk told Californians that the United States would not respond sympathetically if they revolted against Mexico.

8. The United States did not take all of Mexico because its invasion of that country was not successful.

9. The Wilmot Proviso prohibited slavery in the territory taken from Mexico.

10. The Free-Soil Party had the abolition of slavery as part of its platform.

11. The South supported Taylor because he was a southerner and a slaveholder.

12. The Compromise of 1850 passed, despite the opposition of Webster and Calhoun.

13. After 1850 the Whig Party emerged as the one party without sectional divisions.

14. The Kansas-Nebraska Act repealed the antislavery provision of the Missouri Compromise.

15. Northerners saw Preston Brook's attack on Charles Sumner as an example of the barbarism of the South, while southerners believed Sumner had insulted Brook's uncle and got what he deserved.

16. Northerners believed that there the South was involved in a "slave power conspiracy" to take away their liberties.

17. President Buchanan proved a firm and decisive president at the very time the nation needed one.

18. The Republican Party became the party of the "free-soil-free-labor" ideology.

19. The South thought the Dred Scott decision would hurt efforts to expand slavery.

20. With Lincoln's election, the Republicans controlled both the legislative and the executive branches of the government.

GENERAL DISCUSSION QUESTIONS FOR CHAPTERS NINE-THIRTEEN

These questions are designed to help you bring together ideas from several chapters and see how the chapters relate to one another.

1. In the 1790s, two political parties emerged to struggle for control of the new government. By the 1830s, these two parties had disappeared, in name at least, and in their places were other parties competing for the same prize. What had taken place during this time? Write an essay in which you explain the rise, fall, and reorganization of the two original parties, being sure to consider not only what happened to them as organizations, but also what happened to the programs they endorsed.

2. If any one force dominated the era we just studied, it was nationalism. Almost every aspect of American life was influenced by it. The question, however, is what gave rise to this outpouring of national feeling, and what was its effect? Write an essay in which you examine domestic developments in the United States (political, economic, intellectual) during the period between 1800 and 1840; from this examination, determine what it was that convinced Americans that their nation was destined to be great, and how this conviction affected the government's domestic policies.

3. It was during this period that the West emerged as a major factor in the political and economic development of the United States. Just what influence did this section have? Consider the growth of American political institutions and attitudes along with the expansion of the nation's economy between 1820 and 1860—from the standpoint of the West—to determine just how that section shaped, or tried to shape, what took place. Also, examine how the Northeast and the Southeast reacted to the growth of the western regions.

4. Despite having a minority of the population, the south, between 1830 and 1860, was able to block most legislation it felt was not in its best interest. How was this accomplished? Explain how southern politicians protected the "southern way of life" from the will of the majority. What effect did this have on the two-party system?

5. Trace the course of American antislavery attitudes between 1830 and 1860. How did the movement evolve from one characterized by radical reformers with little support to one supported by most northerners? What changes in philosophy and action were necessary for the antislavery forces to accomplish this?

6. What factors gave rise to the reform movement of the years 1820 to 1860? How did this movement reflect Americans' image of themselves, and what effect did it have on American politics?

7. What happened to the Whigs? Examine the evolution of the Whig Party, and determine why it was never able to effectively challenge the Democrats' supremacy. What happened to the Whigs, North and South, after the national party disappeared?

8. Explain the expected and unexpected consequences of early large-scale efforts to manipulate the American landscape.

9. Explain the impact of the "waterpower era" on urban development.

CHAPTER FOURTEEN
THE CIVIL WAR

Objectives

A thorough study of Chapter Fourteen should enable the student to understand:

1. The reasons why all attempts to reach a compromise in the time-honored way failed in 1860 and 1861.

2. The unique problems faced by the newly inaugurated President Lincoln, and his use of executive powers to solve them up to July 4, 1861.

3. The many interpretations of the causes of the Civil War advanced by historians.

4. The ways in which the Confederate States of America compared with the United States in manpower, natural resources, finances, industrial potential, and public support.

5. The significant legislation enacted by Congress once southern members were no longer a factor.

6. The considerations involved in President Lincoln's decision to issue the Emancipation Proclamation, and its reception in the North, in the South, and in Europe.

7. The basic structure of the government of the Confederate States of America, how it differed from that of the United States, and how it dealt with the vital question of states' rights.

8. The efforts of presidents Lincoln and Jefferson Davis to act as commanders in chief under their respective constitutions.

9. How other nations, particularly England and France, viewed the struggle, and how their courses of action affected the outcome.

10. How the American Civil War was part of a worldwide movement to create large, consolidated nations.

Main Themes

1. How the South came to attempt secession, and how the government of the United States responded.

2. How both sides mobilized for war, and what that mobilization revealed about the nature and character of each side.

3. How the North won the Civil War.

Pertinent Questions

THE SECESSION CRISIS (372-375)

1. On what constitutional interpretation was the concept of secession based? Which states were the first to secede, and what was the reaction of the United States government to this?

2. What compromises were proposed to bring these states back into the Union, and why did they fail?

3. What was Abraham Lincoln's opinion on the legality of secession, and how was that opinion reflected in his action concerning Fort Sumter?

4. Lincoln's decision to resupply Fort Sumter presented the South with what dilemma? How did the Confederates react? Faced with this action on the part of the South, what did Lincoln do, and how did the other slave states respond?

5. How have historians answered the question "Was the Civil War inevitable?" Who are the historians answering this question, and what evidence do they present to support their answers?

6. What advantages did the Union have in the Civil War? What were the advantages of the Confederacy?

THE MOBILIZATION OF THE NORTH (375-383)

7. How did the Republican Party act to expand the American economy during the war? To which prewar party was their program similar? Why were they able to enact it, whereas the previous party had not been?

8. How did the Union propose to finance the war? How successful was this? What was the effect on the economy?

9. How did the Union propose to raise troops? To what extent was it forced to use conscription? What was the reaction to this, and why was it so varied?

10. What were the characteristics of Lincoln as a leader? How were these characteristics reflected in his selection and use of his cabinet?

11. What was Lincoln's view of the extent of presidential war powers? Who were the opponents of the war, and how did Lincoln use these powers against them? What was the outcome?

12. For what reason was the "Union Party" created? Who were its candidates?

13. What were the two factions trying to control the Republican Party? What were their goals, and which did Lincoln support?

14. How was this split in the Republican Party revealed in the debate over what to do about slavery? What action did each faction propose? What did Lincoln do, and why?

15. What factors, other than political pressure, brought about the Emancipation Proclamation? What did the proclamation really accomplish? When did full emancipation really come?

16. What role did African Americans play in support of the Union cause?

17. What impact did the Civil War have on the Northern industrial economy?

18. What impact did the Civil War have on women in the North? What part did women play in the war effort?

THE MOBILIZATION OF THE SOUTH (383-388)

19. Explain the origins of the Confederate government. How did its constitution differ from that of the United States? Who were chosen as its leaders, and what problems did they face?

20. How did the Confederacy attempt to finance the war? What problems did it face, and what were the results?

21. How did the Confederacy propose to raise troops for the war? How did these plans compare with those of the Union, and how successful were they? Why?

22. Why was states' rights the "great dividing force" in the Confederacy's war effort? What caused this division, and what was the effect?

23. How did the Civil War "transform" Southern society? How was this transformation like that which took place in the North? How was it different?

24. What impact did the war have on the lives and circumstances of women? Of slaves?

STRATEGY AND DIPLOMACY (388-392)

25. Compare and contrast Abraham Lincoln and Jefferson Davis—their backgrounds, abilities, and objectives. Why was Lincoln more successful at organizing a command system than Davis?

26. What role did Lincoln propose for the United States Navy? How did the Confederacy attempt to overcome this naval advantage, and what was the result?

27. What were the foreign-policy objectives of the Union and the Confederacy? How did each attempt to achieve these objectives, which was most successful, and why?

28. How did the West play a continuing political, diplomatic, and military part in the conflict?

THE COURSE OF BATTLE (392-403)

29. How did advances in the effectiveness of arms and artillery change the way soldiers in the field fought?

30. What major engagements were fought in 1861? What did they reveal about the possibility of an early end to the struggle and about the readiness of the two sides for a major conflict?

31. What was the Union plan for the conquest of the West? How did the Confederates propose to defend this area? How did the campaign advance, what battles took place, and which of the two armies more nearly achieved its objectives?

32. What was the Union plan on the Virginia front in 1862? Who was the general selected to carry this out? Who was the Confederate general he faced, and what was the relative strength of the two armies?

33. Outline the battles fought in the East in 1862. How did Lincoln's action toward his commanders affect the war effort? What were the relative positions of the two armies at the end of 1862? Which side had been more successful in achieving its objectives?

34. Why was 1863 the "Year of Decision"? What took place in 1863 to swing the advantage to the side of the Union? Where did these battles occur? Who were the generals involved? What did the battles accomplish? Why were they so important?

35. What was Grant's grand strategy for 1864? Who was to be in charge of the armies involved, and what were their objectives?

36. How was the Confederacy finally defeated? In what way did the Union forces destroy the South's will to carry on the fight?

WHERE HISTORIANS DISAGREE (376-377)

37. Explain the various interpretations that historians have advanced to explain why the Civil War took place.

38. How have these interpretations followed the general outlines laid down by Senator William H. Seward in 1858?

PATTERNS OF POPULAR CULTURE (388-389)

39. How did baseball become the "national pastime?"
40. What does the popularity of baseball indicate about America at the time of the Civil War?

AMERICA IN THE WORLD (384-385)

41. Explain the nineteenth century worldwide movement to create large, consolidated nations.

42. Explain how the American Civil War fit into this movement.

Identification

Identify each of the following, and explain why it is important within the context of the chapter.

1. fire-eaters

2. Fort Sumter
3. Crittenden Compromise
4. "blundering generation"
5. "irrepressible conflict"
6. Homestead Act
7. Morrill Act
8. greenbacks
9. Copperheads
10. Ex parte Milligan
11. Confederate Conscription Act
12. Joseph Brown and Zebulon M. Vance
13. Monitor and Merrimack (Virginia)
14. Charles Francis Adams
15. "King Cotton diplomacy"
16. Trent affair
17. William C. Quantrill
18. Jayhawkers
19. Samuel Colt and Oliver Winchester
20. U.S. Military Telegraph Corps

Where did each of the following battles occur? Who was the victor, and what was the significance of the outcome?

1. First Bull Run
2. Shiloh
3. Murfreesboro
4. Seven Days
5. Second Bull Run
6. Antietam
7. Chancellorsville
8. Gettysburg
9. Chickamauga
10. Chattanooga
11. Wilderness campaign
12. Petersburg
13. Atlanta
14. Nashville

Document

Daniel O'Leary, a captain in the Union army, took part in the bloody fighting of the Chattanooga and Atlanta campaigns and by the fall of 1864, had seen all of the war that he wanted to see. Having lost a brother fighting for the Union in Virginia and a brother-in-law, who fell in Dallas, Georgia, fighting for the Confederacy, he had every reason to feel tired and perhaps a bit disillusioned. The following is from a letter that he wrote to his wife just after his regiment had withdrawn from Atlanta and returned to Chattanooga, where they were to be discharged. What does his letter tell you about the status of the struggle at this time?

What of O'Leary's attitude toward black soldiers? The fall of Athens, Alabama, was not exactly what he had heard. About 400 black troops were captured, but some contended that the surrender had been the fault of their white commander. Nevertheless, what does O'Leary's reaction to the rumor tell you about the difficulties that blacks faced in being accepted? Also, what does this indicate about what men like O'Leary considered themselves to be fighting for?

What other evidence of disillusionment can you find in this letter? Who was the "Little Mac" whom O'Leary mentioned? How might this reference have been an indication of O'Leary's feelings about the way the war was being run? In general, what does the letter tell you about one group of Union soldiers?

Chattanooga, Tenn.

October 8th, 1864

MY DEAR WIFE

I shall endeavor to write you a few lines under difficulties. My frail canvass house is not proof against the stiff north wind that is blowing, shaking my desk so that it is almost impossible to write even if I had anything to write about. . . .

There has been some trouble along our lines of communications of late. Forrest with a large force of cavalry was between here and Nashville and deprived us of a mail for more than a week, but he had to seek other quarters in which to operate after having captured about 1,500 Negro Soldiers at Athens, Alabama. Another strong force of the enemy has been threatening the railroad between here and Atlanta, but they came to grief. They made an attack on our forces near Allatoona Mountains and were repulsed leaving 500 dead on the field. White soldiers are not so easily captured as their <u>colored brethren,</u> although Republican papers are loud in their praise of the bravery and soldierly qualities of the "down trodden African." Three railroad bridges on the Atlanta road were washed away by the high water occasioned by the late heavy rains and has given us a good rest, there being no trains going from here to Atlanta, and will not be for the next week. . . .

From all accounts the draft is causing a great many to tremble in the North, who were anxious to sacrifice the last man and the last dollar to prosecute the war, but when they are called in it is quite a different thing. I will be glad to hear of some being forced to come out and enjoy the pleasure of being shot at, and see how they like it. I think their love for "Sambo" would grow small and beautifully less in a short time.

I noticed today while in town that the approaching election was the only topic of conversation among the soldiers. They seemed to be pretty equally divided but the Lincoln men made the most noise. They called their brother soldiers who were for "Little Mac" traitors to their country and anything else in that line that they could think of.

Give my love to all the family. . . . Hoping you are well and to hear from you soon I remain your loving husband.

D. O'LEARY

Courtesy of the Kentucky Historical Society, Frankfort, Ky.

Map Exercise

Fill in or identify the following on the blank map provided. Use the map in the text as your source.

1. Border states (slave states that did not secede).
2. States that seceded before the fall of Fort Sumter (with dates of secession).
3. States that seceded after the fall of Fort Sumter (with dates of secession).
4. Western counties of Virginia that remained loyal to the Union.
5. States involved in the campaigns.
6. Towns, cities, rivers, and streams that were principal landmarks in the campaigns.
7. Troop movements of the Union and Confederate forces, with commanders indicated.
8. Battle sites, including (1) names of the battles, (2) dates fought, and (3) the victors.

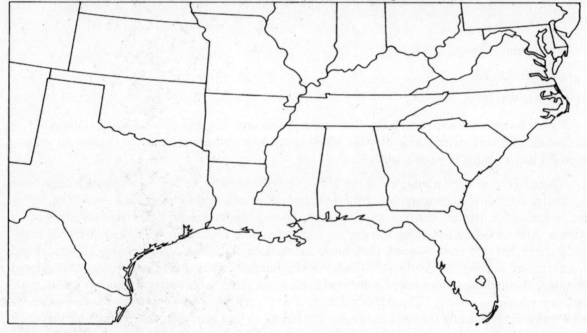

Interpretative Questions

Based on what you have filled in, answer the following. On some of the questions you will need to consult the narrative in your text for information or explanation.

1. Note the order in which the first seven states seceded. Now refer to the map in the text and note the percentages of the population in these states that were slaves. What does this suggest about the way the institution of slavery might have shaped Southern political attitudes?
2. Texas had the lowest percentage of slaves in its population of the first seven Southern states to secede (a percentage lower than some of the states that remained in the Union). What geographic factors might have worked in favor of secession in Texas? Did geographic factors influence the order of secession in the other states?
3. Why did four states that eventually seceded hesitate? Refer to the map in the text to help you form your conclusions.
4. Why did the western counties of Virginia remain in the Union? What does this indicate about how geography shapes sociopolitical attitudes?

5. What effect did the secession of Virginia have on Union war strategy? Why was it necessary for the Union to focus so much of its attention on the Virginia theater?

6. What effect did the choice of Richmond as the capital of the Confederacy have on the South's war strategy? Why was it necessary for the South to focus so much of its attention on the Virginia theater?

7. Why did Lee invade the North in September of 1862? What engagements made this possible? What did he hope to accomplish? What was the outcome?

8. Why did Lee invade the North in the summer of 1863? What engagements made this possible? What did he hope to accomplish? What was the outcome?

9. Why were Chattanooga and Atlanta so important to the Union strategy and to Confederate hopes for winning (or at least continuing) the war?

10. What was the significance of Sherman's March to the Sea?

11. What was Lee trying to accomplish when he was cut off and forced to surrender at Appomattox? From the information on the map in the text, how realistic was his goal?

Summary

Before 1860, references to the nation generally began "these United States are," but after 1865, it became more frequently "the United States is." In that change, one might well see the most important outcome of the American Civil War. The question of the nature of the Union, which had been debated since its inception, was settled—the nation was one and indivisible. The cost had been great, in both human and financial terms, but the war had done more than defeat a secessionist rebellion. It had set the nation on a new course. States' rights, as an alternative to nationalism, had been dealt a fatal blow. The tariff and internal improvements were law and would remain so. Slavery was abolished, free labor was triumphant, and industrial growth and material progress seemed to lie ahead. The war, therefore, was more than a victory for the armies of the Union—the real victor had been the Union itself. Never again would the supremacy of national laws be seriously questioned. The Civil War gave birth to the modern United States. Indeed, it did end an era and begin another.

Review Questions

These questions are to be answered with essays. This will allow you to explore relationships between individuals, events, and attitudes of the period under review. In answering questions 1 and 2, pay close attention to the section in your text entitled "Where Historians Disagree: The Causes of the Civil War."

1. Why did the South secede? What pushed the Southern states over the brink? Examine the events of late 1859 and 1860 in the light of Southern social and economic concerns and from the standpoint of Southern political philosophy. From this, determine why the South resorted to secession.

2. Why war? Reread Document 2 in Chapter Thirteen. Clearly, some Northerners also regarded secession as an answer to the problem of slavery, but why were the majority willing to fight to hold the Union together? Look at the Republican platform for clues.

3. Why did the North win? In an essay some years ago, Richard Current suggested that "God was on the side of the heaviest battalions," but is that a complete explanation? What other factors contributed to the outcome? Bring together these factors, and, after a careful analysis, determine why the North did win.

Chapter Self Test

After you have read the chapter in the text and done the exercises in the Study Guide, take the following self test to see if you understand the material you have covered. Answers appear at the end of the Study Guide.

MULTIPLE-CHOICE QUESTIONS

Circle the letter of the response which best answers the question or completes the statement.

1. By the end of the 1850s the two-party system in the United States:
   a. was the only thing holding the nation together.
   b. still focused on the issues that had created the "second party system."
   c. had reduced slavery to a minor issue.
   d. accentuated rather than muted regional controversy.

2. The first seven Southern states that seceded were:
   a. in the lower South.
   b. the states where the largest concentration of slaves were located.
   c. the home of the most outspoken "fire eaters."
   d. all of the above.

3. Which of the following stands did President Buchanan take after the first state seceded?
   a. No state has the right to secede from the Union.
   b. The federal government has no authority to stop a state from seceding from the nation.
   c. Federal troops should be called out to stop secession.
   d. Secession was a legal act.
   e. Both a. and b.
   f. Both a. and c.

4. Which of the following was true when the Civil War began?
   a. All the important material advantages lay with the North.
   b. The South had the active support of England.
   c. Southern industry was sufficient to conduct a war.
   d. The Union was prepared for a long war.

5. Which of the following was not an advantage enjoyed by the South at the outset of the war?
   a. It would be fighting, for the most part, a defensive war.
   b. Most of the white population of the South supported the war.
   c. Northern opinion on the war was divided.
   d. All of the above.

6. Which of the following was not enacted by the Republican Party during the Civil War.
   a. A new National Bank Act.
   b. Increased taxes on almost all goods and services.
   c. Higher tariffs.
   d. Hard money policies requiring all payments in gold or silver.

7. In which of the following acts did Lincoln not "ignore" the Constitution?

a. Sending troops into battle without asking for a declaration of war.

b. Increasing the size of the regular army.

c. Putting diplomatic pressure on England not to recognize the Confederacy.

d. Unilaterally proclaiming a naval blockade of the South.

8. During the Civil War Northern women:

a. did not become involved in the conflict.

b. tried to get the men they knew to stay home.

c. entered nursing, a field previously dominated by men.

d. did work at home but made no contribution to the needs of employers for additional labor.

9. The Emancipation Proclamation freed slaves:

a. in the North as well as the South.

b. in areas of the Confederacy except those already under Union control.

c. and offered compensation to the masters in slave states that remained loyal to the Union.

d. in the South but offered to return them to masters who declared their loyalty to the Union.

10. The Civil War was difficult on American workers because it:

a. cut off immigration and they had to work harder.

b. drove prices up and cut purchasing power.

c. prevented mechanization, so they had to work longer hours.

d. removed almost all women from the workplace.

11. The Confederacy ultimately financed its war effort through:

a. an income tax.

b. requisitions from the staples.

c. paper money.

d. tariffs on imported goods.

12. The greatest source of division in the South was:

a. the doctrine of state's rights.

b. the difference of opinion over the war.

c. the question of whether to use slaves in combat.

d. over "King Cotton diplomacy."

13. The most concrete legacy of the Civil War for Southern white women was the:

a. recognition that women could do men's work and the opening of more employment opportunities.

b. elevation in status they enjoyed when the slaves were freed.

c. decimation of the male population and the creation of a major sexual imbalance in the region.

d. the loss of status when the slaves were freed.

14. In England, which of the following supported the South:

a. Unenfranchised classes.

b. Ruling classes.

c. Liberals.

d. English manufacturers.

15. The United States was upset when England declared neutrality because:

a. it meant that England might aid the South.

b. it meant that the two sides in the conflict were of equal stature.

c. the South could easily get English loans.

d. such a declaration usually led to diplomatic recognition.

16. The first battle of the Civil War was:

a. Shiloh.

b. the Seven Days.

c. First Bull Run.

d. Wilson's Creek.

17. The bloodiest engagement of the Civil War was fought at:

a. Antietam.

b. Gettysburg.

c. Atlanta.

d. Chickamauga.

18. Sherman's march through Georgia was designed to:

a. find supplies for the Union armies in Virginia.

b. free the slaves in central Georgia.

c. get Lincoln reelected.

d. break the will of the Southern people.

19. "ing Cotton diplomacy:"

a. enabled the South to get all the war material it needed from Europe.

b. worked for most of the war.

c. was a failure.

d. worked for the North.

20. In the Indian territory in the West the Civil War:

a. was hardly felt.

b. was seen as a war between whites, and the Indians did not care who won.

c. resulted in something of a civil war all its own.

d. allowed the Indians to force the United States to give them better treaty terms.

TRUE-FALSE QUESTIONS

Read each statement carefully. Mark true statements "T" and false statements "F."

1. The Crittenden Compromise failed because Republicans refused to give in on the question of the expansion of slavery.

2. Many Southerners believed that the dependence of English and French textile industries on American cotton would force those countries to intervene on the side of the Confederacy.

3. The Republican Party did little to promote economic development during the war.

4. The Union's largest source of financing for the war was taxes and tariffs.

5. In both the North and South, the draft was accepted with little protest.

6. In the North, there was little opposition to the war.

7.   Had the Union not taken Atlanta in September of 1864, Lincoln might have lost the presidency to McClellan.

8.   The Civil War transformed the North from an agrarian to an industrial society.

9.   The Confederate government was composed of the most radical Southern secessionists.

10. Despite many shortages, the South was at least able to grow enough food to meet its needs.

11. Lincoln's handling of the war effort faced constant scrutiny from the congressional Committee on the Conduct of the War, which seriously interfered with his work.

12. Although the war saw many technological advances, it was still possible for armies to fight much as they had for centuries.

13. No European nation offered diplomatic recognition to the Confederacy.

14. Though outmanned on the land, the Confederacy held the advantage at sea.

15. After General McClellan allowed Lee to retreat into Virginia following Antietam Creek, Lincoln removed him from command.

16. After the battle of Chattanooga, the Confederacy's only hope was to hold on and exhaust the Northern will to fight.

17. By sticking to the principles of states' Rights, the South was able to better defend its territory.

18. Because of the way they had been treated by the United States, no Indian tribes supported the Union in the war.

19. Robert E. Lee was the last Confederate commander in the East to surrender.

20. Jefferson Davis was captured with Lee at Appomattox.

CHAPTER FIFTEEN
RECONSTRUCTION AND THE NEW SOUTH

Objectives

A thorough study of Chapter Fifteen should enable the student to understand:

1. The conditions in the former Confederacy after Appomattox that would have made most difficult any attempt at genuine reconstruction.

2. The differences between the Conservative and Radical views on the reconstruction process, and the reasons for the eventual Radical domination.

3. The functioning of the impeachment process in the case of President Andrew Johnson, and the significance of his acquittal for the future of Reconstruction.

4. Radical Reconstruction in practice, and Southern (black and white) reaction to it.

5. The debate among historians concerning the nature of Reconstruction, its accomplishments, and its harmful effects on the South.

6. The national problems faced by President Ulysses S. Grant, and the reasons for his lack of success as chief executive.

7. The diplomatic successes of the Johnson and Grant administrations, and the role of the presidents in achieving them.

8. The greenback question, and how it reflected the postwar financial problems of the nation.

9. The alternatives that were available during the election of 1876, and the effects of the so-called Compromise of 1877 on the South and on the nation.

10. The methods used in the South to regain control of its own affairs, and what course of action it chose thereafter.

11. The reasons for the failure of the South to develop a strong industrial economy after Reconstruction.

12. The ways in which Southerners decided to handle the race question, and the origin of the system identified with "Jim Crow."

13. The response of blacks to conditions in the South following Reconstruction.

Main Themes

1. That the defeat and devastation of the South presented the nation with severe social, economic, and political problems.

2. How Radical Reconstruction changed the South but fell short of the full transformation needed to secure equality for the freedmen.

3. That white society and the federal government lacked the will to enforce effectively most of the constitutional and legal guarantees acquired by blacks during Reconstruction.

4. How the policies of the Grant administration moved beyond Reconstruction matters to foreshadow issues of the late nineteenth century.

5. How white leaders reestablished economic and political control of the South and sought to modernize the region through industrialization.

6. How the race question continued to dominate Southern life.

Glossary

1.   Whigs: A major political party between 1834 and the 1850s. The Whigs were unified by their opposition to Andrew Jackson and their support for federal policies to aid business. The party was strongest among the merchants and manufacturers of the Northeast, the wealthy planters of the South, and the farmers of the West most eager for internal improvements. Abraham Lincoln and many other Republicans had been Whigs before the issues of sectionalism destroyed the party.

2.   veto/pocket veto: The president's refusal to sign a bill passed by Congress. He must send it back to Congress with his objections. Unless two-thirds of each house votes to override the president's action, the bill will not become law. A pocket veto occurs when Congress has adjourned and the president refuses to sign a bill within ten days. Because Congress is not in session, the president's action cannot be overridden. (See the Constitution, Article I, Section 7.)

3.   spoils system: The political equivalent of the military axiom "To the victor belong the spoils." In the nineteenth century, the victorious political party in national, state, and local elections routinely dismissed most officeholders and replaced them with workers loyal to the incoming party. The "spoils" were the many patronage jobs available in the government. At the national level, this included thousands of post office and customs positions. Political organizations especially adept at manipulating spoils to remain in power were often called machines. Civil-service reformers demanded that nonpolicymaking jobs be filled on the basis of competitive examinations and that officeholders would continue in office as long as they performed satisfactorily.

4.   solid South: Refers to the fact that the South became overwhelmingly Democratic as a reaction to Republican actions during the Civil War and Reconstruction. Democratic domination of Southern politics persisted for over a century despite occasional cracks, especially in presidential elections.

5.   Unionists: Residents of the Confederate states who counseled against secession and who often remained loyal to the Union during the Civil War. Unionists were more common in upcountry regions of the South, where the slave-based plantation economy was less influential than in coastal areas of the South. Some Unionists left the South during the Civil War, but many remained.

Pertinent Questions

THE PROBLEMS OF PEACEMAKING (408-412)

1.   What effects did the Civil War have on the economy and social system of the South?

2.   What special problems did the freedmen face immediately after the war? What efforts were made to help them?

3.   What were the competing notion of freedom that existed in the post-war South?

4.   What political implications did the readmission of the Southern states pose for the Republicans?

5.   What were the differences between the Conservative, Radical, and Moderate factions of the Republican Party during Reconstruction?

6.   What were the objectives and provisions of Lincoln's play for Reconstruction? How did the Radical Republicans respond to it?

7.   Describe Andrew Johnson's approach to Reconstruction. How was it shaped by his political background and his personality?

RADICAL RECONSTRUCTION (412-415)

8.   What did the Southern state governments do during the "presidential Reconstruction" of 1865 and 1866?

9. How did Congress respond to the Black Codes and other Southern state actions of 1865 and 1866?

10. What did the congressional elections of 1866 reveal about the public attitude toward Reconstruction?

11. Explain the basic provisions of the congressional plan of Reconstruction of 1867. On what principle was it based?

12. What measures did the Radical Republicans take to keep President Johnson and the Supreme Court from interfering with their plans?

13. Why did Radical Republicans want to impeach President Johnson and why did they fail?

THE SOUTH IN RECONSTRUCTION (415-420)

14. What three groups constituted the Republican Party in the South during Reconstruction?

15. What role did blacks play in southern political life during Reconstruction?

16. What was the balance between corruption and positive accomplishment by the Reconstruction-era state governments in the South?

17. What patterns of Southern education began to emerge during Reconstruction?

18. What changes in land distribution occurred in the South after the Civil War? How were the hopes of blacks mostly dashed?

19. What economic advances did the freedmen make? How did the economic status of blacks compare with that of the average white Southerner?

20. How did the crop-lien system overshadow the economic gains made by blacks and poor whites?

21. How did freedom affect black family life?

THE GRANT ADMINISTRATION (420-422)

22. How did Ulysses S. Grant's political accomplishments compare with his military ability?

23. What were the scandals that came to light during the Grant Administration? What role did Grant play in these?

24. People in what financial condition were most likely to favor expansion of the currency supply with greenbacks? What was done about the greenback issue?

25. What were the diplomatic accomplishments of the Grant administration?

THE ABANDONMENT OF RECONSTRUCTION (422-427)

26. What tactics did white Southern Democrats use to restrict or control black suffrage?

27. Why did Northern Republicans begin to take less interest in Reconstruction and the cause of the freedmen after about 1870?

28. Why was the presidential election of 1876 disputed? How was the controversy resolved by the "Compromise of 1877"?

29. What was President Rutherford B. Hayes's objective in the South? Did he succeed?

30. Compare white and black expectations for Reconstruction with the actual results.

THE NEW SOUTH (427-437)

31. What were the socioeconomic and political characteristics of the "Redeemers" (Bourbons)?

32. How did the policies of the "Redeemer" governments compare with those of the Reconstruction-era administrations?

33.	In what particular products was industrialization in the South most advanced? What factors attracted industrial capital to the region after the war?

34.	How did industrialization in the South compare with that in the North?

35.	Describe the composition of the industrial workforce in the South. What problems did the workers face?

36.	Describe the typical pattern of Southern agriculture in the late nineteenth and early twentieth centuries. What problems confronted most farmers?

37.	Describe the rise of the black middle class. How widespread were economic gains by Southern blacks?

38.	What was Booker T. Washington's prescription for black advancement?

39.	How did the civil-rights cases of 1883 and Plessy v. Ferguson (1896) substantially negate the effect of the equal-protection clause of the Fourteenth Amendment?

40.	What strategies and legal devices did the Southern states use to evade the spirit of the Fifteenth Amendment?

41.	Explain how Southern whites used lynching to control the black population. How did some whites, both Northern and Southern, respond?

WHERE HISTORIANS DISAGREE (424-425, 434-435

42.	How have historians differed over the nature of Reconstruction?

43.	What part has the public played in this debate and why is the era so controversial?

44.	How have historians attempted to explain the origins of segregation in America?

45.	How have social and political development in the United States influenced the debate over the origins of segregation?

PATTERNS OF POPULAR CULTURE (428-429)

46.	How was the minstrel show both a testament to the high awareness of race and the high level of racism in American society before the Civil War?

Identification

Identify each of the following, and explain why it is important within the context of the chapter.

1.	Thirteenth Amendment
2.	O. O. Howard
3.	Thaddeus Stevens
4.	Charles Sumner
5.	Wade-Davis Bill
6.	John Wilkes Booth
7.	Alexander H. Stephens
8.	Joint Committee on Reconstruction
9.	Fourteenth Amendment
10.	Tenure of Office Act
11.	Edwin M. Stanton
12.	scalawag
13.	carpetbagger
14.	Blanche K. Bruce

15.   Hiram R. Revels
16.   sharecropping
17.   crop lien system
18.   Horatio Seymour
19.   Hamilton Fish
20.   "Grantism"
21.   Liberal Republicans
22.   Horace Greeley
23.   Crédit Mobilier
24.   "whiskey ring"
25.   Panic of 1873
26.   "Seward's Folly"
27.   "redeemed"
28.   Ku Klux Klan
29.   Samuel J. Tilden
30.   Readjuster
31.   Henry W. Grady
32.   the "Lost Cause"
33.   Joel Chandler Harris
34.   James B. Duke
35.   standard gauge
36.   convict lease system
37.   "fence laws"
38.   The Atlanta Compromise
39.   Jim Crow laws

Document 1

Read the portions of the chapter that discuss the Black Codes. Also read the section "Where Historians Disagree: Reconstruction." The following selection is taken from the writings of William A. Dunning. Consider the following questions: How does Dunning's account reveal his racist assumptions? How would accounts such as Dunning's lead white Southerners in the twentieth century to conclude that they had been gravely wronged by Reconstruction? Which of the following positions is more convincing? Were the Black Codes a necessary and realistic response to the situation, or were they a thinly disguised attempt to resubjugate the freedmen?

> To a distrustful northern mind such legislation could very easily take the form of a systematic attempt to relegate the freedmen to a subjection only less complete than that from which the war had set them free. The radicals sounded a shrill note of alarm. "We tell the white men of Mississippi," said the Chicago Tribune, "that the men of the North will convert the state of Mississippi into a frog-pond before they will allow any such laws to disgrace one foot of soil over which the flag of freedom waves." In Congress, Wilson, Sumner, and other extremists took up the cry, and with superfluous ingenuity distorted the spirit and purpose of both the laws and the law-makers of the South. The "black codes" were represented to be the expression of a deliberate purpose by the southerners to nullify the result of the war and reestablish slavery, and this impression gained wide prevalence in the North.

Yet, as a matter of fact, this legislation, far from embodying any spirit of defiance towards the North or any purpose to evade the conditions which the victors had imposed, was in the main a conscientious and straightforward attempt to bring some sort of order out of the social and economic chaos which a full acceptance of the results of war and emancipation involved. In its general principle it corresponded very closely to the actual facts of the situation. The freedmen were not, and in the nature of the case could not for generations be, on the same social, moral, and intellectual plane with the whites; and this fact was recognized by constituting them a separate class in the civil order. As in general principles, so in details, the legislation was faithful on the whole to the actual conditions with which it had to deal. The restrictions in respect to bearing arms, testifying in court, and keeping labor contracts were justified by well-established traits and habits of the negroes; and the vagrancy laws dealt with problems of destitution, idleness, and vice of which no one not in the midst of them could appreciate the appalling magnitude and complexity.

William A. Dunning, Reconstruction: Political and Economic, 1865–1877 (1907; reprint, New York: Harper & Row [Harper Torchbooks], 1962), pp. 57–58.

Document 2

The crop lien system, initiated during Reconstruction, continued to be a major grievance of Southern farmers well into the twentieth century. The following selection is taken from The Ills of the South, by Charles H. Otken, a Mississippi Baptist preacher and schoolteacher. Consider this document and the relevant parts of the text, and answer the following questions: Why did the crop lien system arise? What were the consequences of the system on land ownership and crop selection? Could the system be fairly described as a "vicious circle"?

When all the cotton made during the year has been delivered and sold, and the farmer comes out in debt on the 31st of December, that farmer has taken the first step toward bankruptcy. If he is a small farmer, $25, $50, or $75 is a heavy burden to carry. Take these cases: Hezekiah Drawbridge owes $25 at the close of the year; his credit limit was $75. Stephen Goff owes $50; his credit limit ws $150. Buff Tafton owes $75; his credit limit was $250. The year during which these debts were made was fairly good, the purchases were moderate, there was no sickness in these families. The following year similar credit arrangements are made, and they purchase the full amount agreed upon between them and their merchants. From some unaccountable or accountable cause, the crop is a little worse, or the price of cotton is a little less. The winding up of the second year's farm operations finds Drawbridge, Goff, and Tafton with the following debts confronting them, respectively: $65, $115, $155. The outlook is blue for these farmers, and they feel blue. Thus, or nearly thus, this system operates in thousands of cases. Each year the plunge into debt is deeper; each year the burden is heavier. The struggle is woe-begone. Cares are many, smiles are few, and the comforts of life are scantier. This is the bitter fruit of a method of doing business which comes to the farmer in the guise of friendship, but rules him with despotic power. To a large class of men, the inscription printed in large, bold characters over the door of the credit system is: "The man who enters here leaves hope behind," and it tells a sad and sorrowful history. Anxious days, sleepless nights, deep wrinkles, gray hairs, wan faces, cheerless old age, and perhaps abject poverty make up, in part, the melancholy story.

Charles H. Otken, The Ills of the South or Related Causes Hostile to the General Prosperity of the Southern People (New York: Putnam, 1894).

Document 3

Read the section of the text concerning the case Plessy v. Ferguson, which was decided by the Supreme Court in 1896. Included here are excerpts from the majority opinion and from Justice John Marshall Harlan's lone dissent. Consider the following questions: Which opinion is more convincing concerning the implication of the inferiority of blacks in the "separate but equal" doctrine? How does Harlan's dissent foreshadow the arguments of twentieth-century civil-rights crusaders? Is the United States Constitution today truly "color blind"?

The object of the [Fourteenth] amendment was undoubtedly to enforce the absolute equality of the two races before the law, but in the nature of things it could not have been intended to abolish distinctions based upon color, or to enforce social, as distinguished from political equality, or a commingling of the two races upon terms unsatisfactory to either. Laws permitting, and even requiring, their separation in places where they are liable to be brought into contact do not necessarily imply the inferiority of either race to the other, and have been generally, if not universally, recognized as within the competency of the state legislatures in the exercise of their police power. The most common instance of this is connected with the establishment of separate schools for white and colored children, which has been held to be a valid exercise of the legislative power even by courts of States where the political rights of the colored race have been longest and most earnestly enforced. . . .

Laws forbidding the intermarriage of the two races may be said in a technical sense to interfere with the freedom of contract, and yet have been universally recognized as within the police power of the State. . . .

So far, then, as a conflict with the Fourteenth Amendment is concerned, the case reduces itself to the question whether the statute of Louisiana is a reasonable regulation, and with respect to this there must necessarily be a large discretion on the part of the legislature. In determining the question of reasonableness it is at liberty to act with reference to the established usages, customs and traditions of the people, and with a view to the promotion of their comfort, and the preservation of the public peace and good order. . . .

We consider the underlying fallacy of the plaintiff's argument to consist in the assumption that the enforced separation of the two races stamps the colored race with a badge of inferiority. If this be so, it is not by reason of anything found in the act, but solely because the colored race chooses to put that construction upon it.

* * *

It was said in argument that the statute of Louisiana does not discriminate against either race, but prescribes a rule applicable alike to white and colored citizens. But this argument does not meet the difficulty. Everyone knows that the statute in question had its origins in the purpose, not so much to exclude white persons from railroad cars occupied by blacks, as to exclude colored people from coaches occupied by or assigned to white persons. . . . No one would be so wanting in candor as to assert the contrary. . . . In view of the Constitution, in the eye of the law, there is in this country no superior, dominant, ruling class of citizens. There is no caste here. Our Constitution is color-blind, and neither knows nor tolerates classes among citizens. . . . The destinies of the two races, in this country, are indissolubly linked together, and the interests of both require that the common government of all shall not permit the seeds of race hate to be planted under the sanction of law. . . . The arbitrary separation of citizens on the basis of race, while they are on a public highway, is a badge of servitude wholly inconsistent with the civil freedom and the equality before the law established by the Constitution.

Plessy v. Ferguson, 163 U.S. 537 (1896).

Map Exercise

Fill in or identify the following on the blank map provided. Use the map in the text as your source.

1.   Former Confederate states.

2.   First state to be readmitted, including the year.

3.   Last three states to be readmitted, including the years. (Note that the other seven were readmitted in 1868.)

4.   First three states to reestablish Conservative government, including the years.

5.   States in which Conservative government was not reestablished until 1876.

6.   The extent of the crop-lien system in the South in 1880.

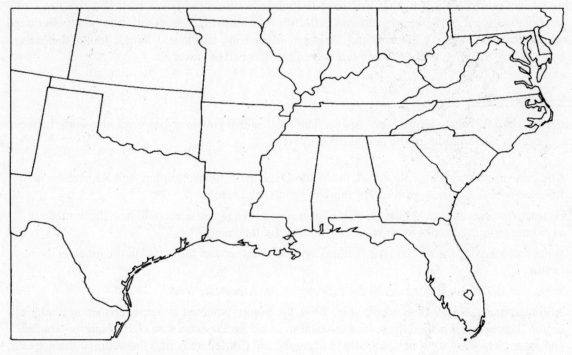

Interpretative Questions

Based on what you have filled in, answer the following. On some of the questions you will need to consult the narrative in your text for information or explanation.

1.   Note the location of the first state to be readmitted by Congress, and explain why it was restored to the Union so quickly.

2.   What did the other ten states have to do to gain their readmissions in 1868–1870? What additional requirements did the last three face?

3.   Note the first three states to experience the reestablishment of Conservative government and explain why the restoration of Democratic Party rule came so quickly there.

4.   What forces delayed the reestablishment of Conservative government in the other states? What episode symbolically marks the end of the Reconstruction era?

5.   Compare the crop-lien system in 1880 to the location of cotton and slaves in 1860. What does this comparison tell you about the nature of postwar agriculture and labor in the New South?

Summary

The military aspect of the American Civil War lasted less than five years and ended in April 1865, but it would take another dozen years of Reconstruction to determine what the results of the war would be. The only questions clearly settled by the time of Appomattox were that the nation was indivisible and that slavery must end. The nation faced other issues with far-reaching implications. What would be the place of the freedmen in Southern society? How would the rebellious states be brought back into their "proper relationship" with the Union? The victorious North was in a position to dominate the South, but Northern politicians were not united in either resolve or purpose. For over two years after the fighting stopped, there was no coherent Reconstruction policy. Congress and the president struggled with each other, and various factions in Congress had differing views on politics, race, and union. Congress finally won control and dominated the Reconstruction process until Southern resistance and Northern ambivalence led to the end of Reconstruction in 1877. Enormous changes had taken place, but the era still left a legacy of continuing racism and sectionalism that was revealed when Southern whites established the Jim Crow system to evade the spirit of the Fourteenth and Fifteenth Amendments. Meanwhile the South continued its colonial relationship with the North, and Southern plain folk, black and white, found themselves trapped by crop liens in circumstances some felt were almost as bad as slavery.

Review Questions

These questions are to be answered with essays. This will allow you to explore relationships between individuals, events, and attitudes of the period under review.

1. Compare and contrast Lincoln's plan, the Wade-Davis Bill, Johnson's plan, and Radical Reconstruction. Consider provisions, motives, goals, and results.

2. Evaluate the successes and failures of Reconstruction. What decision could have been made to avoid the failures? What groundwork was laid for future changes?

3. What factors made the railroad the "central symbol of American progress" in the nineteenth century?

4. What was the ecological impact of the railroad on the American West?

5. Although many changes had occurred by 1900, the South remained an impoverished agricultural region, lagging well behind the rest of the nation. Describe the economic changes in the South, and assess why they were not adequate to bring the old Confederacy into the national mainstream, as some of the region's spokespersons had hoped.

6. Explain the ways in which the Southern white establishment was able to evade the spirit of the Fourteenth and Fifteenth Amendments to the Constitution.

Chapter Self Test

After you have read the chapter in the text and done the exercises in the Study Guide, take the following self test to see if you understand the material you have covered. Answers appear at the end of the Study Guide.

MULTIPLE-CHOICE QUESTIONS

Circle the letter of the response which best answers the question or completes the statement.

1. The Thirteenth Amendment to the U.S. Constitution:
   a. declared that the right to vote could not be denied on account of race.
   b. officially ended slavery.
   c. granted "citizenship" to the freedmen.
   d. provided that states could only count three-fifths (60%) of their black population when determining how many members they would be given in the U.S. House of Representatives.
   e. opened up the West to homesteading by African Americans.

2. The Fourteenth Amendment to the U.S. Constitution:
   a. declared that the right to vote could not be denied on account of race.
   b. officially ended slavery.
   c. granted "citizenship" to the freedmen.
   d. provided that states could only count three-fifths (60%) of their black population when determining how many members they could be given in the U.S. House of Representatives.
   e. opened up the West to homesteading by African Americans.

3. The Fifteenth Amendment to the U.S. Constitution:
   a. declared that the right to vote could not be denied on account of race.
   b. officially ended slavery.
   c. granted "citizenship" to the freedmen.
   d. provided that states could only count three-fifths (60%) of their black population when determining how many members they would be given in the U.S. House of Representatives.

4. Which faction of the Republican Party wanted Reconstruction to punish the former Confederacy, disenfranchise large numbers of Southern whites, and confiscate the property of leading Confederates?
   a. Moderates.
   b. Conservatives.
   c. Redeemers.
   d. Scalybaggers.
   e. Radicals.

5. Which best describes Congressional reaction to the former Confederate states that had set up new governments under Andrew Johnson's "presidential Reconstruction"?
   a. They fully accepted all of the states except Georgia and South Carolina, which had elected no blacks to office.
   b. They conditionally accepted all of the states pending the results of local and state elections.
   c. They refused to seat the senators and representatives from the states and set up a committee to investigate and advise on Reconstruction.
   d. They fully accepted all of the states west of the Mississippi River, but required new constitutions in the others.

6. The "Black Codes" were a set of regulations established by:
   a. the Congress to protect the rights of the former slaves to own property and to find employment.
   b. the U.S. Supreme Court to enforce the provisions of the Thirteenth and Fourteenth Amendments to the U.S. Constitution.
   c. the northern states to prevent a massive influx of former slaves from entering their states and seeking homes and jobs.
   d. the southern states to promote white supremacy and to control the economic and social activities of the freedmen.

7. Which of the following, if any, was <u>not</u> a provision of the Congressional plan of Reconstruction enacted in early 1867?

 a. Dividing the South into military districts administered by military commanders.

 b. Requiring former Confederate states, as a condition of readmission to the Union, to ratify the Fourteenth Amendment to the U.S. Constitution.

 c. Mandating former Confederate states, as a condition of readmission to the Union, to hold a constitutional convention and prepare a constitution providing for black male suffrage.

 d. Declaring that each state must present a plan for distributing farm land to, or providing jobs for, the former slaves.

 e. <u>All</u> of the above were provisions of the Congressional plan of Reconstruction.

8. Critics of native Southern whites who joined the Republican Party called them:

 a. carpetbaggers.

 b. whippersnappers.

 c. scalawags.

 d. white camellias.

 e. filibusterers.

9. Which best describes the extent of "Negro rule" in the Southern states during Reconstruction?

 a. African Americans played a significant political role in several states but never elected a governor or controlled a state legislature.

 b. Some African Americans held local elective offices and a very few were elected to state legislatures but the numbers were politically inconsequential in every state.

 c. In the deep South states where African Americans constituted a majority of the voters due to white disenfranchisement, blacks dominated both houses of the state legislatures and controlled state politics as long as federal troops remained in the South.

 d. African Americans did not actually hold many offices in any state, but they effectively dominated local offices in all but Tennessee and Arkansas through alliances with white Republicans.

10. What institution was the key point of contact in the agricultural credit system for most Southern farmers, black and white, in the late nineteenth century?

 a. Small town banks owned by Northerners.

 b. Large diversified planters.

 c. Finance companies in the larger cities such as Atlanta and Memphis.

 d. Local country-store merchants.

 e. Mail order mortgage companies operating out of New York.

11. In the late nineteenth century, the agricultural credit system in the South encouraged farmers to:

 a. rely heavily on cash crops—especially cotton.

 b. diversify away from cotton toward food grains and livestock.

 c. adopt the use of mechanization on increasingly larger farms.

 d. abandon farming and invest in capital-intensive manufacturing enterprises.

12. Ulysses S. Grant's election as president was largely a result of his being:

    a. governor of New York during the postwar economic boom.

    b. a triumphant commanding general of the Union army.

    c. the popular administrator of the Freedmen's Bureau.

    d. a flamboyant cavalry officer in the western Indian wars.

13. Which of the following, if any, was not associated with the "Compromise of 1877"?

    a. Removal of the last federal troops from the South.

    b. Increased federal aid for railroads and other internal improvements.

    c. Appointment of a Southerner to the cabinet.

    d. Making Rutherford B. Hayes president.

    e. All of the above were associated with the "Compromise of 1877."

14. Which, of the following, if any, is not cited by the text as a reason that Reconstruction failed to accomplish more to promote racial equality in the United States?

    a. Fear that harsh action might lead to resumed military action by the southern states, even though they had been defeated.

    b. Attachment to a states' rights view of the Constitution, even for the rebel states.

    c. Deep respect for private property rights, even for leading Confederates.

    d. Belief in black inferiority by many whites, even Northern liberals.

    e. All of the above were cited as reasons that Reconstruction failed to accomplish more.

15. The "solid" South refers to the:

    a. work ethic values of Southern whites.

    b. courage of Confederate soldiers during the war despite being outnumbered.

    c. steady returns that Northern bankers could expect from investment in cotton.

    d. the fact that the Democratic Party could count on the votes of the Southern states after Reconstruction.

16. In most states, the "Redeemers" or "Bourbons" were typically composed of:

    a. a newly emerging class of merchants, industrialists, railroad developers, and financiers.

    b. essentially the same old planter elite that had dominated antebellum politics.

    c. a coalition of poor, working-class whites and blacks.

    d. white farmers who owned small to medium farms.

17. Henry W. Grady was:

    a. the builder of the American Tobacco Company.

    b. an Atlanta editor who became a leading spokesman for the "New South" idea.

    c. the person principally responsible for Birmingham, Alabama, becoming an iron and steel production center.

    d. the governor of South Carolina who was most vociferous in advocating that blacks should migrate from the South to take industrial jobs in the North.

18. The "convict-lease" system was an arrangement whereby:
   a. Southern states housed Northern prisoners as a way to fund prisons without raising taxes.
   b. a white man convicted of a nonviolent crime could pay a poor person, usually black, to serve his time for him.
   c. the state rented cells to the convicts who then had to pay rent based on pittance wages paid in prison industry.
   d. private interests paid the state for the right to use groups of prisoners to work on railroad construction and other projects.

19. "Jim Crow" is a nickname for:
   a. white Southerners who used violence or intimidation to restrict black activities.
   b. black people who curried favor with whites by acting excessively polite and deferential.
   c. the whole system of laws and customs that kept the races separate in schools, public buildings, housing, jobs, theaters, and the like.
   d. black people who pretended to be friendly toward whites but who secretly undermined white interests.
   e. the African-American culture of dance, music, food, and religion that grew up after slavery.

20. In Plessy v. Ferguson (1896) the U.S. Supreme Court established the general principle that:
   a. states could not prevent blacks from voting just because their grandparents had been slaves.
   b. states could require separate accommodations on trains, in schools, and the like, for blacks and whites as long as the accommodations were equal.
   c. Congress could take away a state's seats in the U.S. House of Representatives if the state refused to allow blacks to vote in Congressional elections.
   d. local governments could use zoning and building codes to enforce racial segregation by neighborhood.

21. Around the turn of the century, which of the following was most likely to attract Northern white support?
   a. Increased enforcement of the Fifteenth Amendment.
   b. Statutes allowing whites and blacks to marry each other if they wished.
   c. A federal anti-lynching law.
   d. Congressional intervention to promote racial integration in Southern public schools.

TRUE-FALSE QUESTIONS

Read each statement carefully. Mark true statements "T" and false statements "F."

1. As bad as the economic and physical situation was for Southern blacks in the aftermath of the Civil War, conditions were even worse for the region's white population.

2. The Emancipation Proclamation ended slavery throughout the South in 1863.

3. Republicans were afraid that the quick return of the Southern states to Congress would lead to more Democratic votes, thereby increasing the likelihood that Congress would establish protective tariffs and subsidize railroads.

4. President Lincoln believed that a lenient Reconstruction policy would encourage Southern Unionists and other Southern Whigs to become Republicans and build a stronger party in the South.

5. John Wilkes Booth acted completely on his own in plotting to murder President Lincoln.

6. Characteristics of Andrew Johnson's personality that hampered him as president were that he was too polite and deferential to assume any leadership initiative.

7. The Tenure of Office Act and the Command of the Army Act were passed by Congress to prevent Southern states from sending former Confederates to Congress or from having them control the state militia companies.

8. Even though the House's impeachment charges were nominally based on specific "high crimes and misdemeanors," Andrew Johnson was actually convicted by the Senate and removed from the presidency for petty political reasons.

9. Despite the end of slavery, most black agricultural labor in the South in the late nineteenth century continued to emulate the gang-labor system in which slaves lived in concentrated quarters and worked in groups under the constant supervision of a white field boss suggestive of the prewar overseer.

10. During the period from just before the Civil War to just after Reconstruction, per capita income for African Americans rose significantly while per capita income for whites dropped.

11. In the 1870s, the expanded printing of greenback paper currency was advocated by those, especially debtors, who believed that inflation would help the economy.

12. In the context of Reconstruction, "redeemed" was used to refer to freedmen who had returned to their original slave plantations as workers after running away during or immediately following the war.

13. The Crédit Mobilier was a railroad construction company involved in scandal during the Grant administration.

14. Hamilton Fish was Grant's secretary of state whose action worsened relations between the United States and Great Britain.

15. Alaska was called "Seward's folly" or "icebox" because of Seward's abortive attempt to sell the territory to the Russian czar as a method of financing the cost of maintaining troops in the South during Reconstruction.

16. In the period from the end of Reconstruction into the twentieth century, the Democratic Party was the political party of the vast majority of Southern whites.

17. In general, the "Redeemer"-"Bourbon" political regimes were inclined to raise taxes to expand services, especially public education.

18. By 1900 the portion of the nation's manufacturing output produced in the South was about three times what it had been on the eve of the Civil War.

19. The portion of Southern farmers who were tenants, cash or sharecrop, increased markedly from Reconstruction to 1900.

20. In the period from Reconstruction to 1900, the crop-lien system helped many Southern back-country farmers in the piney woods and mountains move from cash-crop commercial farming into a ruggedly independent sort of subsistence farming.

21. By the late 1890s, a significantly smaller portion of Southern blacks were allowed to vote than in the late 1860s.

WRITING A HISTORICAL BOOK REVIEW

Writing a book review as an assignment in a history course has at least four important objectives: (1) effective writing, (2) a substantive knowledge about a particular historical topic, (3) the development of a historical perspective and an understanding of the nature and use of historical research, and (4) an ability to think critically about the work of others. A typical summary "book report" can at best teach only the first two objectives. A critical book review goes beyond mere summary to inquire into the overall worth of the work. These are six steps to preparing a review of a historical work. With some modifications, these steps also apply to writing reviews of other nonfiction works.

1. Select a book. Your instructor may provide a reading list, but if he or she does not, you will find that locating an appropriate work can be a very important part of the learning process. Start, of course, with the Suggested Readings after each chapter in the text and with the card catalog or computer database in your college library. Check standard bibliographies, such as the Harvard Guide to American History, and try consulting the footnotes or bibliographies of other works. When you locate a likely book, give it a "once over." Glance at the table of contents and the bibliography, and read the prefatory material to make sure that the book is appropriate to your assignment. Ask yourself if the topic seems interesting, for you will probably write a better review if you have some affinity for the subject. And most importantly, talk to your instructor. He or she has read many books and has probably graded hundreds of reviews, so seek your instructor out for advice.

2. Determine the purpose of the book. The best place to discover this is usually in the preface, foreword, or introduction. What demand did the author intend to fulfill with the book? Did the author write because there was no satisfactory work available on the subject? Did the writer feel that he or she had a new point of view on a well-worn topic? Perhaps the author wrote a popular account of a subject about which previous works had been dull and dry. Determine the audience for which the work was intended. Was the work directed mainly at professional historians, at college students, or at the general public? Ascertaining the author's purpose is important, for, assuming that the purpose is worthwhile, the writer should be judged by whether he or she achieved what was meant to be accomplished.

3. Learn the author's qualifications and viewpoint. Find out the author's academic background. Is the author a journalist, a professor, or a professional writer? Has this writer published other books on related topics? Consult the card catalog; check Who's Who in America, Contemporary Authors, Directory of American Scholars, or other directories. Viewpoint, however, is generally more important than credentials, since an author must be judged mainly by the quality of the particular work you are examining. A Pulitzer Prize-winner may later write an undistinguished book. But many first books, often derived from the author's doctoral dissertations, are outstanding. Knowing the author's point of view, however, may put a reader on guard for certain biases. A Marxist historian will often write from a predictable perspective, as will an extreme rightist. Biographers are often biased for or against their subjects. For example, after the assassination of John F. Kennedy, many of his intimates, most notably Arthur Schlesinger, Jr., wrote biographical works. A reviewer could not adequately analyze Schlesinger's Thousand Days without knowing something about his close relationship with the slain president. Look for information on point of view in prefatory materials, in the body of the book, and in reference works with entries about the author.

4. Read the book. Read critically and analytically. Be sure to identify the author's thesis—the main argument of the book. Look for secondary theses and other important points. See how the author uses evidence and examples to support arguments. Are his or her sources adequate and convincing? Does the author rely mainly on primary—firsthand, documentary—sources or on secondary sources? Consider the author's style and presentation. Is the book well-organized? Is the prose lively, direct, and clear? Take notes as you read so that you can return to particularly important passages or especially revealing quotations. Remember that being critical means being rational and thoughtful, not necessarily negative.

5. Outline the review. The following outline is only a suggestion; it is not a model that you should necessarily follow for all reviews. You may find it appropriate to add, combine, separate, eliminate, or rearrange some points.

I.   Introduction
     A. Purpose of the book
     B. Author's qualifications and viewpoint

II. Critical summary
     A. Thesis of the book
     B. Summary of contents, indicating how the thesis is developed (Use examples. While this will generally be the longest part of the review, you should make sure that your paper does not become a mere summary without critical analysis.)
     C. Author's use of evidence to support the thesis and secondary points

III. Style and presentation
     A. Organization of the book
     B. Writing style (word choice, paragraph structure, wit, readability, length, etc.)
     C. Use of aids (photographs, charts, tables, figures, etc.)

IV. Conclusion
     A. Historical contribution of the book (How does the book fit into the prevailing interpretation of the topic? Does it break new ground? Does it answer a troublesome question? Does it revise older interpretations? Does it merely clarify and simplify the standard point of view? You may need to consult other sources when considering this point. See, for example, the "Where Historians Disagree" sections in your text.)
     B. Overall worth of the book (Would you recommend it? For what type of audience would it be best suited? Did the author accomplish the intended purpose?)

6. Write the review. Follow your outline. Use standard written English. When in doubt, consult The McGraw-Hill College Handbook or a similar reference. If your instructor does not assign a standard format, the following style is generally accepted.

I.   At the top of the first page, give the standard bibliographic citation of the work under review. (Reviews seldom have titles of their own.)

II. The review should be printed or typed double-spaced, with dark print, on good- quality bond paper. The typical review is from 450 to 1,200 words long.

III. If you quote from the book under review, simply follow the quotation with the page number(s) in parentheses. For example: "The author makes the incredible assertion, 'Jefferson turned out to be America's worst president.' (p. 345)."

IV. If you need to cite other sources for quotations or facts, use a standard citation style.
     You may find it helpful to read published book reviews as a guide to the preparation of your own. Most historical journals, including the American Historical Review and the Journal of American History, publish many short reviews at the end of each issue. Reviews in American History, which prints longer reviews, is especially useful. To determine where reviews of the particular book you have chosen have been published, consult the Book Review Digest or the Book Review Index. Assume that your audience is college-educated and well-read, but do not assume that your hypothetical reader has in-depth knowledge about the subject of the book under review.

PREPARING A HISTORICAL RESEARCH PAPER

A research paper helps students develop competencies very much like those that are enhanced by doing a book review. One of the best ways to develop a historical perspective is to actually write some history—even a short research essay. In addition, preparing a paper gives students the opportunity to become more competent in research skills and in the organization of diverse materials into a meaningful essay. The suggestions that follow are of a general nature, designed to enable an instructor to adapt them to the kind of project that best suits the class. These suggestions are directed to students taking the introductory course and who may be writing their first historical research papers at the college level.

1. Select a topic. This should be done with the advice of the instructor. Many instructors have a list of suitable topics to offer their students. If no such list exists, you should consider the following questions: (a) Will the topic help you understand the course? (b) Can a paper on the topic be finished during the term? (Students often bite off more than they can chew. It is better to select a manageable topic, such as "Lincoln's Veto of the Wade-Davis Bill," than one such as "Abraham Lincoln: President.") (c) Is sufficient material available to do an adequate job of research? (d) Does the topic interest you? There are, of course, other factors to consider, but if the answer to any of the above is "no," then the value of the project is lessened considerably.

2. Locate sources. Sources for a research paper fall into two general categories: (a) primary material—sources produced by people who took part in or witnessed the events being researched (letters, diaries, pictures, newspaper accounts, and so forth); and (b) secondary material—sources produced after the fact and generally written relying on the primary sources. To locate these sources, you should first consult a bibliographic guide, such as the Harvard Guide to American History or American History and Life. This will enable you to identify a number of secondary sources whose bibliographies should give you more material (primary and secondary) to look into. You should also examine historical journals, particularly those that concentrate on the field into which your topic falls. You should read related articles, paying attention to the sources they cite, and book reviews, which will tell you of new works on the subject. Once a source is located, you should write its full bibliographic citation on an index card or in a form appropriate to your software. This will make it easier to organize your bibliography during the hectic days just before the paper is due. Consult The McGraw-Hill College Handbook or other similar guides for examples of bibliographic and footnote form. Most colleges have collections of primary material—on microfilm or printed—to aid students in this kind of research.

3. Do the research. The research process has as many approaches as there are researchers, but until you develop the method best suited to you, here are some helpful hints. Begin by reading a general account of the circumstances surrounding the topic you have chosen (if your topic is "Witch Trials at Salem," read a general study of late-seventeenth-century Massachusetts). Then turn to the more specific secondary sources, and begin reading and taking notes. Take notes on index cards, one citation to each card (or the software equivalent). In this way, you will have notes that can be arranged in the order you desire when the time comes to write. Do not worry about having too many notes—better to have too many than too few, which would mean additional research at the last minute. Also, when taking notes, be sure to record the location (title, volume, page) so that you will not have to backtrack to find a citation. If you do the work the first time, you will not have to waste time retracing your steps at the end.

4. Organize the paper. If your research is done systematically, the organization of the paper will all but take care of itself. There are, however, a few hints that might be helpful. First, do not leave this to be done last. Even while you are pulling material together, you should be organizing it into a loose outline. This will show you where gaps exist, will tell you which areas need work, and will often cause you to redirect your efforts in a more productive way. In this way, the process of organization is ongoing, and so when the research is done, the paper is organized. Still, you should prepare an outline just before you begin to write. This forces you to go over all the material once again, makes it fresh in your mind, and gives you the opportunity to make any last-minute adjustments.

5. Write the paper. Again, if the previous steps have been carefully taken, writing the paper is easy. The note cards you have accumulated should be organized to correspond with your outline. However, be sure to pay attention to your thesis so that the paper will not be just a string of note cards. Write a rough draft of the paper, with documentation on a separate page. At this stage, footnotes may be in an abbreviated form, but they should be complete enough for later reference. Beware of the tendency to overquote. As a general rule, you should quote only when the actual wording is as important as the idea being transmitted or when "colorful language" spices up the narrative. In most cases, however, it is best simply to put the information in your own words and cite the source.

For general information on the use of the language, consult The McGraw-Hill College Handbook or another handbook used in freshman English classes.

6. Prepare the final draft. After the rough draft is finished and at least one revision has taken place, the clean copy should be prepared. Notes may be placed at the bottom of each page or at the back, depending on the instructor's preference. The bibliography should be placed at the end of the paper. Other additions-- title page, table of contents, an outline—may be included or omitted as the instructor desires.

By paying careful attention to the directions by your instructor and by following the portions of this guide that apply to the project you undertake, you should develop basic research and writing competencies that will help you in many other classes.

ANSWERS TO CHAPTER

SELF TESTS

Chapter One

MULTIPLE-CHOICE QUESTIONS

1.   c
2.   d
3.   a
4.   b
5.   d
6.   c
7.   a
8.   b
9.   b
10.   a
11.   c
12.   b
13.   a
14.   b
15.   a
16.   d
17.   b
18.   c
19.   b
20.   b

TRUE-FALSE QUESTIONS

1.   F
2.   T
3.   F
4.   F
5.   F
6.   T
7.   T
8.   T
9.   T
10.   F
11.   F
12.   T
13.   F
14.   F

15. T
16. F
17. T
18. F
19. T
20. T

Chapter Two

MULTIPLE-CHOICE QUESTIONS

1. b
2. b
3. c
4. a
5. c
6. c
7. d
8. a
9. e
10. c
11. b
12. b
13. a
14. a
15. b
16. c
17. b
18. a
19. a
20. b

TRUE-FALSE QUESTIONS

1. F
2. T
3. T
4. F
5. F
6. F
7. F
8. T
9. F
10. T
11. F

12. F
13. F
14. F
15. T
16. F
17. F
18. F
19. T
20. F

Chapter Three

MULTIPLE-CHOICE QUESTIONS

1. c
2. a
3. a
4. d
5. d
6. d
7. a
8. d
9. c
10. a
11. b
12. a
13. d
14. c
15. b
16. d
17. b
18. c
19. d
20. d

TRUE-FALSE QUESTIONS

1. T
2. T
3. F
4. F
5. F
6. F
7. T
8. T

9.   F
10.   F
11.   T
12.   F
13.   F
14.   F
15.   T
16.   F
17.   T
18.   F
19.   T
20.   T

Chapter Four

MULTIPLE-CHOICE QUESTIONS

1.   a
2.   a
3.   c
4.   b
5.   c
6.   d
7.   c
8.   d
9.   a
10.   a
11.   b
12.   c
13.   c
14.   d
15.   a
16.   b
17.   c
18.   a
19.   b
20.   a

TRUE-FALSE QUESTIONS

1.   F
2.   T
3.   F
4.   T
5.   F

6.   F
7.   F
8.   T
9.   T
10.   F
11.   F
12.   T
13.   T
14.   T
15.   F
16.   F
17.   F
18.   F
19.   T
20.   T

Chapter Five

MULTIPLE-CHOICE QUESTIONS

1.   b
2.   d
3.   d
4.   c
5.   a
6.   c
7.   b
8.   d
9.   c
10.   a
11.   b
12.   a
13.   a
14.   c
15.   d
16.   c
17.   a
18.   a
19.   c
20.   b

TRUE-FALSE QUESTIONS

1.   T
2.   F

3. F
4. T
5. F
6. T
7. F
8. T
9. F
10. F
11. F
12. T
13. F
14. F
15. T
16. T
17. F
18. F
19. T
20. F

Chapter Six

MULTIPLE-CHOICE QUESTIONS

1. a
2. a
3. c
4. b
5. b
6. c
7. a
8. d
9. d
10. a
11. e
12. a
13. d
14. d
15. a
16. b
17. d
18. b
19. d
20. c

TRUE-FALSE QUESTIONS

1. F
2. T
3. T
4. T
5. F
6. F
7. F
8. T
9. T
10. T
11. F
12. T
13. T
14. T
15. F
16. T
17. F
18. F
19. F
20. T

Chapter Seven

MULTIPLE-CHOICE QUESTIONS

1. b
2. d
3. a
4. b
5. b
6. a
7. d
8. b
9. a
10. c
11. d
12. b
13. a
14. a
15. c
16. a or b
17. b

18.	a
19.	a
20.	c
21.	a

TRUE-FALSE QUESTIONS

1.	T
2.	T
3.	F
4.	F
5.	T
6.	F
7.	F
8.	F
9.	F
10.	F
11.	F
12.	F
13.	F
14.	F
15.	F
16.	T
17.	F
18.	F
19.	T
20.	F

Chapter Eight

MULTIPLE-CHOICE QUESTIONS

1.	c
2.	d
3.	c
4.	b
5.	b
6.	a
7.	d
8.	b
9.	a
10.	c
11.	c
12.	b
13.	d

14.	e
15.	a
16.	a
17.	d
18.	a

TRUE-FALSE QUESTIONS

1.	T
2.	T
3.	T
4.	T
5.	F
6.	T
7.	T
8.	F
9.	F
10.	F
11.	T
12.	F
13.	F
14.	F
15.	T
16.	T
17.	F
18.	T
19.	F
20.	T

Chapter Nine

MULTIPLE-CHOICE QUESTIONS

1.	c
2.	a
3.	b
4.	c
5.	b
6.	d
7.	a
8.	c
9.	d
10.	a
11.	a
12.	a

13.	b
14.	b
15.	b
16.	d
17.	b
18.	b
19.	c
20.	d

TRUE-FALSE QUESTIONS

1.	T
2.	T
3.	F
4.	F
5.	F
6.	F
7.	T
8.	F
9.	T
10.	T
11.	F
12.	T
13.	T
14.	F
15.	T
16.	T
17.	T
18.	F
19.	T
20.	F

Chapter Ten

MULTIPLE-CHOICE QUESTIONS

1.	c
2.	c
3.	e
4.	b
5.	a
6.	a
7.	d
8.	a
9.	b

10. a
11. b
12. c
13. c
14. a
15. b
16. c
17. a
18. d
19. e

TRUE-FALSE QUESTIONS

1. T
2. F
3. T
4. F
5. F
6. T
7. T
8. F
9. T
10. T
11. T
12. T
13. F
14. F
15. F
16. F
17. T
18. T
19. T
20. T

Chapter Eleven

MULTIPLE-CHOICE QUESTIONS

1. c
2. b
3. d
4. b
5. b
6. c
7. c

8. b
9. d
10. d
11. c
12. d
13. b
14. c
15. b
16. a
17. b
18. b
19. c
20. b

TRUE-FALSE QUESTIONS

1. F
2. F
3. T
4. T
5. F
6. F
7. T
8. T
9. F
10. T
11. T
12. F
13. T
14. F
15. F
16. T
17. T
18. F
19. T
20. F

Chapter Twelve

MULTIPLE-CHOICE QUESTIONS

1. d
2. b
3. c
4. b

5. c
6. d
7. a
8. a
9. d
10. b
11. b
12. b
13. a
14. c
15. d
16. a
17. c
18. b
19. c
20. c

TRUE-FALSE QUESTIONS

1. F
2. T
3. T
4. F
5. T
6. F
7. F
8. T
9. T
10. T
11. F
12. F
13. F
14. T
15. F
16. F
17. F
18. T
19. T
20. T

Chapter Thirteen

MULTIPLE-CHOICE QUESTIONS

1.   a
2.   b
3.   c
4.   a
5.   d
6.   d
7.   b
8.   b
9.   b
10.   c
11.   b
12.   b
13.   a
14.   a
15.   a
16.   a
17.   c
18.   a
19.   e
20.   c

TRUE-FALSE QUESTIONS

1.   T
2.   F
3.   F
4.   F
5.   T
6.   F
7.   F
8.   F
9.   T
10.   F
11.   T
12.   F
13.   F
14.   T
15.   T
16.   T
17.   F

18. T
19. F
20. F

Chapter Fourteen

MULTIPLE-CHOICE QUESTIONS

1. d
2. d
3. e
4. a
5. d
6. d
7. c
8. c
9. b
10. b
11. c
12. a
13. c
14. b
15. b
16. c
17. a
18. d
19. c
20. c

TRUE-FALSE QUESTIONS

1. T
2. T
3. F
4. F
5. F
6. F
7. T
8. F
9. F
10. F
11. T
12. F
13. T
14. F

15. T
16. T
17. F
18. F
19. F
20. F

Chapter Fifteen

MULTIPLE-CHOICE QUESTIONS

1. b
2. c
3. a
4. e
5. c
6. d
7. d
8. c
9. a
10. d
11. a
12. b
13. e
14. a
15. d
16. a
17. b
18. d
19. c
20. b
21. c

TRUE-FALSE QUESTIONS

1. F
2. F
3. F
4. T
5. F
6. F
7. F
8. F
9. F
10. T

11. T
12. F
13. T
14. F
15. F
16. T
17. F
18. F
19. T
20. F
21. T